SHAMAN HEART

TURNING PAIN INTO PASSION AND PURPOSE

STEPHANIE URBINA JONES

Featuring: Angela Bard, Iva Enright, Christine Falcon-Daigle,
Maura A. Finn, Robin Friend, Sonja Glad, Tina Green, Emily K. Grieves,
Dhela Griffith, Kathy Guidi, Pamila Johnson, Rev. Annie Mark, Carley Mattimore,
Tiffany McBride, Michelle A. McFarland, John Mercede, Lisa A. Newton,
Jeremy Pajer, Sherrie L. Phillips, Rev. Dr. Ahriana Platten, Mark J. Platten,
Karen Ann Scott, Dr. Ruth A. Souther, Julianne Santini, Atlantis Wolf

"Stephanie Urbina Jones has curated a powerful collection of stories of transformation which welcomes us and encourages us to take the first, or millionth, step on our own path. She understands in her bones how we transcend circumstance—by dreaming our life to fruition from our sacred longings, and we amplify it by honoring the sacred longings of others. Stephanie is both grounded and winged. Her Shaman Heart lifts us up."

–Maia Williams, Co-Director 2004-2020
San Miguel Writer's Conference & Literary Festival

"Here at last is our tribe of healers and visionary ambassadors of Spirit and Wellness that we've longed to consult with! With timely, profoundly relevant stories and deep wisdom, this is just the resource we need for troubled times."

–Francis Rico, Author, Mystic, and Toltec Spirit Guide

"Stephanie Urbina Jones has used her own experience to lead others into new worlds, worlds where we surrender, accept, and are born again. This powerful collection of stories by a diverse group of spiritual leaders has the power to transform the reader. I am one of those readers, and I can follow the feather that leads to a new lightness of being. Everything connects."

–Kathleen Hudson, Ph.D. and Author of
Corazon Abierto—Mexican American Voices in Texas Music

"*Shaman Heart* is a sacred journey of transformation. Reading it is like receiving a solar hug connecting you with your inner sun to shine bright and illuminate the new world. I know this book will touch many and be a gateway to their own healing and a reminder to dance here and now. We are the children of the sun."

–Jorge Luis Delgado, Author,
Peruvian Mystic, and Shaman

"In *Shaman Heart*, Stephanie Urbina Jones and her band of healers and mystics and lovers of living offer a glimpse into their lives and their stories. Each has had the courage to peek into the abyss and not turn away from the pain and the sorrow, as so many of us do. We were taught that there was no coming back from such a peek. These wise ones teach us, through their story and the sharing of their medicine, that within the very heartbreak lies the hidden treasure. (After all, God comes if God comes at all, disguised as our own lives.) These are powerful stories of resurrection and liberation. Reading them will invite you to remember how you too are a resurrection story with your own medicine to offer the world. As one author says:

"I knew I had to resurrect from the inside by rebuilding the truth of who I was."

Take *Shaman Heart* and eat. Take *Shaman Heart* and drink. Read it and learn to bless the world with the gospel of your own story. You are the beloved, no matter what."

–Rev. Roger Butts, Author, *Seeds of Devotion*

"*Shaman Heart* was one of the most wonderful experiences at the Dreaming House. It was my honor to have all the beautiful authors here in Teo as they created this book which will bring light and love to the world. These dreamers became like family, and I am so grateful to be part of their gifts to the universe. I give thanks to all of you, but especially Stephanie and Jeremy. I look forward to the next *Shaman Heart* Author's Journey."

–Alberto Hernandez - Crazy Dreamer -
Owner of the Dreaming House

SHAMAN HEART

TURNING PAIN INTO PASSION AND PURPOSE

STEPHANIE URBINA JONES

Featuring: Angela Bard, Iva Enright, Christine Falcon-Daigle,
Maura A. Finn, Robin Friend, Sonja Glad, Tina Green, Emily K. Grieves,
Dhela Griffith, Kathy Guidi, Pamila Johnson, Rev. Annie Mark, Carley Mattimore,
Tiffany McBride, Michelle A. McFarland, John Mercede, Lisa A. Newton,
Jeremy Pajer, Sherrie L. Phillips, Rev. Dr. Ahriana Platten, Mark J. Platten,
Karen Ann Scott, Dr. Ruth A. Souther, Julianne Santini, Atlantis Wolf

Shaman Heart

Turning Pain Into Passion and Purpose

Stephanie Urbina Jones

Copyright © 2022 Stephanie Urbina Jones

Published by Brave Healer Productions

Paperback ISBN: 978-1-954047-49-5

eBook ISBN: 978-1-954047-55-6

DISCLAIMER

This book offers health and nutritional information and is designed for educational purposes only. You should not rely on this information as a substitute for, nor does it replace professional medical advice, diagnosis, or treatment. If you have any concerns or questions about your health, you should always consult with a physician or other healthcare professional. Do not disregard, avoid, or delay obtaining medical or health-related advice from your healthcare professional because of something you may have read here. The use of any information provided in this book is solely at your own risk.

Developments in medical research may impact the health, fitness, and nutritional advice that appears here. No assurances can be given that the information contained in this book will always include the most relevant findings or developments with respect to the particular material.

Having said all that, know that the experts here have shared their tools, practices, and knowledge with you with a sincere and generous intent to assist you on your health and wellness journey. Please contact them with any questions you may have about the techniques or information they provided. They will be happy to assist you further!

I took a little trip to my closet
and I opened up the door
Skeletons were rattlin'
about settlin' some scores
Hello all you wish I would have
could have should have beens
It's time to turn the page
and turn these enemies into friends

Lyrics from *Bones* by Stephanie Urbina Jones

A PROFOUND AND SACRED JOURNEY

On January 5, 2022, amid a raging pandemic, snowstorms, fires, and canceled flights, leading spiritual teachers, preachers, and healers from around the world came together.

Over seven days, they laid their lives on the altar of the feathered serpent, Quetzalcoatl, and took a leap of faith in the pyramids of Teotihuacan.

Each author, an expert in their field, was invited to surrender through ceremony and initiation while writing and carving out their powerful truths. They faced hell, walked on fire, danced, and breathed into their soul's purpose. They remembered their divinity and awakened their shaman hearts. Through the courage of 26 star seed dreamers, two spiritual adventure guides, and one badass Brave Healer publisher, this powerful collection of real-life stories infused with wisdom, magic, sacred medicine, and tools for personal freedom—26 Tales of Transformation—was born.

www.ShamanHeart.org

Rio de Luz. The vision of the river of light streaming from Teotihuacan's Moon Pyramid is one that has guided me through many dreams. The original creators of the City of the Gods had the hydraulic engineering capacity to literally conduit water down the famed Avenue of the Dead. Every time I've stepped onto the avenue and turned toward the Pyramid of the Moon rising as an echo of the hill behind it, it has felt as if the Great Mother herself is pulling me into her heart. The hill, now known as el Cerro Gordo, the Fat Hill, is in fact called Tenan in Nahuatl, the indigenous language of the region. Tenan means Great Mother. The hill was once a volcano that long ago gave birth to the entire valley, interlacing it with lava tunnels, obsidian, slag, and subterranean rivers. Walking up the avenue toward the Pyramid of the Moon is like walking upstream through an enormous birth canal, following the beat of the Mother's heart back to the source of all that we are. It is a return to Creation.

I approach my art making as an opportunity to embark on a journey, to open doorways and to walk along that fine line that separates the visible and invisible worlds, attempting to build bridges of connection between the two. This is a pilgrim's path, at times treacherous, at times ecstatic, but I am always aware of the symbolic signposts along the way that direct us with specific intention toward the sacred. Something is sacred when it reminds us of our connection to the Divine, when it opens our hearts, when we remember a sense of union with our Creator. Much of my artwork is inspired by the environment around my home in central Mexico, by the 2000 year old pyramids of Teotihuacan, a city created by masters who reminded themselves of their innate connection to all life by adorning everything from simple bowls to massive temple walls with symbols of that connection. The path I walk with my art is intended to lead both me and my viewers toward a deeper communion with Divine Source.

Emily K. Grieves

www.EmilyKGrievesArt.com

DEDICATION

Tell me can you hear it
This longing in my spirit
This whisper from my heart
This prayer in the dark

This book is dedicated to my great-grandfather Manuel Anaya Urbina who had the faith and conviction to follow his heart and crossed the border in 1907 in pursuit of his religious freedom, his divinity, and for a better life for me and generations to come.

And to all the seekers and dreamers,
to all those hungry for something more,
longing for delivery from their pain and a road map to freedom.
To my mother, my father, and ancestors,
whose darkness and light gave me life and seeded my shaman heart.

Thank you.

And to the spirit of Frida Kahlo who inspired me to live as a bold, brave and wildly passionate artist of life.

Viva La Vida!

Lyrics from *Prayer in the Dark* by Stephanie Urbina Jones and Mark Marchetti

TABLE OF CONTENTS

INTRODUCTION

My honey is hot and ready to receive.
To be filled and rocked until the star seed
of my longing explodes into every cell of my being.
They told me I'd be done by now, but THIS is my beginning.

The beginning that came after the ending of giving my power to people
and thoughts that were not my own.
I slayed those dragons, cut those cords, haunted my youth
and all the places I lost myself and went away
because too much pain was too much pain.

That pain gave birth to me.

I was so brilliant, that little girl who rocked herself
and told stories to keep herself safe.

Oh, my precious baby you were born from the stars
you came to be here on purpose, on time,
but not before you traveled the broken road
that shattered your heart and hard shell wide open

You see it was all a part of your destiny.
I know it's so hard to believe
that this was a part of the great mystery. . .school?

Baby, you can't be a twinkling starlet in the sky forever.
You can't make a wish from way out there
and suddenly be delivered into a full, fulfilling, juicy life
that makes you shout from the inside out
like a holy night of unleashed passion
that keeps you coming and coming with waves crashin'

No, you can't have that kind of juice
without being willing to lose. . .control
Without coming to earth and being rebirthed
through pain, shame, caca and rain

To come out shining in the sun great full.

You see my love, you got to feel the pleasure and pain to give birth
Embody it all to find your passion and purpose on earth
And just when you think you think you know it all
Then you're ripe for the lesson you'll learn when you fall

Here you go to surrender again
But now you know sometimes the gift comes when
you're willing to give up and throw your towel in
Strip down, jump in the river and swim

Look up at the clouds, feel the cool summer breeze
Hear the birds as they chirp and sing in the trees
Soon the sun will set the night sky on fire
Stars will twinkle and wink and fill you with desire

In your boat you'll then float down a stream into caves
On the canyon walls the story of your life will play
First a dream then a fetus, fingers, toes you're born
Walking, talking soon your life's growing corn

One by one scene after scene.
The epic awe filled tale of transformation in me,
Through tears and years you will finally come to see
The shaman heart star you were born to be

So look in the mirror see that masterpiece of life
You're a fucking goddess You are Divine
Let your longing explode into every cell of your being
They told me I'd be done by now, but THIS is the beginning

This is the Beginning by Shaman Heart, Stephanie Urbina Jones

On the morning I was tasked to write the intro for this book, my soul first gave birth to the words above.

It was the revolution of my evolution, a celebration and affirmation of having traveled over thirty years into and through the heart of my hurt to bring myself home. It brought me to my knees and to the ancient city of Teotihuacan time and time again, where the first seeds of my faith and freedom were planted and began to grow. Fifteen years later, my life is transformed, and I'm living beyond my wildest dreams.

It was through my dogged determination, devotion, and dedication to my own inner healing that I've become a trusted teacher, leader, successful songwriter, recording artist and co-founder of Freedom Folk and Soul, where we humbly midwife sacred journeys of the soul all over the world. I am a powerful dreamer.

As fate would have it, I turned yet another page of my life when I became an author in the best-selling book *Sacred Death.* As I was writing, I had a vision that I would lead 25 conscious creators on a transformational journey to birth an inspiring book at the Dreaming House in the heart of Mexico.

I knew I had met my fiery match in Laura Di Franco, the publisher and CEO of Brave Healer Productions, when she immediately said, "Let's go."

My husband, Jeremy Pajer, co-founder of Freedom Folk and Soul, and I have been leading journeys to this powerful portal of change for over a decade. Together Laura, Jeremy, and I combined our unique gifts to ignite a bold new dream and create the first-ever Author's Journey. This journey included writing *Shaman Heart - Turning Pain into Passion and Purpose.*

Of all the sacred journeys I've taken and led, none have been more profound than this one.

Welcome to Shaman Heart, my friends. It's an honor to be the lead author of this powerful collection of stories. Many people have asked me, "What is a Shaman Heart?"

The answer is pretty simple: a Shaman Heart is an ordinary everyday human who has learned to see in the dark and walk between the worlds. A Shaman Heart has been through their own sacred initiations and healing crisis and come through to the other side more healed and whole. Whether it's a death of a loved one, divorce, illness or depression we can turn our pain into an initiation and be a sacred witness or messenger in these bittersweet, crossroad moments in life.

From this place of humbled, broken-open wisdom and grace, we can then walk with others and assist them as they journey through their own darkness to the dawn of a new beginning.

I want you to know that I wanted to die from a very young age. I carried a tremendous amount of pain and shame. I didn't know until I got to Teotihuacan, the sacred land of my ancestors, that the desire to die was a call for love.

My own Shaman Heart was awakened there at the end of the avenue of the dead. As I sat and breathed in front of the pyramid of the moon, the darkness I had run from my whole life gave birth to the light within me. I laid my pain and shame on the altar, and there in sacred ceremony; I was reborn.

There within the heart of the hurt is the medicine. Your sacred ache is a sacred call for love. When we have the courage to tend to and honor our truth, with grace, time and attention, we can turn our pain into wisdom, passion, power and purpose.

My deepest prayer is that your soul may be rocked and awakened by these 26 inspiring true-life tales of transformation. As you read, may each story breathe life into your bones and invite you into your own sacred initiation as you follow your shaman heart to live a life beyond your wildest dreams.

All my love and grace,

Stephanie

CHAPTER 1

MANUEL'S DESTINY AND THE FAITH TO FLY

CREATING A MEDICINE WHEEL OF MUSIC

Rev. Stephanie Urbina Jones, Artist of Life,
Healing Arts Minister, Rockstar Shamama

MY STORY

"Don't tell anyone you are Mexican."

The words shot through my body in slow motion and filled every cell of my little being with shame. My skin was white, so nobody knew my daddy was brown. I kept my secret, and by the time I was seven, I was a ghost of a girl. My parents divorced, and my mom remarried and moved us to a small town in Texas.

Seared into my mind were stories and beliefs I told myself that played over and over like broken records.

You are not worthy. You are not wanted. You are fat. You will never be enough. Don't be who you are.

And I can still hear my mom saying, "Don't tell anyone you are Mexican."

Thankfully, my soul wisely flew to a place where I safely disassociated most of the time. I learned to escape in a number of ways, but by far, the most comforting was while rocked in the arms of my favorite songs. I truly believed Carole King when she sang *You've Got A Friend.* Her music was my medicine.

When my mom got me Yamaha lessons, we found out I had perfect pitch. In fourth grade, Mr. and Mrs. Jenkins, my angels and choir teachers, discovered I had a good voice. I sang in the choir at the Methodist church and with my stepdad at St. Mary's.

Everyone encouraged me to sing, and yet no one knew how painful it was when the attention was on me. I sang in the shower, but I could not stand in the spotlight. I was overcome with shame. Even though I wanted to sing, I would freeze and regress to that shameful little girl.

I was blessed to have been raised in this Mayberry of Texas, where I never met a stranger. Weekends were spent four-wheeling, two-stepping, coon hunting, and dragging main. We lived across the street from Pat's Hall, and my favorite Honky Tonk was Luckenbach.

I was in charge of spreading the sawdust and collecting beer tabs, while Margie, the bartender, was my babysitter. I spent many afternoons listening to soon-to-be-famous poets Townes Van Zant and Guy Clark as they carved out their souls with guitars.

My life changed when my dad came to get me after I graduated high school. He took me to Mexico for the first time, and my brown heart exploded with joy, love, and bittersweet sadness for all I'd missed.

I went to college at the University of Texas and joined a sorority. On Father's Day weekend, I was so excited to have mine come join me for lunch. I'll never forget that frozen moment in time when my brown dad walked through the door. You could have heard a pin drop. Everyone stopped what they were doing and turned to stare.

I felt terror, shame, confusion, and anger. I wanted to be loved and liked by everyone, yet I loved my dad. I felt torn between two worlds. It was the same painful, conflicted feeling I had growing up as a child. I knew in that instant that if they had known I was Mexican, I wouldn't have been invited to be a part of this group that had become like family to me. I was crushed. I began to get an inkling of understanding of what my father, and so many others, experienced every day. I wanted to crawl inside my skin once again and hide.

Soon after, I tried out for the musical Godspell, and I froze at the audition. After being hired for my first band, I was fired for freezing on stage in front of 5000 people. I made up my mind to give up performing and decided I'd rather help bring healing music to others and just work in the music industry.

My first job was at BBA Agency in Austin. We handled the calendar for the Elephant Room, and so I booked myself for a happy hour. I stepped down into the basement bar and was greeted by a cloud of smoke and red velvet curtains.

With the amazing David Webb on piano, three vodka sodas, and almost tipping over, I sang *Crazy* to three people and the bartender. One of them was my dad, who said, "Mija, you were born to sing."

I made my way to Nashville and gratefully discovered a gift of writing. I was soon hired as a staff writer for Sony ATV. I purged my pain and began carving out stories in song. I loved my job hanging with my best friends, being paid to dream, drink coffee, and write in my pajamas.

Sadly, during this time, my beloved abuelita passed. Before she did, she shared her vision for my life and said, "Mija, you will be a messenger sharing the beauty of our Mexican culture with the world."

Within a few months, I felt the pull to know more about my roots and rich heritage. I returned to Mexico.

It was 6:30 a.m. when the bus pulled into San Miguel de Allende, a pueblo magico built on crystals. I stayed with a family and was immersed in their life and school each day. My soul danced as I wandered through the cobblestone roads. Many afternoons, I ended up in the jardin staring up at the clouds and the pink cotton candy-colored Parroquia against the blue sky and listening to mariachis serenade lovers.

I was in heaven. I spent hours studying, listening, and wondering how and why my great-grandfather Manuel left this magic in Mexico.

His story haunted me since I was a child. My grandma used to take me to see him every time I came to visit. He always welcomed me with a silver dollar and a smile behind his thick, black-rimmed glasses.

He died when he was 105. Amazingly, at 102 years of age, he got on a plane and flew to Italy to meet with the Pope. We have a picture of them together, and I've always wondered what they talked about.

Grandma told me he was born in Mapimi Durango, Mexico and that he'd been called at a young age by God. At 16, he made his way to Rome to study and become a priest. There, within the Vatican walls, something profoundly painful happened. No one knew what it was.

Within two years, he came back to Mexico only to then leave his country, family, and faith to follow his heart across the border in El Paso. He went on to become a Baptist minister traveling and preaching the gospel.

Grandma told me, "He crossed for religious freedom, his own understanding of divinity, and a better life for generations to come."

During my time in Mexico, more and more of my childlike wonder reawakened as I remembered and replayed the first precious years of my life with my dad and familia. I can still smell the homemade tortillas and hear the mariachis rehearsing in the neighborhood at 115 North Cibolo. I had the time of my life.

One day in San Miguel, I opened the all-Spanish newspaper and there it was, the only phrase in English, *A Gathering of Healers*. I didn't know what that word meant, but I knew I had to go.

When I opened the door to the casita, a tiny Mexican woman welcomed me. Before long, we were lying on the ground as she drummed, made music, and invited us to breathe. I dropped into a deep dream state, and suddenly, there he was—my great-grandfather Manuel.

He explained what happened in Rome and why he came to the US. He expressed how proud he was of me. Like my grandma, he said, "Mija, it's time for you to make music, tell stories, heal, and reawaken the faith in your heart."

I woke from this experience and felt clearer and more alive than ever in my life. I cried so many tears. I felt so light. I wrote the song *Revolucion en*

Mi Corazon before heading back to Nashville. Soon I mortgaged my home for the first of four times to make records. My destiny was calling.

The years and pages of life turned. I married and birthed a beautiful young daughter. I seemed to have it all but truthfully suffered with debilitating depression and thoughts of suicide. I tried countless ways to unburden my heart, from tried and true traditional religion to 15 years of talk therapy and recovery.

I knew all about my wounds, but I could not change the deep grooves I was stuck in. I understood if I did not change, I would burden my daughter with this history. As fate would have it, I was invited by a cosmic cowboy, Lee McCormick, who I'd met ten years before, to join him and his group at a place called the Dreaming House in the Pyramids of Teotihuacan, Mexico. I knew I had to go.

The road of my life took a turn in this ancient city of mystery where it's said that "Man Becomes God." I knew about this womb of recreation after reading *The Four Agreements* by Don Miguel Ruiz.

Not long after, I took the Initiates Journey through the marketplace of my mind and hell before taking a leap of faith. I stalked my life and made my way down the avenue of the dead. I walked with my wounds, cried, prayed, and came undone.

I unraveled years of stories and trauma. It was a pilgrimage of pain and the beginning of the resurrection my heart.

As I climbed to the top of the pyramid of the sun, I said to Lee, "I can't do this. I can't change. It's too late. I am so ashamed."

He turned me around and said, "Stephanie, you're addicted to suffering."

My knees went out. I crumbled to the ground as the truth rocked me. I realized the broken records of shame and pain, *you're not good enough*, and *no one wants you*, came from inside me, by me, the storyteller.

I had used my imagination to cast spells and tell lies, unknowingly hurting myself over and over again. Yes, my parents and their parents did and said some unfathomable things, but now it was my responsibility to take ownership of my life. I was shaken to my core yet empowered by realizing I could take the needle off the record and change.

On top of the pyramid of the sun, I heard a voice that said, "You will be a fiery angel. You will use your voice as a sword to cut through the darkness." Light filled every cell of my body. Freedom never felt so good.

I returned to Nashville with a passion and belief that I could and would transform my life. I hunted my pain to find and rescue the little girl who had dissociated and gone away.

Although my first marriage failed soon after my return from Teo, it sent me into the depths of a healing crisis. I welcomed all kinds of alternative experiences, therapy, and ceremonies to heal and release my trauma.

Magic unfolded, and a few years down the road I met my current husband in a medicine wheel during a weekend retreat. Jeremy is a Toltec teacher who was adopted into the Lakota tribe. He carries many spiritual and sacred rites of passage in the medicine bag of his life.

Soon I was immersed in vision quests, sweat lodges, firewalks, breathwork, Toltec dreaming, and sacred journeys that helped me get into my body. I learned to heal, remember, and release the pain and suffering I carried since childhood. I brought more and more of myself home to wholeness.

Within a short time, I harnessed my thoughts and was rarely depressed. My life rapidly transformed. Jeremy and I were married in a medicine wheel, and soon after, created Freedom Folk and Soul to walk with and guide others as they healed their lives. We now lead sacred journeys all over the world.

Who knew back then that once again things were about to change in a big way. One phone call became the cosmic breadcrumb that connected the dots between my music, my faith, my passion and my purpose.

"Hello?" I cautiously answered the phone call.

"Hi, this is Raymond Gutierrez. This is a strange question, but I'm wondering if you happen to be related to Manuel Anaya Urbina.

I froze. After a few moments, I replied. "Ummm, yes I am. He was my great-grandfather."

"Well, you see, I was wandering in an antique store and happened to come across this old bible with his name in it. I recognized your name as Stephanie Urbina Jones, the singer, and wondered if there was a connection."

I didn't know what to say as tears filled my eyes.

Over one hundred years later, the same bible Manuel had crossed the border with was handed to me just before I made history carrying our Mexican roots to the heart of country music. As I transformed my sacred wounds into my sacred medicine, I was invited back into the spotlight.

On Oct. 2, 2018, I made history as the first artist in the ninety-three years of the Grand Ole Opry to sing and bring the heart of Mexico and mariachi into the center of that sacred circle on that hallowed stage. In that moment, my pain turned into my passion and purpose. Although one hundred years apart, mine and Manuel's dreams had come full circle.

Like a bird in the sky with my heart open wide and the faith to fly
Like an unbridled horse on an unchartered course to a better life
With hope in my soul his corazon made of gold
I believe I can do anything
His story lives on in me
I'm so grateful to live and be free
Manuel's Destiny

Lyrics from *Manuel's Destiny* by Stephanie Urbina Jones, Mark Marchetti & John Mabe

THE MEDICINE

Music is medicine. Through good and bad times, the song remembers when.

This ceremony is an invitation to create a soundtrack ceremony in song to honor the life and music that made you. Designing an intentional record is a powerful act of self-love. It's a fun and courageous way to call back and remember who you are. Use the compass of your shaman heart and let the music play.

STEP 1

Find a private space to create an altar. Within that altar, create a medicine wheel (a circle with a cross in it).

STEP 2

Open sacred space by putting on some relaxing background music. Light some sage or copal. Call in your ancestors and guides to be with you.

STEP 3

One by one, read the description of each of the seven directions below. Take a few minutes with each one, and journal what that direction means or represents to you.

Ask the great mystery for a song or two to honor that sacred time in your life. After you've prayed, journaled, found a song, and come to a completion or intentional pause for that direction, light a candle in that part of the medicine wheel. This is to mark how you've illuminated, honored, and commemorated that time in your life with song. Repeat this as you go through the seven directions and Medicine Wheel of Music.

After you're done, thank your ancestors and make a playlist of your Medicine Wheel of Music soundtrack. Play it often to honor how far you've come. You are turning your wounds into your medicine.

THE SEVEN DIRECTIONS AND MEDICINE WHEEL OF MUSIC

THE WEST

Find a song that represents this crossroad moment of you taking responsibility for your life. This is the place of introspection and adulthood. Choose a second song to represent surrendering into the water. Go with the flow and be carried.

THE NORTH

Find a song that represents where you come from—your ancestors and family of origin.

THE GREAT BELOW

Find a song that represents the love of the great mother who will never abandon you. She will hold you through it all.

THE EAST

Find a song to represent your new life, new beginning, innocence, and childlike wonder.

THE SOUTH

Find a song to represent your sacred rebel, passion, identity, and desire.

THE GREAT WITHIN

Find a song that represents your commitment to love, honor, and respect yourself.

THE ABOVE

Find a song that represents the dreamer, infinite possibility, and freedom.

Turn off the lights, crank up the music, and dance to your Medicine Wheel of Music. Celebrate who you are and how far you have come!

Stephanie Urbina Jones—Singer, teacher, writer, sister, friend, mother, wife, and lover of life, Stephanie Urbina Jones brings her passion and experience of living a life of creative freedom to people all over the world. This rockstar shamama has a passion for transformation and is a living example of not only dreaming but bringing those dreams to life. Whether she is writing a song, performing, or leading sacred journeys of transformation as co-founder of Freedom Folk and Soul, Stephanie is following her heart and chiseling out her soul. She sees herself as a kind of midwife, guiding folks on their journey of self-discovery, healing, and transformation, empowering those who seek to live a life of passion and purpose.

Stephanie has spent over 25 years in pursuit of her personal freedom. She has studied, prayed, walked, talked, worked, and turned over stones in the road and in her heart to heal and create a life of humility, passion, and purpose.

A true "walker between the worlds," SUJ shares inspiration in music from her albums, including "Shaman Heart," a transformational journey in song with audiences and fellow journeyers everywhere.

SUJ is a #1 Billboard Country Music Songwriter traveling with her Honky Tonk Mariachis, sharing joy and her history-making "Country Music with Chili Peppers" all over the world.

To learn more about Stephanie Urbina Jones and her work in the world:

Websites: www.freedomfolkandsoul.org
www.stephanieurbinajones.com
www.shamanheart.org

Facebook: https://www.facebook.com/Freedomfolkandsoul.org

Instagram: https://www.instagram.com/freedom.folk.and.soul
https://www.instagram.com/stephanie_urbina_jones

To see Stephanie's history-making moment on the Grand Ole Opry:
https://vimeo.com/293257898/eeaa184c13

CHAPTER 2

BEFRIENDING DOUBT

BEING THE MESSENGER YOU WERE BORN TO BE

Jeremy Pajer, CCDC, Healing Arts Minister,
Personal Freedom Coach

God, what did I sign myself up for, to write in a book—you don't write.

Mind going completely blank. Heart racing. Disassociation setting in.

You know what you need to do? Back out of this project! There are plenty of writers on it. What were you thinking?

Okay, Okay. What's a good excuse to get out of this? Think, think.

It's not a good time. There's too much going on in my life right now. My stepdad is really sick, and my mom needs me.

Ahhh, maybe I will get sick and won't be able to do it. That's a legitimate excuse.

It's too much. You don't know anything anyway. You're a fraud. Who do you think you are, writing a book? You have nothing to share.

Deep breath. Another deep breath.

Hello, old friend. I hear you. I know you're scared. Just pause, breathe. I want to thank you for all the times you've done your job to protect me when it wasn't safe to be seen, to be heard, or to be vulnerable.

I know it was hard to grow up in an environment where you thought you were never enough. I know you got hurt many times when you just tried to be you.

You are just doing the job I assigned to you, so thank you. Take a slow, deep breath. We've got this. We've crossed this threshold many times. We've been seen and shared our truth, our message, and we are still here. We're okay.

It's been a dream of ours for 20 years to write. Feel that desire. Breathe. We've got this. We're okay. It's going to be okay. We're going to do this.

We're going to share our message with the world. Yes, it is a risk. Yes, it might hurt. We've been hurt many times, and we are still here.

So just write.

I've got to be honest. I've spent many years learning, listening, and soothing this voice in my head. I call this befriending doubt. Here I am, walking into the fire once again as I try to write this chapter.

Inside of me is a terrified little boy who doesn't think he's good or worthy enough and doesn't feel safe expressing his truth. This boy was shut down, not validated, and taught to do what he should, not what he wanted.

It was painful and scary to be me, so I created this beautiful part of myself to keep me safe, and he's gotten really good at his job. So much so that if I don't listen to him, I will disassociate, and there will be nothing in my head.

I mean nothing—no thoughts, a complete state of frozen, as if I haven't spent the last 20 years learning, teaching, sharing, and helping people walk through their pain and turn it into their medicine. But in that moment of panic, there is nothing. It's real, and I know I'm not alone.

MY STORY

One of my earliest memories is of being in the classroom as a little kid. I watched this lady sharing in the front of the room. I remember what it felt like to have someone give me their full attention. She took the time to come over to my desk, kneel beside me, and help with something I didn't understand. Throughout school, I had a secret desire to be a teacher from that time on. But even at that young age, I had this voice of doubt deeply ingrained inside me.

You're not smart enough to be a teacher. That's not who you are. You're destined to run the family business. You know how to do that. There is too much risk. Teachers don't make enough money...

This secret desire, along with the doubt, continued through school. I couldn't even fully admit to myself that this was my dream.

I grew up in Massachusetts. My parents divorced when I was two. My father's side of the family was Italian, and he owned a deli, banquet house, and a few other businesses. He was the patriarch, an angry, dominating, and controlling man.

My mom was French Irish, and early on, I deemed my mom not capable of taking care of us or even taking care of herself. Through the painful experience of being in both homes, I learned to put my needs aside. I took care of my mother, while at the same time, I became the good, little, perfect soldier in my father's home for fear of his wrath.

The combination of these things led to my internal doubt and complete lack of sovereignty. There was no room for what I wanted if I was to remain safe.

It's important to point out that this isn't about blaming my parents. I like to say the real problem with my parents is that they had parents. No one gets out of childhood without some wounds, and my parents were tasked with teaching me and giving me something they never had.

My father was an incredible man, and he passed on much wisdom and life skills that helped me become who I am today. My mother taught me how to love unconditionally. No matter what I did or who I became, she just loved me.

I had to go back and find that little boy. I had to let him feel those traumas, get angry, get sad, and grieve those lost and wounded parts. In doing this, I've accepted and forgiven my situation. All of it needed to happen to be who I am today.

Having grown up in a family where my father took over the business from his father, and me being the only son, I was expected to follow in my father's footsteps. I felt an incredible amount of pressure to continue in the family linage.

I was expected to grow up fast and work in the family business at a young age. There wasn't a place for me to have my own dreams. Having such a powerful, controlling, and rage-full father, I lived in a constant state of fear.

It was terrifying. I never knew when he would fly off the handle. Rather than develop a true sense of sovereignty or independence, the safer, easier thing to do was what I was told. Of course, I had to figure out what was expected before he even expected it.

I believe this was the birth of the perfectionist in me. If I did everything right, if I did everything perfectly, I wouldn't get yelled at. Any chance at having a voice, or anytime I tried to be free, it was shut down and met with more rage. I made some agreements to just do what was in the safe zone, not take risks, not be me, and not move towards anything other than what was expected.

At fifteen, I worked in my family's deli every day after school. I was groomed to take over for my father. In addition, three or four nights a week, I'd work at our banquet house. I looked like I was twelve in my chef coat that was too big for me and my frog-patterned chef hat.

I was responsible for running the kitchen. I directed all the kitchen staff and fed hundreds of people. I worked hundred-hour weeks in high school.

When I was sixteen, my father came to me with a choice. He said, "You can take over the deli when you turn eighteen, or you can go to college, and I will sell the deli."

I already knew how to run the deli, and I could make $100K a year doing it. As hard as I tried in school, the best I could do was Cs. Of course, this was another reinforcing factor that I wasn't good enough.

There wasn't really a choice for me. It was too big of a risk. The truth is, I was a very capable young man, with no lack of intelligence or ambition as long as I stayed within the parameters of what I deemed safe.

I took over the deli from my father, and at eighteen, I ran the entire business. By twenty-two, I was successful. I made a lot of money and bought my own house. I owned a brand new truck, boat, jet ski and had a trophy girlfriend.

I had the best of everything. I made it in life and in the eyes of the world and my family. I was the hero child. I also had a $500-a-day drug habit. I was in deep pain, terrified, and desperately wanted to be someone else.

At twenty-three, I found myself in a hospital bed, having just overdosed. The last thing I remember saying to my girlfriend was, "I can't get high enough to kill the pain."

I was living an inauthentic life. I was just doing what I could to keep my head above water. Getting high was my way to avoid, disassociate, and not listen to that voice of *you're not good enough* in my head. It didn't matter how successful I was.

There I was, heart monitor beeping, tubes running in all directions, my parents and family members looking at me with such concern in their eyes. And me, lying there confused, scared, and full of shame. I could do many things in my life, but I couldn't stop getting high every day, no matter how hard I tried. At that moment, lying there in that hospital bed, I finally surrendered.

A week later, I found myself 1500 miles away from home in a treatment center in Tennessee. Confused and full of fear and doubt, I was broken and willing enough to listen. They offered all kinds of holistic healing modalities, from yoga to sweat lodges to Toltec Shamanism.

This stuff was far out of the box for me and how I grew up. Remember, the life I came from resembled a Sopranos episode. My only exposure to anything spiritual was when my sister did Reiki. We all thought she was the weird one.

But I was willing to try anything. I said, "Tell me what I need to do, or I am going to die."

I showed up and did everything offered to me. Who knew it would be the road to my dream?

By the third weekend, two amazing Toltec teachers came to present. They were so full of love and acceptance for who I was. All my brokenness and bad decisions didn't matter to them. We fell in love with each other, and for the first time in a long time, it felt okay to be me.

A few weeks later, they returned and taught a workshop with about 40 people. They said, "Hey, we have an expert on this subject in the room. Jeremy can you tell us about…"

I have no idea what the question was, but I immediately went into full panic, face beet-red, heart pounding out of my chest, and hands and face sweating—complete terror. I stuttered out some words.

I had to do it *right,* and it wasn't okay to be seen except from behind the deli counter, where I was safe. These teachers had somehow seen me and pushed me to be a teacher from the beginning.

My childhood dream of becoming a teacher began to resurface. I remembered how it felt when that educator gave me her attention, love, and grace. I've spent the last eighteen years doing my best as a teacher to be that conduit of unconditional love and acceptance and helping people walk through their pain with grace.

What I needed most from my teachers was acceptance, love, and empowerment for who I really was.

For years, I would step out in front of a group and feel that same panic I felt that first night I was asked to teach. I thought and accepted that I would always feel that panic at the start of each group I led.

I soothed myself, held myself, took a deep breath, and stepped out in front of groups over and over again. I never let it stop me from living my soul purpose. I spent years learning how to befriend that part of myself, acknowledge that I am scared, grab my own hand, and say, "It's okay. We are going to be okay."

I still feel doubt in the days leading up to a class or when I get triggered, like when asked to write in this book. I greet the doubt like an old friend and say: *We are going to share our message, our story, our experience, and we can't do that wrong.*

Somewhere, a deeper passion began to emerge. I sat watching two students of mine at the front of the room. They fumbled their words, trying to do the teaching "right."

I looked up and said, "Stop. Take a deep breath, look around, now tell me what your experience of firewalking has been? What has it done for you?"

In that moment, I watched two teachers be born. This was a defining moment for me. It awakened a passion for helping people become their own messengers, to share their personal experiences. I've gone on to help many people find their medicine and become the best teachers they can be. From my experience, our biggest obstacle is our relationship with our doubt.

In summary, my secret desire to be a teacher was ultimately bigger than my doubt. We've all had a lot of pain, and that pain can lead us to our purpose and passion. Follow your heart. Follow your desire. Follow your longing to be the messenger you were born to be. Grab your hand, listen to that scared part of you, acknowledge the fear and step forward anyway.

THE MEDICINE

I've learned many tools to deepen my relationship with doubt and how to step into it with grace—firewalking, arrow breaking, meditation, breathwork, adventure therapy, and more. These are all powerful ways to work with doubt, but I've chosen to share this simple exercise. It can be profoundly helpful in understanding and moving through doubt.

What you will need: a notebook or a few pieces of paper, a pen, and a quiet place you can sit and can write.

Sit and allow your eyes to close. Take five slow deep breaths. Think of something you are afraid to do. Something that makes you feel doubt.

Then just listen without judgment. Allow that part of yourself to say whatever it needs to.

There may be a whole lot of reasons why you don't want to hear the words or why you can't. Those excuses will come. Just listen. Just breathe. Give that part of yourself full attention. This may be the first time you have fully witnessed this voice.

I invite you to have a conversation with that part of yourself. Listen closely and hear the wisdom of your inner truth.

This is where the paper and pen come into play. You, the one listening, will write with your dominant hand and then let the voice of doubt respond with your non-dominant hand.

Begin to have a conversation between these parts of yourself. Go back and forth as if you are talking to a separate person. Notice the feelings that come up. Perhaps grief, anger, or sadness. Feel them. Don't edit, and again, don't judge. Let the conversation take you wherever you need to go.

When you feel you have come to a place of completion in the conversation, allow your eyes to close. Take five deep, slow breaths. There is a terrified child that created this doubt to protect itself.

Imagine you walk up to that part of yourself. Imagine or remember that child. Look into their eyes. Wrap your arms around them. Let that part of you know that it's okay to be scared. Let them know they are not alone; it will be okay. They are going to be okay.

Finally, take a few more deep breaths and gently allow yourself to come back to the present moment. Open your eyes and notice where you are. Notice how you feel and what has come up for you.

What have you discovered about yourself and your doubt? Write your thoughts in your journal or draw a picture to express your experience.

You have begun the process of befriending your doubt and the first steps toward healing the old trauma that birthed it.

Jeremy Pajer is truly a master of transformation and a leader in the field of personal freedom. He has spent the last 19 years dedicating his life to spiritual growth and the healing arts. His approach to transformation and helping people embrace their humanity is practical, down-to-earth, fun, and loving. One of the things Jeremy is most passionate about is teaching people how to find their own wisdom and become the best teachers they can be.

Jeremy co-founded Freedom Folk and Soul, A Transformational Community of The Healing Arts, in Nashville, Tennessee. He is a lead facilitator in powerful and transformative workshops, classes, journeys, and trainings. He guides people on their journeys of self-discovery, self-healing, and self-expression, from Nashville to Dallas to the pyramids of Teotihuacan, Mexico, and many places in between.

He loves to share his wisdom, creativity, and playfulness as an Ordained Minister of the Healing Arts, Adventure Counselor, Master Breathwork Facilitator, Toltec Teacher, and Personal Freedom Coach. He brings his love and knowledge of Firewalking, Breathwork, Native American Ceremony, Toltec Wisdom, 12-Step Traditions, and Shamanic Practices to people all over the world.

Jeremy leads powerful firewalks, pouring sweat lodges, facilitating journeys and trainings in the US and abroad. He coaches people on their individual paths to freedom. He has studied and apprenticed with many masters from countless traditions throughout the years and loves to share all he has been given.

A true shaman and healer, Jeremy is committed to the individual's growth, transformation, and freedom. He brings his openness and authenticity to every field and is an authentic man of service, heart, and generosity.

To learn more about Jeremy and his work in the world:

On his website: https://www.FreedomFolkandSoul.org

On Facebook: https://www.facebook.com/Freedomfolkandsoul

On Instagram: https://www.instagram.com/freedom.folk.and.soul

Or email him directly:

freedomfolkandsoul@gmail.com or Pajer720@msn.com

CHAPTER 3

PRAYING WITH A PAINTBRUSH

A MANDATE OF CREATIVITY FROM THE VIRGIN OF GUADALUPE

Emily K. Grieves

MY STORY

"I love your sculptures! I'm an artist myself, a painter." I'll never be sure why I said those words, but they changed my life. I picked up a serpentine mask, mottled dark green carved into a heart-shaped face with broad lips and long eyes, and held it in my hand for a long time. Black obsidian spheres, wands, and warriors of all sizes sparkled at me from the tables in the shop.

"Oh, you can paint the mural!" Alberto turned with a beaming smile to Lee, one of the leaders of the retreat I was on, exclaiming, "She can paint the mural!" Lee squinted, focusing on me in the dimly lit room filled with stone sculptures, and repeated, "You can paint the mural!"

"Yeah, sure, I can paint the mural." My words came out in a nervous squeak. *I have no idea what you're talking about!*

Our Toltec spiritual retreat leaders, HeatherAsh Amara and Lee McCormick, had invited us to a fiesta to celebrate our last night on a journey to the 2000-year-old pyramids in Teotihuacan, the City of the Gods. In this place, humans awaken to their divine potential. I had just spent five days walking the sprawling avenues and plazas. Leaning up against the walls of temples, fragments of white stucco and red oxide paint still shimmering with mica on the stones, I'd poured my heart into stalking my limiting beliefs and dreaming a greater life into being.

It was July, and the high mountain desert was a green paradise of nopal cactus blooms and wildflowers unfolding to the nourishment of a rich rainy season. Everything seemed so much more alive here. The bright red breast of the vermillion flycatcher posing on top of a fence post, the cacophonous horn of the propane gas truck driving down the street, the hundreds of angles of steel rebar sticking out of half-finished concrete rooftops, the wild twisting of purple morning glories clinging to the stone wall. This place was extraordinarily awake and awakened my senses to how very asleep I'd been in my ordinary life back home.

My ordinary life was riding the bus across the Bay Bridge every morning to San Francisco's Financial District. It was trudging through the dark canyons of office buildings, riding the express elevator up to the 49th floor of the Bank of America building to file folders away in the archives of my ever-so-thrilling existence as a legal assistant in commercial real estate. I'd hung a couple of my paintings in my grey cubicle, and I had my angel cards in a bowl for anyone to pull. My coworkers in their suits and ties, pencil skirts and stiletto heels, may have seen me as the weirdo of the 49th floor, but they still furtively came by to read messages from the angels. When I announced, "I'm going on a spiritual journey to Teotihuacan, Mexico," the folks in the office didn't know where that was, thinking it must be near Los Cabos and would I go marlin fishing? I had planned the trip for over a year, but I was met with blank, confused stares when I told anyone about it.

I tried to break free of the corporate world many times but always caved in and stayed to pay the exorbitant rent in the Bay Area. Even though I had an art degree, making art and anything creative was always relegated to after-hours hobby status. I never even had the space for it. In one apartment,

I had my easel set up in the bathroom. In another, it was in the closet. After my marriage broke up, I pined for a creative breakthrough and to move elsewhere—anywhere else. I'd drive through the leafy streets of Oakland, imagining myself pulling up roots. I had no idea what would come next, but I prayed and finally went on that trip to Teotihuacan. I tacked on extra days to visit the Basilica of Guadalupe in Mexico City. The trip changed me, and I changed everything about my life.

I'll never forget the day I first arrived at Teotihuacan. We loaded into a van at the Mexico City airport and, after an hour's drive, crested a hill, and the Pyramids of the Sun and Moon burst into view. It took my breath away. To this day, so many years later and Teotihuacan now being my home, my heart still flips in my chest when I see that view. On that first visit, we spent every day exploring the immense grounds of the pyramids, melting our limiting beliefs and merging with powerful energies every time we touched a stone.

One of the most potent experiences I had was standing in the Palace of the Butterflies—an open-air temple that had been used as an observatory long ago, a place to look into a pool of water on an obsidian floor and see the reflections of the stars above. Lee stood in a doorway that opened to the western hills and guided us into a deep state of dreaming while awake. He said, "When I step aside, whatever you see in this doorway is your true spiritual essence." He stepped away from the portal, and I saw the Virgin of Guadalupe.

It has taken me years to begin to understand what it means to have Guadalupe as my true spiritual essence, but back then, I just took a deep breath and felt my mind melt a little more, felt my heart crack open a bit wider with hope for a richer life. The Virgin of Guadalupe would become the voice of my intuition, and I have learned to listen!

When the group leaders took us to that fiesta on our last night, I sat in the sprawling gardens of what would become the Dreaming House retreat center and watched dusk fall with a soft indigo wash across the sky. The stars blinked on, inviting me into a warm night. I felt at home. The Pirul trees arched their branches over me, draping their sweet peppercorn scent into the moist grass. The place was so foreign and familiar to me at the same time. The soil itself seemed to be reaching roots up into my feet, pulling on me to notice the land, to hear the mourning doves and great-tailed grackles weaving their twilight cooing and cackling into a new soundtrack for what home means.

That was the moment I approached Alberto's shop, a dim room filled with old wooden tables, cracked yellow paint heaving under the weight of sculptures, and his huge toothy smile lighting up the space. As I looked around at the room full of obsidian, I could see my reflection in the smooth polish of every piece. It must have been the clarity with which I saw myself at that moment that allowed me to speak the words to Alberto, "I'm an artist." Those words changed my life.

After our exchange, when Alberto invited me to paint the mural, Lee mentioned he would be returning in a couple of months with another group and said, "Why don't you come back down and paint that mural? Why don't you come to live in Teotihuacan for a while?" The whole thing seemed surreal and impossible to me as we wrapped up the journey, and I headed into Mexico City to make my pilgrimage to the Basilica of Guadalupe. When I got back to my little Oakland apartment, traffic careening by outside on MacArthur Boulevard, it was like walking into a stranger's house. *Who lives here? Who reaches for the toothbrush in this way? Who puts the milk in the fridge like that?* I seemed to have become my own witness, observing my old patterns and movements from a different person's perspective.

As I navigated this bizarre new reality, slogging back through the dark financial district to my corporate cubicle, the offer to return to Mexico and paint a mural kept nibbling on my mind. *I need to pray about this. I need to ask the Virgin of Guadalupe.* I drove out to the redwood forest near Santa Cruz on a Sunday afternoon, wandered along a moist path soft with needles, and found a circle of dark wine trunks into which I could wrap my prayers. "Virgin of Guadalupe, Tonantzin, Revered Mother, am I supposed to move to Mexico to paint a mural?" The forest hushed around me for a long moment, specks of pollen suspended in refracted sunlight, and then the answer came. "Yes!" The "Yes!" was loud and clear, vibrating between my ears and echoing inside my skull.

I immediately began the fearsome process of packing up a life in the US and preparing to move to Mexico. I gave away belongings, sold furniture, gave notice on the apartment and at my job. People thought I was crazy. "Isn't it dangerous there?" "Aren't you afraid of being kidnapped?" I filled the dumpster with bags of trash, tears streaming down my face as I slept on the couches of friends. Fear rubbed at my nerves like sandpaper. *How will I make a living? I don't even speak Spanish!* Those voices were powerful, but I clung to the voice that told me, "Yes!"

When the logistics of an international move became overwhelmingly complicated, I prayed to Guadalupe again, and she said, "When you were a little girl, and you were going to go on a trip, did you worry about any of the details? No, you let your father and your mother take care of everything, and you just showed up on the day of the trip. Now let your Father and your Mother take care of everything!" *Oh yeah, surrender and show up, follow the guidance I've been receiving since I said those words, "I'm an artist!" The Virgin of Guadalupe gave me this mandate when she told me she is my true spiritual essence. All I have to do is keep listening to her. If she wants me to paint the mural, she'll help me get there.* And like magic, every problem resolved itself.

I showed up at the airport on the day it was time to go and flew down to Mexico City with all my worldly possessions in three suitcases, one of which was filled with art supplies. I suddenly realized nobody even asked to see my portfolio. They didn't know if I knew how to draw a stick. But there I was in Mexico, riding to Teotihuacan again, pyramids rising into view, and I was coming with paintbrushes this time.

Coming back to the Dreaming House felt like coming home. The mourning doves gurgled a greeting from the peppercorn trees, and the soil at the roots turned up scuffed bits of orange pottery shards, 1800 years old. I started piecing together a mosaic in my mind of all the fragments of my previous life that I would rearrange into a masterpiece of the future that began when I declared myself an artist. Creative opportunity quickly arose as it turned out the mural I'd been invited to paint was for a structure that would never be built. Meanwhile, Alberto said I could paint whatever I wanted wherever I wanted. *This was an artist's dream come true.*

Alberto showed me into the salon where we'd eaten savory mole rojo on our fiesta night. "This will be the meeting room for groups when they come. We have a figure of La Virgen del Carmen that we want to put against the back wall. Maybe you can paint some clouds behind her or something."

I sat alone in the room, staring at that big white wall. Suddenly a hush fell over the room, specks of dust suspended in the light falling through the dirty windowpane, and I heard the voice of Guadalupe speak to me again. "You must paint the vision you had of me in the pyramids on this wall!"

It was a clear mandate rushing in my blood, pumping through my body, swelling in my heart. I exhaled, knowing that I must take on this mission, never waver from it, and never step off the path. This was my path to knowing my true spiritual essence, and the path was painting.

I spent the next year painting that immense mural of the Virgin of Guadalupe appearing to me in the portal of the Palace of the Butterflies. During that year, I learned how to speak Spanish from the construction workers building rooms at the Dreaming House. I studied the original Teotihuacano murals and dreamed into their symbolic meaning, painting reproductions in the guest rooms. I studied Guadalupe, seeking to understand her hidden meaning, how the indigenous cosmology is woven into her image and story, and the significance of her invitation to come to her homeland and make it my own. The mural became the first of many times I would paint her. She kept adding on to her mandate: "Paint my image again! Teach others how to paint my image! Make every creative act a prayer! Pray with your paintbrush!"

I realized painting wasn't just about making a pretty piece of artwork. It was an act of devotion and a way to heal myself. With every brushstroke, I felt more of my old life flow out of me. All the frustrations of every "no" I'd ever been told and all the ways I'd made those "no's" mine, the limitations I'd created for myself out of all the negativity I'd consumed and the ensuing insecurity, unworthiness, low self-esteem and depression, everything that bound me to that grey cubicle on the 49th floor—it all went into the paint and flowed out of me and into the prayers that became her image.

When it was time to paint her face, I prayed to her, "Please use my hands to paint yourself. Please paint yourself as someone I might see on the street. Please show yourself to me." And she became a woman I might see at the fruit stand or waiting at the bus stop. She became every woman. She became a reflection of us all. She became my true spiritual essence.

After all these years, I still listen to her voice every day. I dip my brush into the sky-colored Manganese blue of her mantle and bring it to the rough fibers of the canvas. I gather my prayers and listen to the rushing tides of blood in my heart. Her "yes" lives there.

THE MEDICINE

Being creative doesn't require any art experience. It simply asks us to be intentional. Intentional Creativity® is a method I learned from my teacher, Shiloh Sophia McCloud, that has helped me use painting as a way to create the best version of my life. Creativity can be prayerful, devotional, and healing when we set our intention and bring awareness into the present moment and our feelings. We can use our creative acts to release limiting stories and beliefs from our past and manifest our dreams for a full, rich life experience. We can use simple mark-making, symbols, and colors to create portals to understand ourselves and our true essence more deeply.

Here's an easy example of Intentional Creativity. All you need is two pieces of paper, a pencil or pen, a glue stick, and some colors. Colored pencils or crayons will work just fine! This simple exercise is about taking a limiting belief and actively shifting it in a visual way. When our bodies feel our creative action and our eyes perceive it, these little changes become more real and permanent to us.

Take a deep breath and feel your connection to your own heart. Focus your awareness on some negative voice inside your mind that limits you and tells you that you're incapable or unworthy. Start small. It doesn't have to be a big one! Listen to what the voice says and notice how you feel as you listen to it. Are you ready to let it go, realizing it doesn't serve you and holds you back?

Starting with the words "My limiting voice tells me I can't...," begin to write on a piece of paper and fill the entire sheet. Get it out. When your page is full, place your hands on the paper to bless it, giving all your love to that part of you that was able to release the words. Now choose some colors and color over the written words in any way that feels good to you—no need to make any distinct form. There is no wrong way to do it. Allow the color to caress and soothe the words.

When you are complete with the color, take the paper and tear it into tiny bits, intentionally breaking your agreement to believe in those limits anymore. Try speaking out loud as you tear the paper, declaring, "This is not true! I no longer need to believe this!" When you are finished, gather the paper bits into your hands and hold them to your heart. Ask your heart, "How do I feel now that I've let that old limit go?" Listen for an answer, give your feeling one word: gratitude, curiosity, certainty, passion, etc. You'll know your heart's answer. It's usually the very first thing that pops into your mind before your mind begins to think.

Now take the bits of paper and arrange them on your second piece of paper into a type of mosaic, noticing how fragments of words and color become a new whole. Glue the pieces down to the paper, keeping your heart's word in your awareness with each piece you add. Finally, choose a darker color and write your heart's word in large letters across the entire paper mosaic you've made. You now have visible evidence of your heart speaking to you and honoring you for your courage to release old limitations and embrace the creative voice of your own true essence!

Emily K. Grieves is an artist, healer, and certified Intentional Creativity® Teacher. She received a BFA degree in art from the University of Montana in 1993 and studied art history in Berlin, Germany, as a Fulbright scholar. She explores symbolism, dreaming, and devotion in her artwork and teaches others to incorporate healing intention into their visionary and creative practices. As of 2004, Emily makes her home in Teotihuacan, Mexico, where her paintings are influenced by the cosmological imagery of the ancient pyramids and her relationship with the Divine Mother. She is a member of Musea, an international organization that promotes Intentional Creativity. Together with her husband, she owns the hotel and retreat center Villa Las Campanas.

Here are some resources to help you connect with Emily and the Intentional Creativity community:

www.EmilyKGrievesArt.com – I lead private Mystical Mother painting retreats in Teotihuacan, Mexico, and co-facilitate Book of Dreams retreats with fellow author Iva Enright. Book of Dreams is a powerful process of creative journaling to explore dreaming practices and intuitive development.

www.musea.org – Explore Intentional Creativity with Shiloh Sophia McCloud and the global community that provides education in an art movement dedicated to self-expression as the path to consciousness and compassion in the world.

www.villalascampanasmexico.com – We host retreat leaders who want to bring creative groups to visit the pyramids of Teotihuacan. I also offer Intentional Creativity sessions to visiting groups.

www.thedreaminghousemx.com – Join a Toltec power journey with the many exceptional teachers who visit each year and see my original mural of the Virgin of Guadalupe.

CHAPTER 4

RING, RING! IT'S YOUR BELOVED

HOW TO PICK UP THE PHONE WHEN SPIRIT CALLS

Atlantis Wolf

"Don't go wasting your emotion, lay all your love on me."

- ABBA.

MY STORY

Dove Mountain, North Carolina

"*I'm so sorry, Marcelene,*" I say, thunderstruck, kneeling in bed as I hold my wife's slack body. "*Forgive me. Forgive me. Please forgive me.*"

Marcelene's Spanish hair, long and black, curls in cascades and gleams in the afternoon light of the Egyptian sun. Her hair is catching my tears because I am holding her against me. My face is in her hair as I hold her small waist and wide hips against my bare, sun-bronzed chest and white schenti skirt, her alabaster body wrapped in a cerulean blue sari with a ribbon of gold bangles sewn to the hem.

"You flew too high," she says as her azure eyes close. *"Too far away,"* she whispers and dies in my arms.

I hold her body tight to my skin as I howl and wail from a wound that doesn't bleed, rocking her body and mine, inhaling her Kyphi perfume, pulling the frankincense, myrrh, lily, and blue lotus flower notes into my body, trying to inhale all of her.

"With the gods as my witness," I say, turning my weeping face to the sun, *"I ask you to take all my power from me, from this lifetime as Caesar, and from all future lifetimes. Forever."*

I hold Marcelene, wishing I could press her ebbing body into mine and revive her. *"I'm so sorry,"* I whisper into her hair. *"Forgive me, my beloved, forgive me. Please forgive me."*

The breathwork music ends, and I'm holding Rita, my co-journeyer, on top of my body, her leg between my legs, rocking her and sobbing as she holds me, whispering, *"Forgive me, Marcelene. Please forgive me."*

It's May 2019. I'm in the mountains of North Carolina attending Linda Star Wolf's Shamanic Healing Initiatory Process (SHIP) in a Shamanic Breathwork ceremony. The ceremony focuses on shadow work, finding the parts of your inner landscape you fear the most and the hidden and cloaked parts of your psyche that you ignore to live a normal life.

Linda instructed us to treat our shadow parts as rooms we could peek into as we walked down a long, dark hallway. I ran to the end of the hallway, the darkest room, to discover a past lifetime in the Upper Kingdom, a land of sand, pyramids, and Egyptian temples. My wife, Marcelene, died of a broken heart. She watched my rise to power corrupt the heart of the man she loved.

Teotihuacan, Mexico

It's January 2022. I'm in the mountains of Mexico, another land of sand, pyramids, and, now, Toltec temples, on the same latitude as Egypt, over the ocean that held Atlantis, with Stephanie and Jeremy on a collaborative book project and retreat. I met them when they held the May 2019 SHIP fire walking ceremony. Their Toltec Sacred Journey Breathwork is about to begin. I'm in a windowed, second-floor room, covered in a chevron pattern of yoga mats, blankets, and Kleenex packs.

I close my eyes and let the music carry me into a non-ordinary, deep, meditative state. My journey begins at a vortex, a tube of multi-colored light smears moving in a spiral as I travel through the center, going back in time to collect and claim my power from lost lifetimes. The message is to use my body as a guide. Map the pain.

The chronic pain at the apex of my right shoulder blade burns first, taking me back to Egypt and lifetimes as a stone cutter and scribe. I learned the value of humility and service in those lifetimes through physical labor. I learned how to write hieroglyphics with the god Thoth as a spirit guide. I pull the pain off my shoulder like burnt, charred wood, placing it in an offering chalice as big as my torso, suspended under and around my rib cage. It was alive, full of orange fire, red and black embers, yellow copal chunks, and myrrh sap. The stem stood in my belly, and the base was positioned between my hip bones. The fire crackled and sparked. The copal smoke spiraled around me, thick and aromatic. Just inhaling it felt like a sacred ritual.

The throbbing in my back between my last rib and right hip took me back to China and my life as a rice farmer, stooped all day in all weather with wooden tools. I learned patience and respect for the elements of water and air that could feed a crop through the harvest or raze the field overnight in a storm. I burned my conical rice hat in my chalice.

An ache in my sit bone, the ischial tuberosity at the bottom of my right hip that looks like an eye, led me to Spain, where I was told there was an injury related to childbirth, but details would re-traumatize me, so they remained hidden. I broke off the curve of bone with my hand, placing it in the chalice. I imagined my DNA helix remembering how that bone felt before the trauma, growing a new bone with that pre-trauma blueprint, first out of aquamarine crystal to hold the shape, then osteoclast cells to harden it.

A deep, spiky wound, like a burr, below my shoulder blade required help from Archangel Michael, who warmed the right side of my back under his hands, lifting the scapula bone the way a mechanic lifts the hood of a car. The wound took me back to an indigenous lifetime in a rainforest, a poisoned spear injury. I learned my dad in this lifetime caused the injury, and our historical narrative is coming to an end. I asked a bumblebee to help me. Directed by a fairy, he sucked the toxin from the wound with his straw-like tongue, spitting it with a sizzle into the chalice fire.

The last pain was at the front of the right side of my hip at the iliac spine, a lifelong pain. When I asked about the story behind this pain, the left side of my back and my front side transformed into a black rock in a sweep. I arrived in the darkest corner of the deepest shadow realm, a tormentor of souls because I was tormented, filled with despair, and unable to die. The hip pain was what the unborn son Marcelene carried when she died. The revelation was unbearable. The message was that after I relinquished all power for all lifetimes, I took my own life. I sentenced myself to this dark place, bound to the wound that I caused the death of my wife and our son, unable to forgive myself or ask for grace. I cupped my hands around my son, dropping the pain like a stone into the chalice. I held his tiny, unborn body against my chest, making room for him in my heart. I pulled a cloak of rock around us, entombed in sadness. Unreachable.

I stayed in the pause, a bubble in time, inhaling and exhaling at the pace of whales. I heard the sound of thrumming and pounding. The rock around me cracked and broke, revealing my fetal-tucked body and folded black wings. Strong hands pulled me up and then closed. I heard the crunch of scorched earth below sandaled feet and felt the awareness of being carried in masculine arms. I lost consciousness.

The journey jumped back to feeling Archangel Michael's hands on my back. My body felt warmer, turning to liquid gold with gold wings and sandals. He gave me a sword which I took in my right hand, then switched to my left, sitting down at a desk and writing words in gold. The center of the vortex began to pull away from my view. I watched myself at a writing desk, moving through time, the colors of the spiral vortex still swirling around me.

Sitting at the desk, I heard a voice say my name and smelled the scent of blue lotus flowers. I turned my face up from the book. Marcelene's face was connected to mine in profile, a single line between our forehead, nose, and chin, our lips locked in a lover's kiss, reunited.

At the end of the retreat week, looking out the window on the way to the airport, not listening to the other now-friends in the van, I felt the grief and loneliness of a returning reality without an embodied beloved. I shifted into my female wolf form, in spirit, and opened a dimension of space, howling for my missing mate, sending a sound-flare into the ether, a tether to guide my beloved back to me, as we passed under the sign that said Salidas (Departures).

Hometown, Home State

Returning after the Mexico retreat felt like arriving backward in time. My mind and spirit had moved forward in light-years, but my clients, kids, and cats expected the familiar, known, and predictable version of me. On a trajectory to catch up with my spiritual quantum leap, even my body felt conflicted and halted.

As I tried to fall asleep, all my emotions found me.

Like a dragon retreating into a concealed mountain cave, pulling boulders down behind him to block the entrance, I laid in an emotional cave-corner, peeking at all my angels and demons through the keyhole of light before closing my tear-filled eyes. *Leave me be, leave me be. All of you, please leave me be.* Sadness fell on me like heavy northern snow, thought by thought, flake by flake until I was entombed in a sunless shadow realm.

In the place between sleep and dream, vision and prayer, I heard the approaching footsteps of The Spartan, my spiritual guide who arrived six months ago, unrequested, while I was working on a client and looking into the spirit world. He had walked from behind the green female dragon who sits on a nest of golden eggs in the middle of my office space, wearing sandals, a blood-red flowing wool cape, a bronze helmet, and carrying a sword. Standing on the other side of my massage table, he got down on one knee, sword held across his chest, head bowed, and said, *I pledge myself to you.*

What the heck do I do with a spartan?

He arrived with a spirit lion. The lion sits left of me, The Spartan right of me. All the time.

He arrived again later in a meditation, carrying me in his arms over scorched, crunchy black earth. It was the sound I remember. The sound woke me from unconsciousness, the rhythmic sound of each foot stepping on bits of volcanic rock, moving with unstoppable motion. I awoke, charred and sooty, with black angel wings. When I told him I didn't need to be carried, he ignored me, walking through the darkness up an incline.

I don't remember ever being carried. Being carried for a minute feels nice, I thought. Wait! Where are you carrying me?

I turned my head, squinting into the distance, hearing a crowd of voices. *Caesar! Caesar!*

No, no, no! I thought. *I can't go back.*

Unperturbed, he continued to carry me. I was too weary to fight him. I surrendered to my return to the place and time where I needed to relearn how to master personal power.

And now, in my bed at home, dismembered and dizzy with heavy emotions from the Mexico retreat, I hear his footsteps in my mind between the waking and dreaming worlds. Like a foster kitten over-handled on adoption day, I'm too weak to protest him scooping me into his cupped hands and holding me close.

Being held by my sacred masculine counterpart, the last sluice gate rises, opening a torrent of tears, the final hidden aquifer of salt and water, clearing away every rock in my fortress until I'm bare—a small ball of black light, a thousand specks of inky, shiny darkness. I exhale with a threshold breath, becoming a misty cloud of shadow, the vacuum between stars, and the silence in the void.

A clawed, black hand covered in flinty, craggy scales rises to hold space in front of The Spartan's cupped hands—my guardian dragon, my oldest, most beloved friend. Two open hands, ivory and angelic, beam white-gold light through The Spartan's body to the back of his cupped hands—my mom, my angel twin, who died 13 years ago.

The black specks of mist, flip over, gold. They coalesce into a pulsing, sparkling ball, collecting and condensing to form a baby. I return to life, rebirthed in love, looking at The Spartan with a last memory of sadness. He sings to me, "Don't go wasting your emotion. Lay all your love on me."

He continues to sing, close to my ear, as I lay against his chest, smiling, glowing. I grow into a newborn, then an infant. He rocks me, and I grow into a toddler, then a child. He tosses me into the air, and sparks of color cast in all directions, gleeful. He puts me down. I walk away, a few steps, then I turn to run toward him so he can toss me again, higher. Again! I walk away as an adolescent, turning to run toward him as a young woman. He cups his hands, ready for my foot, launching me into space where I burst apart into balls of colored light, a trail of gold sparks behind me, and disassemble into a hundred constellations. I dance and flash in time to the song he sings. I remold myself back into a single form, returning as a woman flying down into his arms, ready to be held.

I stand in front of him as he leans against the cave wall. He spreads his cells, legs wide, and whispers, *Soften your heart and remember.*

I feel the boundary of my standing body against his skin, our thighs and trunks pressed together, his arms around my shoulders, his open hands on my back, my palms on his chest, my left cheek over his heart. I breathe, eyes closed, and let my heart expand, allowing the sensation of its strength and power to stretch the connection between each cell in my body until I slide between his spaces, eased below his surface. I sink inside the chamber of his ribcage, surrounded by his thrumming heart, my legs inside his legs, my womb encircled by the golden chalice of his hip bones, mingled and merged.

This is real sex, I thought, *activating cellular memories of our lifetimes together before Earth.*

I fall asleep in my bed, warm and smiling, glowing.

Finally, close enough.

THE MEDICINE

So, you've had a tremendous, heart-breaking, mind-expanding spiritual experience. Now what?

How do you take a spiritual experience home, transform the event into real-life action, weave the spiritual blast to another dimension into the fabric of brushing your teeth and making coffee in the morning? Take three steps: activate, integrate, and activate again.

STEP 1: ACTIVATE

Greet every spiritual experience with awe and wonder. Having one spiritual experience is enough to open the neural pathways in your brain, inviting new ways of thinking into your daily experience.

I activate spiritual experiences by meditating, daydreaming, walking in the woods, and engaging in breathwork. Find what softens your resistance and allows your inner healer to connect with your ancestors, spirit guides, and animal allies. If you need help, come to one of my workshops. I make a living helping people connect to spiritual realms.

STEP 2: INTEGRATE

Start with a simple drawing exercise. Take two packs of drawing paper, one black and one white, a set of pastel chalks, and a box of crayons. Sit comfortably and breathe three times, in through your nose and out your mouth. Imagine an experience you had that was difficult to describe in words. Gather all the feelings, sensory details, and colors. Draw a representation of the experience. Place the page across the room and gaze at it. Notice any new details? Ask a sacred friend for feedback. They may have insight for you. Meditate on the page so new messages and stories can unfold. Repeat until the experience feels complete.

How do you express yourself? Is it journaling, singing, painting, sculpting, playing an instrument, or something else? Take the path of creativity that feels easy to you. Every time we create, we are alive. The force of life moves through us like a flower that channels Earth's energy up to its stem and opens into the sun.

Bring your spiritual experience into the physical world in any way, or every way, that feels satisfying to you. Then share it with someone you trust. Ask for feedback. See what they see in your expressive self. Let them give you insight. Bringing a sacred witness to the table will open you to further personal investigation.

Find your muse and practice your craft. We need your medicine in the world.

STEP 3: ACTIVATE AGAIN

I had a client once tell me that he had a night-long sweat lodge experience where he shape-shifted into a black panther and stalked his prey in the jungle. When I expressed my astonishment and asked about his next sweat lodge session, he said, "Oh, I haven't done another one. That was 23 years ago."

Like going to a tropical island for a much-needed rest, keep returning for more. Find other modalities that turn on your spiritual senses. Keep mining your hidden stories and past lifetimes. You are the most interesting person you will ever meet. I guarantee it. If you think other people have deeper or more vivid journeys than you, come back to your lane and spiral deeper into your own interior. All the answers are inside you, waiting to open like an infinite line of gift boxes.

And if you are my Marcelene or The Spartan, come find me. I'm flying through time and space looking for you. Although reunited in spirit, I'm looking for you embodied, my beloved.

I'm Atlantis Wolf, and I believe in you.

Atlantis Wolf is a Shamanic Life Coach, workshop leader, and author who helps people heal using licensed medical massage techniques, emotional release therapy, and spiritual guidance. Her joy is helping people discover their personal power by walking with them into their interior labyrinths, dark castles, and hidden stories. She's available for podcast interviews, retreats, and public speaking events.

Atlantis grew up on a single-lane dirt road, sure her mother was an angel in human form, whistling to birds and asking herself one question: What am I supposed to be doing on Earth? She continues to walk into the forest at sunrise in all weather to ask that question every day.

She holds dual degrees in Civil Engineering and English with a minor in Environmental Engineering. She has worked as a civil engineer, technical writer, business analyst, project manager, licensed massage therapist, certified Emotion Code practitioner, marketing consultant, and entrepreneur.

She is a Shamanic Breathwork Facilitator and Ordained Shamanic Minister by Linda Star Wolf, founder of Venus Rising Association for Transformation and certified as a Reiki Master by William Lee Rand, founder of the International Center for Reiki Training.

She was spiritually asleep until events around her mother's death awakened her gifts to see and communicate with spiritual beings, power animals, and galactic dragons, remembering her past lives as an Egyptian healer, Toltec curandera, and Ayurvedic traveling shaman. She is the Dragon Medicine Woman.

Atlantis is an Aquarian, a single mom to four kids, three cats, and a hot cocoa connoisseur. She lives on Turtle Island.

Web: AtlantisWolf.com

Email: DragonMedicineWoman@gmail.com

Instagram: @DragonMedicineWoman

YouTube: Atlantis Wolf

CHAPTER 5

THE GIFTS OF FRIDA'S GARDEN

THE STEWARDSHIP OF LIMB LOSS AND POST TRAUMATIC GROWTH

Michelle A. McFarland CRM, CMT

MY STORY

Oh, that poor dear.

Floating in space and time, I instinctively recognized the unfolding in the scene beneath me. I'd seen enough TV to know that the girl, lying in her hospital bed below, was in deep trouble. Her swollen, bruised, and disheveled body was lying still, her remaining clumps of hair caked with a mixture of dried blood and red dirt. Her neck elongated, held in position by a thick coiled brace. Bloated arms strapped to the bed, legs akimbo suspended in the air. Her poor legs, the left, bent at an odd angle wrapped in a cast, and the right, half of it gone. What remained was a stump, bound heavily with a combination of bandage and tape, her bed surrounded by a team of doctors and her mother—a mix of terror and desolation etched into her face.

"We're gonna count to three, and when we do, I want you to take a deep breath, then cough."

This is just like TV. That poor girl is fucked.

I could see that this unfortunate female had been through a catastrophe. They were preparing her body for extubation. When the count concluded, they would pull the tube lodged in her throat that had kept her in suspended animation for five days.

"One."

I sensed I was witnessing the beginning of her transition, the clumsy preparation of her broken body to resume its operation.

"Two."

I took a deep breath in support of her soul from my observation point high above in the corner of the room.

"Three!"

In that cringeworthy moment, I was no longer the ethereal observer. As the tube was pulled, I could feel it rake and scrape my esophagus. I violently aggregated back into my physical body with a choke and gasp. I am that unfortunate female. As if a marionette, my glass skeleton excruciatingly stretched and suspended, unceremoniously welcomed back into the world— my spirit, thrown into a new domain of excruciating pain and unslakable thirst. I was confused and horrified. I was immediately flooded with terror, disbelief, and uninvited remembrances of the accident, the week before.

My nightmare began with a scream. I jolted awake from my position in the back seat, witnessed the tilt of the horizon through the front window, then felt weightlessness. Next came the endless pounding wash cycle of the slow-motion roll-over and over.

Oh shit, this is happening! Fuck! This is bad. Holy fuck! When will this stop?

Our possessions were suspended in the air as they rattled about the cabin. The screech of twisting metal, the shattering of glass and bone, the tearing of my skin, and the splintering of my existence as the truck bounced and slid to a stop, upside down, more than 300 feet off-road on the flat desert floor. My waking memory as my eyes opened to a red swirling cloud of dust was a mouth full of crunchy dirt, gasps for clean air, and complete silence. A scan of my twisted body revealed only paralysis and pain. I couldn't determine my orientation—only that I was clinging to consciousness, mortally wounded, and trapped in the wreckage of the truck, unable to move, concerned I'd been left behind.

Where is everyone?

"Hello?"

Maybe I can try to move to help myself untangle from my position. How could they leave me here?

"Hello!"

Nothing.

Surely Joe and Kendall would never leave me. They must have gone for help.

"Hello! I'm here!"

Just then, I sensed movement. I wasn't abandoned at all. My sweet angel of mercy, Kendall, appeared as if an apparition, reaching toward me, her outstretched hand piercing the veil to reach mine.

"I'm here, Michelle. I'm with you."

"Oh, thank God! And Joe? Where's he?"

"He didn't make it."

No! This isn't happening.

There in the middle of the desert, the post-crash portal dissolved, my happy-go-lucky life faded to black.

In that hospital bed, my first few minutes of new consciousness were stark and filled with desolation, my mouth caked with residue—red clay from the desert floor. I tried to speak, but nothing came out. From my view, I could see the many concerned faces peering back at me, trying to give words to my lips. It was a cacophony of confusion. None of the helpful suggestions were anywhere near close to my immediate need.

I'm thirsty! Why can't you understand? Can't you read my lips? Wouldn't you be thirsty too?

I tugged against the bed rail and implored the group with my eyes. I tried motioning to drink in several ways, all the while mouthing "thirsty!"

Understand me. I'm fucking thirsty!

The doctor agreed to loosen my restraints, a whiteboard thrust in front of me, a pen placed in my hand. I scribbled the word "thirsty" or tried to at least and then observed their confusion as they tried to decipher what I had written. As the second hand continued to sweep the clock, my mother stepped forward.

"Michelle, do you want water?"

Yes, please, yes! Water!

There was much conversation. Water wouldn't be allowed. Instead, I was presented with a sponge-tipped stick, dipped in water, then inserted into my mouth and swirled around, the dampening followed by suction. It was a small win, several swirls of the stick followed by hoovering ensued, and then my clarifications began with a coarse whisper.

"Is it true? Is Joe dead?"

"Yes, you've been in an accident. He did not make it. Your leg has been removed. You are in traction, have a crushed hip and shattered pelvis. Tomorrow you will have another surgery."

"Will I walk again?"

"I don't know."

My life was over, replaced by a cavernous sinkhole of death and loss. I could do nothing but surrender. I had heard and experienced enough.

Today fills me with curiosity and anticipation. A special day indeed. I'm enjoying my 12th year post-trauma, traveling in Mexico City on retreat and walking (yes walking) through the gates of Museo de la Casa Azul to commune with my Mentora en Dolor, my mentor in pain, Frida Kahlo. In case you don't know, Frida is globally revered for her art, turning her pain into purpose and her rebellious nature. She is also an amputee like me. Her spirit greets me at the gates.

"Welcome, Mija. I've been waiting for you. Come inside and make yourself at home."

As I step into her world, I'm captivated. How did she do it? How the hell did she thrive in 1940s era Mexico, with no accommodations, handicapped bathrooms or placards, hell—no sidewalks, no elevators! None of the modern medical support systems I rely on. Her replacement parts, braces, and medical contraptions were fabricated of wood, metal, and leather, and yet, she did it all, with strength and grace, wearing kick-ass, defiant, red leather boots adorned with colorful stitching and jingle bells. Amor!

In the first few galleries, her talent, diversity, and brokenness are celebrated. Intertwining expressions of her life give breath to young Frida, her family, her beloved Diego, and her connection to the natural world. Portraits of a seemingly whole-bodied Frida adorn the walls, each portrait more curious than the next. Her portraits suggest a woman with a secret. Brow topped gleaming eyes exude easy confidence, arms crossed, hands cradling her mid-drift. Perfect skin, rouged lips topped with a trace of mustache, simple embellishments of shell, and bone grace of her strong slender neck. Her braided hair, interwoven with purple yarn, adorns her head like a crown. There is zero hint of her pain and no illusion to the mantle of inadequacy of the physical handicap she is saddled with. Frida is a vision of strength and mystery; defiant of expectation, her legacy speaks to me—a collection of cultural ideals, artistic exploration, and socio-economic values.

I can't help but compare my post-trauma experience and feel a strong connection. As an independent woman, I have a world-class medical team, a strong and supportive family, and the most generous friends one could hope for. Yet still, in post-trauma shadows, I've struggled with depression, body dysmorphia, the queer comfort of self-isolation, and the sorrow and rage my cells hold. Grief and a deep sense of loss are constant companions. The carefree version of myself shelved—a voluminous collection of unfulfilled passions, hopes and desires. I grieve my inability to effortlessly rise to greet friends and family with a heartfelt hug, the feeling of sweat on my skin as I ecstatically dance, the spontaneity of skinny dipping, taking stairs two at a time, and invitations I'll never receive out of deference to my mobility. Above all, I mourn the absence of a confidant, someone with an organic understanding of the unique challenges that living in a continuum of recovery presents.

"Mija, this world was not made for people like us. We must carve our pathway. We have no choice but to adapt, to transform our pain and disembodiment into medicine that works for us. Do not be afraid. There will always be sacred universal support cradling you in your decisions, no matter how difficult they may be, as your Corazon Inmaculada continues to grow."

Intrinsically I accept there is no cure for what ails me. No one is coming to save me. I will never spontaneously grow a leg, and as I age, I imagine existing will only become more difficult. I am a healer and possess a rich toolbox to curate my evolutionary unfolding, I am an adolescent in my post-traumatic growth, and I have a lot of catching up to do! I peel back a new layer with each sunrise and greet the day with self-inquiry.

Where do I begin?

Living in the light of my post-trauma transcendence, I have an increased capacity to love and let go, a supremely deepened sense of gratitude, an increased sensitivity to detect and support others in their unique suffering, and a closer connection to spiritual realms. In the years of transitioning into my differently-abled worldview, I've embraced meditation, traveled the globe, climbed pyramids, walked on fire, explored the worlds of shamanic journeying, and risen to new heights personally and professionally—all through the unique lens of limb loss. I have come to know and channel the healing power of love and universal energy.

"Michaela, with intention, desire, and wholeheartedness, you will continue to grow in your capacity to be all things that have been intended for you on your earthbound journey. Each day you begin your walk of exploration anew, on your path into the unknown."

As I continue to move through the casa, each room holds more treasures: the kitchen with its wood-fired cooking counter and curio cabinets chock full of idols, dishes, and mementos. Frida's bedroom—a place of creation and transformation on so many levels with her bronze death mask resting in its rightful place atop her pillow, and at the foot of her bed a terracotta *urna funeraria* holding her cremains. Her studio—its tables topped with boxes of crushed metal paint tubes, glass bottles of pigment, brushes, and palettes, and her fabulous glitter collection. In position before her easel sits a mirror and a throne fit for a queen of generations, her oxidized metal wheelchair; two essential tools leveraged in the co-creation of her identity. The studio is her portal—its large white paned windows overlooking her magical garden, the centerpiece of Casa Azul.

As I step into the garden, I'm transported into Frida's interior world, her source of inspiration and safety, her doorway to transformation. Brightly painted blue walls, an expression of love, fortify the perimeter of this magical container. I see short stubby fan palms flourish atop a carpet of impatiens flowers, and thickets of bamboo stretch toward the sky. Untamed bougainvillea vines shimmy up the ramparts and tall palm trunks, incorrigible in their wildness, cascading sprays of fiery pink flowers as they climb. Plump geranium and lush fern co-mingle. The garden is alive with color and sound. I sense the energy and movement of Frida's menagerie, beloved playmates Xoloitzcuintle and spider monkey; trusted confidants, eagle, and fawn. Birds of paradise stretch their necks and sing to the sun. A red-light district of prickly nopal cacti showcases bulbous, engorged pinkish-red fruit. Bundles of spider plants spinning webs of variegating tendrils dangle from the limbs of the royal purple foliaged jacaranda trees. Unorganized placements of striped canna lily, tips bursting with sensuous eruptions of orange and fiery red seemingly kneel in deep repose before the steps of the courtyard pyramid, an altar laden with ceremonial artifacts of pre-Columbian Meso America. In pilgrimage to myself, I intentionally traverse the wide stone path, slowly soaking it all in; step by step, my holy longings become seeds as I meander the courtyard. I reach the fountain and sit in quiet contemplation. I gently close my eyes and feel a soft serenity wash over me. With imagination, I'm transported and presented with the gifts of Frida's garden, her portal of transformation.

"Hola Chiquita. Have some maize; the ducks love it."

Frida places a hand full of colorful corn kernels in my outstretched palm.

"You've intuited my secret; the garden is where I come to disassemble. I feed my sorrows to the water and watch the ripples of regeneration give birth to nuevo sueños. You too must feed your seeds with your sorrow, unworthiness, and self-doubt, whisper your holy longings into these kernels with love and kindness, and watch them sprout and mature into magnificent creations. Till and fertilize your soil thoughtfully, mi Chiquita, infuse it directly from your open heart, caress and massage the earth as a lover's body ripe with anticipation. Plant seeds of joy and happiness, adore your seeds of resurrection and strength, and water them daily with intention. Your interior garden is your haven, your dream world. A place where spirit speaks encouragement when the grip of pain and darkness falls.

Listen to the slow and constant motion of growth here and know that you are growing too. The answers to your curiosities lie in the garden of your sacred heart, but you must be still enough to receive this wisdom. Listen closely to the whispers of the flora as they speak in tongues encouraged by the wind, then harvest your sueños with zest! Greet each day with wonder, take each glorious step with intention and above all Chiquita, Viva la Vida!"

THE MEDICINE

Dear reader, you are about to embark on a journey, a Curative Art Process (CAP). To begin, gather supplies: Paper, canvas, paint, brushes, pastels, pencils, crayons, collage items, glue. Anything you can creatively leverage to give birth to your experience. Give yourself the gift of time and find a quiet space in which to practice.

Get comfortable in any position that works best for you. Gently close your eyes. Begin with a few slow deep breaths, in through your nose, out through your mouth, allowing your body to release any tension. Let the weight of your body be fully supported as you continue to breathe and relax.

Imagine yourself walking slowly along a path. It's a pleasant path, any kind that you wish. It's a beautiful day, and you feel relaxed and happy. Soon you come upon a gate. This gateway leads to a special place where you feel welcomed, safe, and comfortable. Push the gate open and allow yourself to enter. As you cross the threshold, you step into an enchanted garden. Visualize and observe the colors and objects that surround you. Feel the gentle rays of warm sunlight filter through the canopy above. Everything peacefully co-exists in this place.

You're encouraged forth by the gentle call of birdsong, each step an invitation of discovery. Begin to explore with your senses and know that you can travel the world in as little as an acre. What do you see? Strong, bold colors and shapes? Muted combinations of soft light? Fluid silhouettes? Are edibles ripe for the picking? What will you harvest when the time is right?

Continue to take deep rhythmic breaths as you commune with your unique oasis of extraordinary beauty and peace. Everything in this place grows exactly as you wish. Here is your eternal garden; you cultivate the bond between your inner and outer worlds. Connectedness to this space provides a foundation to grow your dreams and intentions.

Continue forward now; in the next few steps, you come upon a bench at the foot of a fountain.

On the bench sits a basket of colorful seeds, awaiting your intent. Plant your seeds in the earth beneath you, imbue them with your dreams and longings of transformation. Each seed gives birth to inspiration, sow these seeds of exploration and curiosity, fertilize them with your unique and diverse viewpoint. Spend the time here that is necessary for you to rejuvenate and self-care.

Slowly walk back through the garden towards the open gate when you are ready. There you are returned to the path that led you to this place of contentment. As you make your way back upon the path to the here and now, remember you can return to your private refuge to harvest your seeds of love and hope any time you wish. Take another deep inhalation, and as you exhale, open your eyes.

It's time to begin your Curative Art Process by bringing your garden to the page. Use your art supplies to recreate your vision. You don't have to be an artist to bring your visualization to the page—do your best and allow your intuition and creativity to guide you. Give life to your dream garden or interior world, manifest and refer to it often. There are no rules. This is your perfect vision, the garden of your imagination. You can complete this process as many times as you like.

Suggested CAP Modifications: Record the CAP Garden script above for guided playback. Add background music or solfeggio frequencies to journey by. These frequencies can unlock and unblock clogged energy or stabilize overactive energetics.

Michelle A. McFarland CRM, CMT. A lifelong seeker and intuitive empath born and raised in the heart of California's wine country, Michelle's unique journey includes turning personal tragedy into active integrative healing. Through the lens of limb loss, she seeks to balance the challenges of survivorship with the gifts of her personal death experience. Her transpersonal exploration continues to illuminate and inform her deeper understanding of attaining full aliveness through experiential practice and philosophies influenced by the Shamanic wisdom of the North and Central America's indigenous oral traditions, coupled with Ancient East Indian Buddhist, Vedic, Hindu, and Yogic meditative spiritual practices. As founder of Shaman's Apothecary Healing Arts, Michelle shares her love and knowledge of ancient, esoteric, and mystical realms in addition to intuitive hands-on therapeutic healing of body, mind, and spirit through modalities including but not limited to; Mastership Usui Reiki, guided Shamanic, meditative and Curative Art journeys, and breathwork facilitation.

When not working or dreaming into her next adventure, you can typically find her holding court around a campfire, somewhere along the California coastline, sharing laughter and a habanero margarita with her friends and her trusty terrier Gracie by her side.

Interact with her on these platforms:
Website: www.shamansapothecary.com
Instagram: @shaman_michelle
Email: shamansapothecary@gmail.com

CHAPTER 6

HEARTBREAK TO HEART WARRIOR

EMBRACING THE STRENGTH AND WISDOM WITHIN

Carley Mattimore, MS, LCPC

MY STORY

What? You want me to go to South Africa? To the White Lions? What do you want of me? How can I help? I don't know what to do. I don't have the money. I can't do that!

The messages were clear, but the doubts, insecurities, and fears came vigorously, challenging my expanded growth.

We were wedged together in this small holy room with shamanic statues of Isis, Anubis, drums, feathers, and talking sticks. We were body next to body, seekers diving deep into our pain to bring it up for transformation. The speaker was the renowned Andrew Harvey, a mystic and scholar.

I listened closely and clung to every word this gregarious man said. I extracted every nugget of wisdom for survival during the dark times he predicted were unfolding on the planet. It was also a call to action, a mandate to stand as warriors of truth, to support our earth during its dismantling. It was October 2011.

I sat on the floor in the small sanctuary, right up in front, close, personal, and within inches of the speaker who stood as he delivered his message. My knees, as I sat cross-legged, almost touched his shoes. Andrew paused before calling on me, my hand raised high, ready, and poised to share when he mentioned the White Lions of Timbavati.

Then, he called on me, "Yes, you."

Energy like a bolt of lightning sprung from his energetic field into my heart, blasting it. Great sobs of grief came tumbling out of me. A flood of tears, snot, and animal-like sounds erupted from somewhere deep within my core.

For days, when I connected with my heart, I felt gut-wrenching pain as more tears flowed out of me. In a Shamanic Breathwork process, I received a clear directive from the White Lions and Maria Khosa, Lion-Queen of Timbavati, to come to South Africa to meet with the lions. In my vision, I experienced the horror and pain of their capture. I experienced the terror they felt at being imprisoned in a canned camp, waiting to be shot by a trophy hunter who paid as much as a hundred thousand dollars to kill the king of beasts.

A canned camp is a horrific, for-profit industry where lions (and other animals) are socialized and raised to be shot and killed for sport. In my breathwork, the medicine woman, Maria, assisted me in the healing necessary to embark on this next part of my journey and soul purpose.

Before this awakening, I reluctantly signed up for the Shamanic Healing Initiatory Process (SHIP) in March 2011. SHIP is a month-long training program to become a certified Shamanic Breathwork facilitator to fulfill a vision my husband John Malan had in 2005. Little did I know opening the door to my own dark, dense energy of repressed pain would facilitate the flow of channels within me. The cleared pathways in my energetic body would allow me to hear the messages from my soul, encouraging me to step into a higher octave of my sacred purpose.

I experienced the traumatic loss of those I loved and still love. I was 20 years old when my father and 13-year-old sister died in a car and semi accident. My beloved husband died in an automobile accident nine years later, leaving me with two small children to raise.

I worked with the profound grief stored in my body as other wounds from childhood came bubbling to the surface to examine, feel, release, and let go. Many stories, beliefs, and patterns developed through the lens of not being good, powerful, or smart enough, keeping me small and contained.

I began to understand a new reality and a new story using Shamanic Breathwork and other modalities, including ritual, teachings, bodywork, writing, guided meditation, group processing, art, etc. This work supported my body, mind, and Spirit in transforming pain into purpose. I moved dense, tar-like energy in my body and my kundalini life force energy soon moved through me like a fountain.

The doubts were still challenging the uncertain-but-demanding calling growing within me.

Who do you think you are? You aren't enough! You aren't strong enough, brave enough, smart enough, or good enough!

This was not the first time I had a breakdown and break-through moment. Many years earlier, I was faced with a second big trauma.

A man asked, "Ms. Mattimore, can I come in?"

"No, I don't know you."

"I am the coroner. There has been an accident."

I paused ever so briefly and said, "My husband?"

"Yes."

"He's dead?"

"Yes."

It was 1985 when I received the knock at my front door, where a middle-aged heavy-set, dark-haired man in a frumpy suit stood solemnly. I had opened the door a crack.

I crumpled inside instantly, a wail of pain forming into a mass of raw emotion surging through me in the guttural scream of death. Our four-year-old daughter ran down the stairs, with her friend, to see what happened.

"Mommy, did Sherah bite you?" Our one-year-old daughter was still nursing. I gently responded, "No, honey, there has been a car accident. Your daddy died."

She said, "Mommy, no, can't the ambulance put him back together?"

Each cataclysmic moment is just that, a moment out of time and space. They set life in motion for the next part of my journey. I live it and walk through it, gathering pieces of my experience to guide me on my path. The unprocessed grief from my traumatic experiences of loss was stored in the crevices of my body, lodged in between conscious and unconscious memory.

My heart closed just a little bit more. I tucked my pain away in secret compartments of my being until the time was right for me to excavate and transform the suffering to deepen my service work in the world.

Thus, when the lions called, I went into a deep process. I faced my resistance and fear, moved through it to come out on the other side, and found trust. I now hear my trusted friend, mentor, and guide, Mandaza Kandemwa's wise words, "If you are called, you must go." A soul's directive is a big deal. We always have a choice. Not listening can cause one to retract and shut down.

Every action has a purpose. I surrendered and signed up for Andrew Harvey's Warriorship Trip to the Global White Lion Protection Trust in April 2012. I found myself at the Drakensberg mountains in what can only be understood as a magical moment. They are also referred to as the Dragon Mountains in South Africa and are located on the 31st Meridian, the sacred spine of the continent of Africa.

It was on April 16th, the 36th anniversary of my father and sister's death.

The year previously, I performed a ritual where I pulled a dragon out of the cave, which represented a lost soul aspect of myself that went into the darkness to cope with this trauma. It was a reclamation of the pain I stuffed deep inside of me. As I did this, I sang "Puff the Magic Dragon."

Now sitting in the back of the van, a year later, my fellow journeyers spontaneously sang, "Puff the Magic Dragon." I wept with the symbolism and healing that enveloped me.

Later, as I lay on a concrete table in a small enclosure on White Lion land in the Heartlands of Timbavati, an intuitive bodyworker asked me if I was feeling any blocks in my body.

I said, "Maybe my sacral area as I am having some digestive issues."

As he placed his hands on my body, he exclaimed, "There is so much power in your sacral! It's not closed; it's your heart that is blocked."

He said, "The passion and power in your sacral are coming up through your body but stopping at the heart. Instead, it's going down your arms carrying the imprint: "Why bother no one listens anyway?"

I tried to argue with him. "But my heart is open!"

He said, "A crack in the heart can feel so big."

It was the beginning, and I knew it to be true. The warrior within had given up her power through lifetimes of pain and suffering, detached and resigned to her fate.

When I expressed this imprint on the last day of my warrior's training, the message I took away was: *It doesn't matter whether anyone listens or not. You must speak your truth. And you must always pass this truth through the heart.*

Through seven trips to the White Lions during almost the same number of years, I followed my soul's calling to each next step in the journey of my inner warrior. Each of my visits to Africa expanded my understanding of why I was called to Africa and the significance for each of us to do our healing work to transform personal and collective trauma.

Cataclysmic and synchronistic moments and deep psycho-spiritual work with my pain ushered in a new vision of my work. From this place of deep healing, I proclaimed the truth of who I am: *I am a warrior of truth, love, and light.*

I'm here to be of service to the personal and collective transformation of pain, the unprocessed grief stored in both humanity's and the Earth's bodies.

This includes a comprehensive understanding of the role of the heart-centered shamanic warrior born from transcended pain. This evolution enables us to return to wholeness and grow boundaries from the inside out as individuated, unique, authentic, heart-centered beings. Only then can we know and operate from an interdependent model supporting each other and all of nature.

This is the way.

THE MEDICINE

I would like to offer you an integration ritual for your heart warrior within. One that not only holds the truth of who you are but has the courage and conviction to guide you to your next right step as you put it into action, following your own soul's guidance.

Humans have used rituals for many thousands of years to put our intentions into the world for the Great Mystery to hear (you can substitute your own higher power's name). Rituals are the sacred container for our dreams, helping them come into manifestation. In this cauldron, they gestate and give birth to the holy of holies, the creative life force energy of creation.

The intention of this ritual is to connect with our inner heart warrior to ask for guidance and support so we can access our inner wisdom, strength, and courage to say "yes" to the call when it comes. This is also to find the strength and wisdom to digest, process, and move through our cataclysmic moments, feel them fully, ask for assistance from seen and unseen worlds, know we are never alone, and walk through them.

You will need the following items for your ritual:

- A ceremonial cloth.
- Something to hold the space for the Four Directions: East/Air: Feathers, South/Fire: Candle, West/Water: Bowl of water, North/ Earth: Plant or soil (other items that represent the elements can be used, of course.)
- Something to hold the space of the Great Above and Great Below or Heaven and Earth: (example: stars for the Great Above, a globe for the Great Below.)
- Something to hold the space of the Great Within: Half of a small melon (seeds removed) and a spoon.
- Offerings for your Inner Heart Warrior: These can be things like rice, juice or beer, small candies, egg, tobacco, herbs, etc. Let the spirit guide you to what these should be. These can be placed in small bowls.

To prepare for your ritual:

You can perform this ritual either inside or outside. Chose a space and a time where you will be uninterrupted and can go inward into a sacred connection with your Inner Heart Warrior. It is recommended that you smudge the area with sage or another sacred plant to clear the space for your ritual. You can also do this through intention.

- Lay your cloth down in front of you.
- Place the four things representing the four elements of air, fire, water, and earth on your cloth in the direction they represent, East, South, West, and North. Light your candle.
- Place the Great Above and Great Below items on your cloth, centered above and below.
- Place your melon to represent you and your heart warrior in the center of your cloth. Place the spoon next to your melon.
- Place your offerings in front of you in their small bowls.

Sit comfortably in a meditation pose, close your eyes, and go inward. Take three deep breaths in through your nose and out through your mouth. On the inhale, bring in life force energy to your heart space, and on the exhale, breathe out any congestion, fear, doubt, or blocks. Begin to open your heart space more and more with each inhale and exhale. Connect now with your heart warrior, the part of you that feels and hears the truth within, your inner knowing, and is ready to act for your next right step.

When you feel you have a connection with the Sacred open your eyes and use your spoon to carve out a piece of the melon and eat it, it represents your willingness to connect with the flesh of our inner warrior. Remember to chew slowly and deliberately, savoring the sweetness of your connection to your warrior within.

Take a pinch of one of your offerings, for example, the tobacco, and place it inside the melon. With each offering, say a prayer or intention personal to you. Allow yourself to be open to Spirit's guidance to heal your heart and help you on your journey. Do this with as many prayers as you feel called to offer, holding reverence with each offering.

Take your melon bowl in both hands and lift it up to Great Mystery when you feel complete.

Breathe in gratitude, return the melon to your cloth, place your hands on your heart, and smile to complete your ritual.

Now take the melon with the offerings and place it somewhere special. It can be outdoors under a tree, on a riverbank, in your compost pile, wherever it can be offered up to the Great Mystery and released through being eaten by wild creatures and its decomposition process.

Click the link below to witness this ceremony.

https://youtu.be/MMfW80QyEp8

Carley Mattimore is a psycho-spiritual midwife supporting the birth of a New Humanity as a warrior of the heart, psychotherapist, and healer. She is co-author of Sacred Messengers of Shamanic Africa, a book about her personal transformation and awakening to a bigger story for humanity, Earth, and Cosmos. Her upcoming book is on the new paradigm unfolding for the heart-centered warrior.

Carley and her husband, John Malan, are co-founders of Aahara Spiritual Community of Venus Rising in the Heartland of Springfield, Illinois. She is a shamanic minister, master shamanic breathwork facilitator, White Lion Leadership Academy graduate, and Lion-hearted Leadership practitioner. She is a Healing Touch practitioner and Shamanic, Usui & Tibetan Reiki Master.

Carley leads psycho-spiritual workshops, including her new signature program, birthed through the development of her own warrior, called the Shamanic Warriorship Path. It is a new paradigm of warrior energy for these times.

Carley and Judith Corvin-Blackburn also facilitate a Shamanic Multidimensional Mystery School: Becoming a 5th Dimensional Being on Earth. Other workshops include the Shamanic Healing Initiatory Process (SHIP) and Shamanic, Usui & Tibetan Reiki Training.

Carley loves giving inspirational talks sharing her passion and supporting clients' and groups' personal transformation using a shamanic understanding.

Carley and her husband are spiritual adventurers who offer transformational journeys to sacred sites in Africa along the 31st Meridian for personal and collective transformation.

Carley is the mother of five strong and independent daughters in a blended family and grandmother of eight wonderful grandchildren. She lives with her husband John and their two cats. She loves to garden, be in nature, make wholesome food, travel, and connect with people all over the world.

To learn more about Carley Mattimore, click below.

Website:
https://www.carleymattimore.com/
https://www.aaharaspiritualcommunity.org/

Facebook:
https://www.facebook.com/carley.mattimore
https://www.aaharaspiritualcommunity.org/

Instagram:
https://www.instagram.com/carleymattimore
https://www.instagram.com/aaharaspiritualcommunity

Other links/resources:
https://www.youtube.com/channel/UCx-JuWpNNUcrvdr0ap-TNUQ

CHAPTER 7

SOUL WEAVING

HEAL ANCESTRAL TRAUMA THROUGH CHANNELED AWARENESS

Dr. Ruth A. Souther, Hypnotherapist, Spiritual Counselor

MY STORY

"I don't know who I am," I sobbed. "I don't know *what* I am."

The wail tore out of me from the depths of my core as tears poured down my face. It was the first honest thing I said to the circle of people now staring at me. My face flamed with embarrassment for those tears. I'm not a crier, and yet I could not stop the flow.

The mirror cracked, and awareness oozed out.

I am lost in the arctic tundra with no compass or map to guide the way. I am overwhelmed with painful loneliness and bitter cold. My nose bleeds from the sting of harsh winds, and all I can smell is. . .nothing. My uncovered flesh aches and is unmoving. I see nothing except blinding snow.

"Awwoooooo. Awwoooooo." I release a primal howl, one last call to my people. No one answers. Grief crushes me from the inside out.

I face my own death, abandoned and afraid. I can only surrender. I fall face first into frozen oblivion.

When I woke up, I was lying on the floor with those same concerned folk gathered around me. Each reached out to touch me, hold my hand, or stroke my hair and fevered face. Dizzy and confused, I made my way back to my chair with their help.

What just happened?

My soul told me who I was in no uncertain terms. And it wasn't a little midwestern white girl raised in a rural Methodist church. I didn't know what to do with this manifestation. *Was it even real? Had I hallucinated? Had I been hypnotized? Under a spell? Why did this feel familiar?* I remembered that dying woman as if I had lived her life and her death.

I took a chance with that long-ago class. The language was scary but brought shivers of excitement and a strange, thrilling recognition. The teacher spoke of breathtaking concepts:

"Magic is simply changing your consciousness at will. Your intention is everything, and yet, you must do the work, or it's an empty prayer."

Prayer had always meant asking for help from some invisible, omnipotent being. It was never about creating possibilities or living my truth. It was about taking handouts if God felt generous that day.

"The Akashic archives, the records of your past lives, are open to you," the teacher continued. "All that you've ever lived, and all you will ever live are within your reach when you learn to shift your conscious awareness."

The teacher told stories of past lives and retrieved memories from the edges of the collective unconscious. She brought forth an aching desire from my heart of hearts. The message was terrifying but crystal clear. To quote from The Charge of the Goddess (by Doreen Valiente, Starhawk adapted version):

And you who seek to know Me, know that the seeking and yearning will avail you not unless you know the Mystery: for if that which you seek, you find not within yourself, you will never find it without.

The Mystery.

"I *am* the mystery," I spoke the words aloud, my voice filled with awe.

I felt dizzy. Events began to make sense. I've always had flashes of other existences. I thought I just made them up. The stories came in dreams, both day and night. They weren't all sad; some were funny, and some profound. Some presented ancient rituals honoring the Earth, and others touched realms beyond my imagination.

Magic became both real and surreal. The portals to other times opened, and strange things happened. To say I had no fear would be a lie.

Although the confusion did not cease in that moment, I began to understand the concept of lost pieces of soul returning home. It turned out that it wasn't always my past lives I saw but others who needed to speak. Unconsciously, I invited these energies and memories to use my body as a conduit. This is called channeling in some circles, possessed in others, and ultimately became my soul purpose.

Long ago, in the hills of Missouri, another woman stepped into me. I was taken by surprise and could only let her anguish pour through me. Her tears fell from my eyes, and she spoke through my lips. It was a language I had never heard, and those with me, even the experienced facilitators, were worried. I could hear them asking if I was okay, but I could only respond as this unknown female.

Some of her language was clear: "No, no. . .please. . .help. . ."

The plea was not for herself but her family. Her agony was heart-wrenching, and yet there was nothing I could do but let her shrieks be heard. Her pain was visceral; I felt every bit of it. Her people were tortured and murdered, and I relived all of it. I wept and screamed and beat my fists on the ground to no avail. It repeated the horrors of my vision in the arctic circle.

Was she me in a different time? Or had I always been her, now in a different body? In the moment, it didn't matter.

I spoke in faltering English, pouring out my terror. My wrists and ankles are torn open and bleeding from the ropes. I could no longer stand. The ugly scent of death is in my nostrils. Despite my begging, I was dragged through mud and coarse grass. Finally, the strain was too much, and I gave up. I died.

This time I didn't ask what it was. I knew it was a soul memory, and another piece clicked in. I realized then it was my duty to invoke the past. From that point on, I decided to make it a conscious invitation.

During a mystery school event in Missouri, I summoned Lilith, an ancient goddess who once walked the Earth as a human. I expected wicked joy and the freedom to exist under my own rule. I thought I would be empowered and dripping with rich layers of newfound authority.

But no. Lilith, too, was grief-stricken. She was meant to birth the human population and couldn't fulfill that duty. Everyone misunderstood her flight into the desert. She was ashamed, dishonored, and humiliated, so she fled and was blamed for everything. Once again, I railed against the dark powers, cried, and cursed until I was wrung out and left an empty shell.

I failed. I cannot exist within these bounds. My heart aches with the lost souls of my children. I wept as staggering grief overtook me. I could barely walk with the weight. My body hunched over, and my eyes blurred. I prayed it would be the end of me, so I might be with my little ones. But, alas, such was not the will of Gaia. I survived.

Lilith did not die like the others. She gathered herself bit by bit to overcome her tragedy. She gained strength and power and became the voice for those too weak to speak for themselves. She became my patron goddess. To this day, she empowers me to do my work in the world. She is fierce, dynamic, and funny. Was it because I offered her my voice? Possibly. There is no doubt she continues to be heard.

As I recovered the core of my spirit through the essence of channeled wisdom, I realized why I'd never been in harmony with my surroundings. Human pain is ancient. It collects in the unconscious, and somehow, somewhere, through someone—through every willing and courageous heart—it must be healed. The bubble must burst and bleed and finally scab over to restore the balance of humanity.

I found my tribe then, and they've reappeared over and over whenever I'm in need. I trace the patterns of the Earth with my feet and trust my intuition that I'll be led to the right place. Soul magic has never failed me.

This is both my pain and my purpose. It's my passion. It's who I am. It's what I am. This gift of channeling other energies humbles me, and I freely offer it out.

I experienced being out of sync with others for most of my life. It seemed I was dancing to a beat no one else could hear. I didn't connect, even though I did a good job of faking it. I didn't think I was heard or, if heard, was greatly misunderstood. It was alienating and painful to speak a symbolic language. Half the time, I didn't even know what I meant.

The right words were just out of reach, and the concepts were hidden in the recesses of my mind. The sensation felt like a cartoon character trying to run fast and getting nowhere. Nothing fit, as if I was wearing an itchy sweater that should be ripped off and thrown aside.

If you have ever felt this way for any reason, there are deeper mysteries waiting to be discovered. Healing those lost parts is critical, whether they're in your ancestral DNA or another reality reaching out. In the Medicine section, I've provided one method to support you in connecting, or reconnecting, to ancient wisdom.

THE MEDICINE

Heal ancestral traumas through soul weaving.

If possible, record this meditation in your voice with soft music in the background. Allow pauses to happen naturally and add more words as they come to you. Listening to your voice is a powerful tool. I encourage you to do this to build confidence. Record as many times as necessary to get the rhythm of your voice. Give yourself time. Don't rush the process.

Find a quiet space, preferably darkened, where you can allow your body and mind to fully relax. Lying down is helpful but not necessary if that is uncomfortable. If you feel anxious with your eyes closed, concentrate on one spot. A corner where the ceiling meets the wall is ideal.

Listen to the music and permit yourself to drift. Let all other sounds in the room blend and fade away. Set aside any concerns. Let your mind go blank. Inhale slowly and exhale slowly. Allow this deep, slow breath to continue as long as you need. Each time let yourself sink deeper until you can imagine or remember your soul's story.

Now picture a gold thread attached to your center. This is your soul thread. Let it come forward from any part of you that is willing. Keep breathing and drifting as you feel the thread tighten. Feel it as it vibrates with life force. Hear the thrum as it connects to those who came before. Reach out and touch the thread. Let it guide you to another place and another time.

Feel secure and protected as you hold onto the thread—it will always bring you back. Know that you are safe, and all that you see is in a different time and place. You are here to bring healing energy. You are here to weave a new story. Your soul is here to weave magic, release old wounds, and bring peace to the ancestral realm.

Breathe. Call to the ancestor who wishes to appear.

Breathe. Do not judge who emerges from the mists of time.

Breathe. See that person form in front of your eyes.

Notice the details. Female, or male, or neither?

What clothing are they wearing? Any jewelry?

What does their hair look like? Is there a hat or head covering?

Can you see colors? If so, what are they?

Breathe in their scent. Let it inform you about this presence.

Do you have a sense of age? Of the time you are in?

Ask if you may place your hand on their chest. Wait for permission.

Invite them to place their hand on yours.

Synchronize with them—pulse with the beat of their heart.

Connect on the soul level of trust. Let them know you are here for them.

Allow the current of emotions to begin. Notice the strongest sensations. What are you feeling? If there are tears, let them flow. Release any sounds that may bubble up.

Commune with this person.

Ask questions.

Hear the response.

Ask if they will receive healing energy from you. If they are willing, offer comfort and love.

Open yourself to receive the same from them.

Weave your stories together.

Let the fabric of life be restored to its full beauty. Let it become strong and flexible.

Keep this link open with them until you have completed the soul weaving.

Now take a deep breath. Slowly and gently pull your hand away from your ancestor's heart. Give gratitude for all you have learned. Thank them for receiving your healing. Accept any appreciation in return.

You see your ancestor fading back into the mists, and you know you must return to this time and this space. There are others waiting to see you, but not now. Not in this visit. It is time to return.

Follow the gold thread back. Allow it to pull you into your physical body. See the thread as it winds back into your essence, preparing for your next journey.

Inhale. Exhale. Slowly bring your focus to the present. Open your eyes and blink a few times. Notice your surroundings. Feel the weight of your body. Wiggle your fingers and your toes.

When you are ready to sit up, be cautious until you are certain you are completely back from your journey.

As soon as possible, write down your experience. If there are missing pieces, they often appear later as you process, or in your dreams. Keep a journal handy for these moments of awareness.

Drink lots of water and eat grounding food—protein is good for bringing you all the way back. Rest, and give gratitude for the gift of your ancestors.

Dr. Ruth A. Souther is a Metaphysical & Natural Arts practitioner in Springfield, IL. She is a Hypnotherapist, a Master Shamanic Breathwork Facilitator with Aahara Spiritual Community, Master Reiki Practitioner, Ritualist and Minister. She holds a Masters in Shamanic Intuitional Practices and a Doctorate of Shamanic Psychospiritual Studies through Venus Rising University.

She has written The Heart of Tarot (an intuitive guide to the cards); Vega's Path: The Elemental Priestess/Reclaiming the Elemental Priest (a year-long process), and three novels: Death of Innocence, Surrender of Ego, and Rise of Rebellion. The fourth, Obsession of Love is forthcoming, as well as Vega's Path: The Universal Priestess.

Ruth is an Initiated Priestess through Diana's Grove and has taught with the Reclaiming Collective of San Francisco at Missouri and Texas Witch Camps. She has studied Tarot and Astrology since 1990, teaches classes in both subjects, and provides readings in person and online.

She created Vega's Path Priestess Process in 2012, designing it with her personal spiritual and elemental experiences as a guide. She is a facilitating member of The Edge of Perception (public ritual/ceremony collective) and The Sanctuary of Formative Spirituality, a NFP church.

Ruth is a contributing author and board member/Chief Editor of Crystal Heart Imprints—an independent co-operative press that supports and guides both authors and artists in their creative projects. She is a facilitator/teacher at Naked Magik, an annual celebration of metaphysical practitioners, authors, and artists.

Reach Ruth at 217-341-2768 or ruthsouther52@gmail.com

www.vegaspath.com

www.facebook.com/vegaspath

www.formativespirituality.org

www.facebook.com/relaxedstateofmind

www.aaharaspiritualcommunity.org

www.crystalheartimprints.com

www.facebook.com/crystalheartimprints.com

www.nakedmagik.com

CHAPTER 8

THE REFLECTIVE VEIL

WAIT UNTIL YOU MEET YOURSELF

Robin Friend

Before reading my chapter, I want you to know you are whole. In life, you're embarking on a journey of uncharted travels. Your final destination is undoubtedly guaranteed by the Divine, by life itself—whether in this lifetime or the next, you will reach your destination. Trust, courage, and most of all, love are tools you'll want to keep with you. May they become your eternal companions. Shadows linger at the curves of your path, yet you'll travel on. You are brave. You're transforming fear into a charge that empowers you in the name of Divine Love. You, my friend, are turning pain into purpose.

MY STORY

There she is. Steadfast and determined. Her eyebrows angled at the curves of her face. Furrowed and fierce, each tiny hair strand carefully following an invisible template forming a mountainous peak above each eye. Are her eyebrows reaching for the sky? I dare stare into the deep intensity of her wise eyes as they penetrate my being. She holds her gaze without a flinch, without skipping a beat in the rhythm of her heart, without a shadow of doubt present. How does she do this and be me?

Studying the image I see in the mirror leaves me in awe. Can I reach through the reflective veil and join you there long enough to learn your grace and confidence? I can be you since I am you. Right? Can I be that fearless goddess in the mirror?

I'd spent hours talking through my upcoming dream job interview during a stellar performance of mirror role-play starring me and the fearless goddess I could pass for. I was beginning to feel as steady as she who looked back at me with a soft encouraging smile. *Oh yeah, we've got this!* Just one more practice question before calling it a night. "What qualities do you feel you'll contribute to this role that best reflect your leadership?"

My Apple watch rings suddenly. "Who's calling this late?" *Incoming call from. . ."*Me?"

Puzzled and curious how I'd managed to call myself, I answered, "Hello." No response. "Hello?" The line remained open, yet still no reply. After eleven seconds, it disconnects. "I wonder what that was all about?" The solicited response met me from within; *Everything is going to be okay.* The hairs on my arms stood straight up in the air as the antenna of my physical body received the loaded message. Although, I had no idea what was in store.

Nine months later, I lay calmly in the bed, watching the clock tick. Looking around the room, I examined the patient information board hanging to my left. *Caring for others as we would care for those we love.* Alright, I was in good hands. *My comfort plan; My pain goal; What's important to me?* All three of those spaces were left empty on the board. No worries. I was confident I could comfort myself. I could manage pain. My motto was: *This will all be a memory one day.*

I researched and chose the best physician for my journey, and although he was gone for the holiday, I was confident all would go well. I'd recently committed to remaining ten steps ahead of any signs of instability. Since saying "yes" to this calling, my world toppled to and fro. It did not all go according to my carefully thought-out plan; we had an early scare in the beginning, bedrest followed, my twelve-year career ended abruptly. This has, by far, been the most demanding pregnancy of the four. I blamed it on the in-vitro fertilization meds (IVF).

I admit I was ready to complete my assignment as a gestational carrier. My body was ready. After dedicating my days to gladly spoiling my womb mate, I'd finally see his face and the joy of his mother once she held him. The unbearable-unless-I'm-sitting-up-while-sleeping heartburn would end. The inability to fit my foot in a shoe due to excessive swelling would go away, and I'd get to place my finger in the tiny hand of this precious being I've sung to, played Mandarin for, and carried inside of me. It was so peaceful being there with just the two of us. Our own little zen party before everyone arrived.

Hours later, I tightly closed my eyes and visualized the face of the fearless goddess I've known all of my life, staring back at me through the reflective veil. *I am her. She is me.* I squeezed the white sheets with sweaty hands, reminding myself to breathe despite the excruciating pain, and hearing my silent scream with each draw of air. *I am her. She is me.*

I turn to my sister-in-law and softly admit the inevitable, "Something is wrong. Call the anesthesiologist." A simple procedure was performed to speed up labor by manually breaking my water. The instrument used punctured me within. With every breath, I felt my womb ripping open, and for the first time, I felt my body broken. My sister-n-law stood in shock. I'd given birth to my three daughters without ever having the assistance of an epidural. Me rising off of the bed in pain during the procedure indicated what neither of us wanted—a complicated delivery.

Orders were entered. Time passed. Heart rates dropped. Monitors alarmed. Oxygen was provided. Through it all, the on-call physician continued to check my cervix like she was preparing the turkey for Thanksgiving dinner. Hand in. Hand out—no gentleness in sight. No empathy was found at the foot of my bed in this room gone cold and sterile. My body was taking too long, according to her demeanor. She stretched my cervix. I gripped the sheets. I could still feel my body failing the assignment to birth this little one.

She ordered to increase Pitocin administration—a synthetic version of oxytocin, the hormone the body naturally produces to induce contractions. I felt the massive earthquake of my womb and worried if my body would crack open under the pressure. There was a clear presence of tension that existed between her and other staff members. *Why me?* I mouthed. *Why not?* I had no logical answer for the voice within, so I again silenced myself. The nurse spoke on my behalf, and the on-call physician overruled us all with her unwavering authority. She walked out of what felt like the darkest of rooms with her head held high while I lay lost. Unseen, unheard, I disappeared into the invisible hollow of the hospital bed.

"PUSH!" The on-call physician bolted.

"I'm pushing."

"PUSH MORE!"

Defeated, I cried, "I'm trying. I've never had an epidural before, and I don't know how much harder you want me to push. I'm pushing as best as I can."

"TURN OFF THE EPIDURAL!"

My eyes widened. The sterile room immediately became silent following the demand to remove the only medicine that stood between me and excruciating pain once again. I had no voice. I looked on with fear filling my eyes as my mind prepared me for the womb-ripping pain returning soon. We all waited for an eternity.

I lay on my back, legs bent and opened wide, breathing cautiously. Unsure of how intense the pain would become, I stared, waiting for a miracle. There was no conversation; everyone met with their own thoughts in silence. *Deadman walking.* It felt like an execution rather than birth. There was the long wait for unbearable pain, the long wait for the next demeaning statement to match the dissatisfied expression of the medical professional between my legs, and the long wait for this child to be born. It has to get better after delivery. I rubbed my rounded belly and reassured my womb-mate that he would be born into love. The pain resurfaced at a new intensity, and I pushed the life out of me into him.

The pain subsided. I was sore and bruised within, but I survived. Time was now passing in my favor. Just as I prepared to dump this experience in the painful memory log, I could feel something was still off. *Wait.* I peered around the room. To the left was a new mother learning how to hold her newborn son with my sister-in-law's assistance. To the right was the nurse organizing and preparing to transport us to our comfy rooms. In the center was the physician seated between my still open legs. My knees bent and reached for the sky. Exhausted and ready to rest, I studied the focused disposition of the physician.

Something is wrong.

I wanted to be so angry with her after this entire ordeal. I wanted to be free of her.

Wait, something is wrong.

I wanted out of there! *Wait.*

I closed my eyes and felt the fearless goddess standing at the reflective veil.

See her.

I opened my eyes and looked at the woman who sat before me. I saw her. I saw the fearless goddess in her, just as I've seen her when I stand in the mirror. I exhaled and gently said, "Is everything okay?"

My voice startled her. It shocked me too. It was the first time I'd found it since I'd been there. She shared that my placenta had not detached from the uterine wall, and she'd need to insert her hand into my uterus to remove it manually. I had a retained placenta. It had been thirty minutes, and acting quickly was essential to avoid life-threatening complications such as infection or excessive blood loss. I nodded in acceptance.

She spoke to the nurse, "Increase the epidural." The tension was finally sliced with the sharpest of knives. The epidural had been removed. What once was a focused disposition now appeared perplexed. One might imagine someone so poised had earned her share of problem-solving awards, but she was now under increased pressure. The rapid-fire of problems kept going. The voice of my sister-in-law met her next, "Is she supposed to be losing that much blood?"

In the midst of all of the tension, the umbilical cord attached to my retained placenta leaked blood onto the bed and floor. Without a child on the other end, life was leaving me. I trembled uncontrollably. I felt the panic sink into the room. Everyone's face read confusion and disbelief. Bodies moved swiftly. Conversations flowed rapidly. An anesthesiologist appeared. Another medical professional appeared. And another. The room was filled with unfamiliar faces and a stretcher to take me to the operating room. I was cold. No amount of blankets warmed my chilled body. I could see the concern in their eyes.

I tried my best not to recall dramatic scenes I've seen on film when the character dies after a series of unfortunate events, or the alarming reports of African American women being three to four times more likely to die from childbirth than non-hispanic white women.

Is this where it ends? Was I called to do this and then die? My daughters aren't here. My parents aren't here. And life is leaving my body.

I was spiraling in my thoughts. I knew these halls. I'd walked them a hundred times as an employee years ago. Wearing the patient lens wasn't quite what I'd expected. I can only look up. It became the longest journey of speckled ceilings, smiling pictures hanging on the walls wishing me on my way, surgical masks floating above me in frequent motion and constant chatter, and all I could think was, *Is this it? Are these my last moments in this life?* Tears soaked the sides of my face. From within, I heard, *Everything is going to be okay.*

And just like that, those who were opposed began working together to save my life. We entered the operating room, and the professionals who once glared at one another with disdain and distaste moved in harmony to prep me for my procedure. Seven women surrounded me in the operating room. I wasn't sure how I managed to be granted a woman's circle for my allegory, but it was indeed magical. My nurse from labor and delivery remained fixed to my side as a guardian angel. The on-call physician now smiled with enthusiasm and began to softly outline the details of the procedure I was preparing to undergo. After being informed I would also need a DNC to scrape out the contents of my uterus, I drifted my eyes upward to watch the words dance above my head as I sought comfort. On cue, my nurse asked, "Is it okay to share your birthing story?" I smiled humbly.

I'm not invisible anymore. They see me. They hear me.

Beaming from the connections found in our unspoken pain, each of the seven women delivered their birthing stories free of competition. One had given birth to twins. Another had foregone IVF and birthed multiples, also. Each of them took turns sharing their incredible birthing journey. The fearless goddess who stood at the reflective veil was present in each of us. We were connected in a web of light reflecting the beauty of birth.

We spoke proudly of the wonder we met in the journey of birthing, even coupled with loss.

Our stories included tragedy as well. The circle that formed around my stretcher was sacred. A circle of loss and gain. A circle of joy and pain. A circle of motherhood. A circle of life. At the foot was the on-call physician. She touched my leg, and I jumped—my body's reflexive response to the day's events. To my surprise, she smiled and said, "Everything is going to be okay."

At my head, an anesthesiologist grinned and held a nurturing gaze with me as she softly stroked my crown, "You're in good hands, Robin." I exhaled and closed my eyes in relief. We all made it through the pain.

The fearless goddess stood at the reflective veil steadfast and determined. She holds her gaze without a flinch, without skipping a beat in the rhythm of her heart, without a shadow of doubt present.

THE MEDICINE

I've replayed the events since they've occurred, curious of how things might have turned out if I never found my voice or if I found my voice sooner. Those results are debated, but none are certain. I'm certain it's important to always have access to my voice. Absorbing the sound of others and entertaining the voice of the ego is easy. It takes practice to be with your voice. Often, I didn't know how my own voice sounded. I learned to be polite by muting my voice. I learned to make room for others by disappearing. I learned to help another by sacrificing myself. I'd rarely listened to my own voice. I couldn't hear it over all of the noise. Exercising my will to wait for me to catch up with what was going on around me was foreign. I didn't want to be left behind. I wanted to fit in. I wanted to be loved. So I rarely used the word "wait" to gather my thoughts or hear my voice.

My voice is my truth—the expression of my original self. My voice is connected to the fearless goddess who stands at the reflective veil.

I used to react quickly, responding how others wanted, then mirroring it for myself. Now I exercise my will to wait and meet myself before meeting the needs of others. It's one of the easiest and most empowering techniques I've ever practiced. I found my voice simply by saying, "Wait."

"Wait" isn't harsh, nor is it a plea. It's a gentle command to honor yourself. "Wait" is a graceful reminder to connect with your sovereignty.

Let's practice using a simple scenario that could result in our voice being lost:

A: I'm here to get my hair colored today.

B: What a treat! What color? You'd look great with platinum blonde and highlights. Let me show you some pictures!

A: Thank you, but wait. I have a color in mind. I even have a photo.

B: Okay. Let's see. Nice! I can brighten and incorporate more color to accentuate your features! It's what I do, trust me!

A: Wait, that sounds amazing. Let me process that for a moment. Excuse me; I'll be right back.

A is removing herself from the flow of energy she's receiving. It's exciting, although it's loud. She is no longer able to hear her own voice without the influence of others. *B*'s enthusiasm is overshadowing her own. *A*'s questioning her decision and the role she's chosen to play in this experience. *B* nor *A* has caused any harm. Both just currently wear two separate lenses. And *A* wants to choose from the place of her authority.

Does she silence herself and ignore her first choice?

Does she change her mind and walk away altogether, escaping the disappointment of *B*?

A's mind provides numerous outcomes and a plethora of questions.

A: *Wait*

Her mind pauses and begins again.

A: *Wait*

The mind delivers a long pause.

A hears her voice during the long pause. She feels her truth. She returns to *B* and calmly presents her decision with grace and ease.

If only I'd learned to say "wait" much earlier in life. "Wait" honors my free will to choose with informed consent. I can ask questions from my place of truth. I can wait to see my original self in the reflection of others. We're all connected by the fearless goddess that stands at the reflective veil. We just have to practice patience and wait to see our true selves.

Robin "Cue" Friend is the founder and Creatrix of Eleven Eleven Candles and More. She started her journey as a spiritual practitioner when she began creating unique intention candles to deliver peace to every being. As a Master Intention Candle Artist, she aligns the body with the soul using subtle all-natural products that compliment the senses instead of overwhelming them. Not only does she create light in her candles, but she also sparks the brilliant light of her clients for them to see and love. She freely explores her abilities while balancing her time with her three daughters, dancing and singing in the bamboo forest near her home, and being with water—it's her element. She is a skilled energy worker and works diligently to further expand her gifts. She now serves as a healing artist, medium, and peacemaker priestess, offering an array of products and services, including sacred ceremonies, high vibrational intention products, intuitive consultations, and custom intention candles.

Cue is deeply connected to translating indigenous practices and ancient wisdoms into our modern society to elevate our thinking, our actions, and our view of self at a higher level of consciousness.

You are invited to visit the online store or connect with Cue at:

https://www.eleven-eleven-candles.com/

Facebook @elevenelevencandles

Instagram @elevenelevencandlesandmore

CHAPTER 9

MANTRA, MUDRA, AND MORE

STAYING CONNECTED TO YOUR HIGHER SELF DURING TIMES OF CRISIS

Kathy Guidi

"The truth is that our finest moments are most likely to occur when we are feeling deeply uncomfortable, unhappy, or unfulfilled."

- Scott Peck

MY STORY

Sitting in the darkness, I wait for the medicine to come on. I'm at an ayahuasca ceremony and have just drunk a cup of the thick medicinal, earthy-tasting elixir. Back at my seat, I silently chant the mantra "om mane padmi hum" 108 times while thumbing my mala beads. The mantra helps focus the mind, calm the nerves, and slow the breath, so I'm ready when the hallucinogenic effects of the brew begins.

Mother Madre Ayahuasca, I have come for more healing. What is next for me to see? I begin conversing in my mind with this master teacher plant. Within 45 minutes, the descent into the plasmic field commences, and we're off on a multiple-hour journey deep into the psyche.

The journey isn't always pleasant as this medicine is a purgative. I lay back on the mattress, feeling the uncomfortable rumblings in my belly. "Let's look here," she says as we navigate deeper into the recesses of my heart. *Whoa. I'm not so sure I want to look.* "But you must," she whispers to me. "Surrender, trust, and let go."

Peaking into this chasm I feel sadness, exhaustion, loneliness, and truths that have been tucked away and ignored for some time. I'm suffocating by the weight bearing down on me. My soul longs for a deeper loving partnership, it's yearning for some adventure, and my spirit wants to be free. I no longer wish to remain married to my husband of 24 years, nor do I wish to remain shackled to the maintenance and running of our beautiful retreat center. We've lost our connection, and I've lost my spark. The realization of these truths is crushing. *How do I get myself out of this?*

I sit up and hold the 'Have No Fear' mudra, opening my chest, slowly rocking back and forth. Finally, a wave of nausea, like a torpedo fired from a submarine, jettisons itself from deep within my gut, up through my esophagus, and out my mouth into the waiting bucket. Several excavations of vomit are removed from deep within my root chakra. Old stories and emotions come out. Exhausted, I collapse onto the mattress.

Beautiful visions of vines and trees alive with vibrant colors traverse my periphery. The visuals are stunning, and the message I take is: If you step through the pain and live your truth with integrity and authenticity, then beauty will be yours. The beauty of life, purpose, and living a life worth dying for is waiting on the other side.

In the next day's sharing circle, the tears stream down my face as I grasp the talking stick: "I love our property. I have put so much of myself into it for the last ten years, holding the energy for retreats, maintaining the gardens, and doing the catering. But the truth is I don't want to do it like this anymore. My spirit wants to fly, and I need to make some big changes." I purposely hold back my feelings about my husband. Shame permeates my body as I admit these truths. I feel exposed and a failure. Yet a sense of relief washes through me as I say these words aloud. *This is the first step,* my inner voice says.

The full crisis erupts like fiery lava flowing down a volcano two weeks later. Night after sleepless night, I'm jolted awake, wide-eyed in the blackness, full of fear, staring into the abyss, emptiness overtaking me as I realize I'm in the fires of transformation again. The serpent has been unleashed, and there's no going back. *You are ready for this initiation. Listen to your heart, and go slowly.*

My husband tries to soothe my wracking sobs as we sit on the couch, and I blurt out, "I don't think I can do this anymore, not this way. We've been through this dance over and over, and we're not making progress on healing this core wound of ours. I need to separate, to disentangle our energies, and stay within myself, to hold my own counsel, find my own spark, and re-negotiate everything."

I can't believe I'm saying these words. It's as if another version of myself is speaking through my mouth and looking out my eyes. He's shocked at first but knows what I say is true. We agree to meet every morning for a heart-sharing where we can speak honestly about how we're feeling. *Yes, speak truthfully. Lay all the cards out on the table and see what's there. You will then have a place to work from or leave from,* the inner voice says.

But this is painful, I shout back into my head. *I'm not used to operating fully from my heart, putting myself first, listening, actioning. I don't know how to do this.*

But I do know. I know I want to move into a higher octave of me, one fueled by love and truth. I come across bell hooks' words on love in action. Love, she says, is a combination of trust, commitment, care, respect, responsibility, and truth-telling. *Yes, you are to walk this talk and create a partnership and life where these are at the forefront of your relationship. Love is the only way through.*

All of this is happening in the weeks leading up to the creation of this book, and I honestly don't know if I can fulfill my obligation of producing my chapter. I give an eye-roll to the universe for the profound way in which she moves us into position on the chessboard of life, unfolding things perfectly for our learning and growth if we're willing to flow with her undulations.

Nonetheless, I still have my doubts. I fire off an email to Stephanie. "I'm not sure I can participate in this book next month as I'm literally falling apart, not sleeping well, can't get a grip on my mind, and feel like I'm going crazy. I think I'm going to separate from my marriage and property." Understanding, nurturing, and empathic, she supports whatever decision I need to make to take care of myself. And she gently encourages me to stay with the project and stay connected from afar with the group who are going to the pyramids of Teotihuacan for a week-long initiation and writers retreat.

Vacillating with indecision, I wonder if I can bear my soul while bearing my pain and write this story while the story unfolds! It's difficult to get the words out, to see them appear on the page without causing a cascade of tears to erupt.

I take my mala beads and go sit in our Temple of Venus. Perched on my meditation cushion, I connect my in-breath and out-breath, slowing my body down, turning inwards, and soon the mind follows. I pray and hold council with my guides. *How am I going to write this story?* I ask.

You are strong enough to take this journey and tell your story. Your tender shaman heart is ready for this expansion and embodiment of truth and love. Stay connected to us, and you will not be led astray.

Easier said than done.

The initial days unfold in agonizing slowness, and I often feel I'm outside of myself watching someone else's life. I have a quick sob or two throughout the day as the realization dawns on me that I've crossed over a threshold of my own limitations, birthing myself anew.

The tears slowly recede after the first three weeks and come less frequently. My daily practice keeps me grounded and anchored to my higher self. Without this strong foundation, my mind would descend into the lower frequency vibrations of the ego-mind and cast blame with all the 'should-haves' towards him and myself. But staying connected to my higher self allows for wisdom to come through.

You need to purge. You need to declutter the physical items from your life so that the energy can move.

You need to get closure on what you no longer want and call in what you do.

You need time and space to break the cycle of patterning that you and your husband are stuck in.

You need to get new systems in place to manage the property and run the retreats.

You need to follow the spark in your heart and go do the things you keep saying you want to do.

Disentangle from him and get to know yourself again.

By weeks five and six, I'm in motion; the force of the universe is flowing through me. I'm moving my train forward, and there's no room for any heavy baggage. And it's not to say I don't have bad days, but for the most part, I'm holding myself steady and upright.

I held a fire ceremony on New Year's Eve, burning pieces of paper, closing chapters of my life, and visioning in the new. My husband and I are stable, conversing, and allowing each other space, taking things one day at a time. We are sitting in ultimate presence, not looking backwards, nor looking too far forwards, as we deconstruct our marriage not knowing what awaits us. I have so much respect for him for traveling this new path we're on.

Bags of clothes, books, and other detritus stuffed into closets and garages have been purged, and already the energy is flowing. We've met with another couple interested in living on our land for half the year, and we're calling in for a regular groundskeeper.

I'm taking care of myself, having massages, and regularly leaving the property for solo time. I've made the intention to take myself away on fun trips to re-ignite my soul, and already the sparks of desire are starting to bubble up.

What does it mean to truly live with a shaman heart? We don't need to know the outcomes; we just need to be present with our truth today and engage from that place in moving forward. The path towards wholeness and healing requires putting one small step in front of the other. Trust, surrender, let go.

THE MEDICINE

The practice shared below is what I'm using right now to keep myself centered as I navigate my current crisis. Allow yourself 45 minutes to an hour to do all three components: Mantra, Mudra, and Toning. To realize the benefits from these, commit to doing the full practice for at least one week.

These exercises are best done first thing in the morning or in the evening before bed and not on a full stomach. You will want to be in a quiet and peaceful place where you won't be disturbed and where you can make some noise.

Sit comfortably in a chair or cross-legged, keeping the back straight and relaxing your shoulders and neck. Your eyes can be closed, directing your inner attention towards your third eye or half-open gazing toward the tip of your nose.

MANTRA

Reciting mantras aloud has a harmonizing and healing effect on the physical, mental, and emotional energy body. A mantra can be any set of words repeated multiple times. Depending on the length of the mantra, the repetition is usually 27, 54, or 108 times. Using a mala (prayer beads) allows for ease of counting. A mala has 108 beads.

I have chosen the Tara Nyurma Pamo Sanskrit mantra, which roughly translates to "the swift heroine who liberates one from fear and obstacles and increases bodhicitta (awakened heart)."

Take a few breaths to ground yourself: inhale, belly inflates; exhale, belly deflates.

When ready, using your mala or other means to count, repeat the below 108 times. Take a deep inhale through the nose, and on the exhale, repeat the mantra for as long as your exhale allows. Take another breath in, and repeat, until you complete 108 repetitions.

As you're chanting the mantra, visualize any fear or obstacles melting away, sliding down your body and received by the earth. Imagine your heart expanding with each breath and repetition, connecting to something greater than you, whether it be God, Divine Source, Great Mystery or whatever word resonates.

OM TARE TUTTARE TURE BODHICHITTA SVAHA

(phonetic pronunciation: Ohm Taray Two-Taray Turay Bodi-cheetah, Swaha)

Or, if you prefer an English mantra, try this:

Liberate me from my fears and connect me to my awakened heart.

When finished, pause and scan your body for a minute or two before moving on to the mudras. Notice how you feel.

MUDRA

A mudra is a yoga movement involving the arms, hands, and fingers. Holding them in specific positions positively affects one's overall well-being, and a daily practice helps to release old and unhealthy energies. It will charge up your vital life force energy.

I have selected four mudras to help lift out of lower vibrational feelings and emotions: The mudra of Happiness, Self-Confidence, Compassion, and The Inner/Higher Self.

Do these mudras in the following order and each for a minimum of 90 seconds, working your way to three minutes or longer. Inhale and exhale through the nose, taking deep, slow breaths centered at the solar plexus. As you breathe and hold the mudra, you may bring a mantra or affirmation to mind or remain empty, focusing on the breath.

HAPPINESS MUDRA:

Sitting with a straight spine, bend your elbows and bring your arms to your sides, away from your body. Elbows are just below the level of the shoulder. Palms face forward. Stretch the index and middle fingers and bend the ring and pinky fingers, pressing them into the palms firmly with the thumbs.

I am capable of being happy, feeling happy, and embodying happiness. I am a beautiful soul radiating light and love.

SELF CONFIDENCE MUDRA:

Sitting with a straight spine, lift your hands up to the level of your solar plexus with elbows bent to the sides. Bend the middle, ring, and pinky fingers and touch them back to back. Extend the index fingers and thumbs and press them together. The thumbs are pointed towards you, touching at the solar plexus, and the index fingers away from you.

I have the power, courage, and determination to create the life I want and to have the things I want.

COMPASSION MUDRA:

Extend your arms out to your sides with your arms parallel to the ground, palms facing forward, and with fingers stretched out. Inhale and slowly turn your head to the right, exhale and slowly turn back towards the center. Do this four times, then do the same for the other side. Repeat.

Even though it's taken me this long to come to my understanding, it's okay. I love me. Even though I feel angry, I have compassion for who I was and who I am becoming. Even though I didn't have the strength or courage to make changes before, I do now, and all will be okay. I am being guided every step of the way.

INNER/HIGHER SELF MUDRA:

Cup your hands by placing the tips of your index, middle, and ring fingers and the balls of your hands together. Then with the fingertips of the thumbs touching, bring them towards the touching fingertips of the pinky fingers, creating a cathedral-like formation—a triangular window forms above the tips of the pinky fingers.

Bring your hands out in front of your forehead and gaze through the opening without blinking for as long as you can. Then lower your arms and hold the mudra an inch or so below your chin.

The triangular window is the window to my soul, which sits in a giant cathedral of love. I travel through this window into the great cosmos beyond connecting to my higher self and deep wisdom. I know what I need to do.

TONING

We're going to tone the vowel sounds "Ooo, Ohh, Ahh, Ehh, Eee" (U, O, A, I, E), which link to the body's chakra energy centers. The order starts from a low "Ooo" sound (base chakra) up the scale to a higher-pitched "Eee" sound (crown chakra).

The focus of this component is to make a sound that helps release and move any stuck energy in the body. Don't think too much as you make the sounds. Just flow through them, pausing as long as you need between each one. Take a deep in-breath through the nose, and use your slow out-breath to tone.

Put your hands below your belly button onto your root/sacral chakra. Sound "Ooo" three times.

Next, place your hands above your naval onto the solar plexus chakra and sound "Ohh" three times.

Moving up, shift your hands on your heart chakra. Tone "Ahh" three times.

The hands next go to the throat chakra. Sound "Ehh" three times.

Place the palms of your hands above your brow, the third eye chakra, and relax your fingers onto the top of the head, the crown chakra. Tone "Eee" in a high pitch three times.

Pause and feel.

Lastly, using your hands to guide you through the five chakras, sweep your hands from base to crown while toning quickly, "Ooo, Ohh, Ahh, Ehh, Eee." Hold the "Eee" for as long as you can while simultaneously lifting your arms into the heavens and imagining a portal of white healing light beaming down through your central channel from crown to root. Do this a minimum of three times.

Pause and feel.

I hope you feel grounded, connected to your higher self, and ready to face whatever lies in front of you today. Remember, baby steps.

Hop on over to my resource page for a free PDF printout of these exercises with photographs of the mudras and some audio files to help guide you: https://birdsongretreat.nz/Shaman-Heart/

Kathy Guidi is co-creator and kaitiaki (steward) of Birdsong Retreat & Sanctuary, a place for wellness and spiritual healing. She is a certified Shamanic Breathwork facilitator and Ordained Minister through Venus Rising Association for Transformation, a Reiki Master, a retreat facilitator, caterer of plant-based nourishing kai (food), an Earth honoring ritualist and apprentice in the Pachakuti Mesa Tradition of Peru, and a spiritual mentor. She holds bachelor's and master's degrees in business and finance.

She is an all-around WOW-girl (ways of wellness) seeking to optimize body, mind, and spirit. She left a well-paying corporate and urban lifestyle in San Francisco for greener pastures in rural New Zealand, where she has been living with her husband on a ten-acre slice of paradise since 2006. In the early days, the retreat and sanctuary were for their own healing, then slowly became a place for friends and travelers to find respite. Since building their Temple of Venus, they have been hosting and facilitating small boutique transformational wellness events focusing on shamanism and shamanic practices.

She is passionate about earth stewardship, sacred relationship/ayni with all things and beings, and helping people with their journeys towards wholeness. In this second phase of life, her passion centers around personal development, understanding the psyche, healing our internal wounds, and becoming conscious, heart-centered humans.

You can find her dispensing wisdom to friends and guests from the garden, from the kitchen, or from the comforts of their cozy couches. She offers group shamanic breathwork sessions and co-facilitates women's retreats.

Connect with her on the following sites:

Website:
https://www.birdsongretreat.nz
https://www.kathyguidi.com (coming soon)

Facebook:
https://www.facebook.com/BirdsongRetreat
https://www.facebook.com/KathyGuidiWOW

Email:birdsongretreat@gmail.com

CHAPTER 10

ACCESSING YOUR INTUITION

THE CURE FOR INDECISION

Sonja Glad, DPsS, LCPC

MY STORY

"Good morning, girls," I call out as I approach the chicken coop and pull the cord to raise the door.

"How're you doin' today, Lola? Want a piece of bread? How 'bout you, Spots? I see you're ravenous, Queeny," and she rips another big chunk of bread from my hand. "You don't have to fight over it, Seamore and Little Lady. I have plenty!"

I hear tires crunching on the gravel drive, throw the rest of the bread to the girls, and pull on my gloves. I turn to greet my best friend, Liz.

"I'm so glad you were able to come for a walk this morning, even though it's only 18 degrees out."

"Me too," replies Liz.

We start walking down the drive and turn left onto the country road where I live.

"I can't imagine the sky being any bluer than it is right now," Liz exclaims.

"I know! There's not a cloud in the sky! Check out the hoar frost on the needles of that Scotch pine! It's so beautiful!"

I inhale deeply and feel ice crystals forming in my nostrils. I pull my hands up into the sleeves of my winter coat. Even with gloves on, I feel that tingly feeling in my fingertips.

"So, how's Jake doing?" I ask.

"Well," Liz responds and proceeds to tell me about her son's struggles with being a business owner in these tumultuous COVID times.

After the update, she asks me how I've been since our last walk together. I pause. "I've been having trouble sleeping."

Liz waits me out. She knows I sometimes need a little extra time to form my thoughts into words. I love her for her patience with me. As I go into my head, the cold, the azure sky, and the beauty all around me seem to fade. I notice the tension building in my shoulders. It feels like my previously crisp thoughts are now jumbled.

"I don't know what to do."

"What to do about what?" Liz asks.

"I can't decide what to do." I feel Liz looking at me. I turn my head towards her, and she smiles encouragingly. "It's hard enough leaving my wife, my grandchild, all my friends and family, and closing down my private practice, all to follow this pull to Hawaii, for who knows what purpose, but I'm doing it. And now I'm stuck. Do I transport my car there, or do I leave it here? I keep going back and forth. I would love the security of at least having my own wheels. But then it makes it so real that I'm going to be gone for so long. Does having my car with me somehow take away from the real experience of going and trusting that I can survive on my own? But then what about the expenses?"

Now I'm on a roll. The floodgates of worry have opened, and like an erupting volcano, words come spewing from my mouth. "I can't afford to rent or lease a car. Do I hitchhike to get places, like I've seen people do there? How safe is that? What if I get robbed? Raped? Killed?"

"Whoa, Sonja! I think you're getting a little ahead of yourself. How 'bout we take a few breaths." She starts taking a few deep, audible breaths, and I join in.

The world opens up a bit, and I see the oil and chip road beneath my feet. I hear the sound of our footsteps. First one, then the other boot strikes the ground. I realized my mind had become a runaway train. *But all those things could happen,* I reason.

I've gone into my head again. I've shut down.

"Sonja, didn't you teach me some sort of strategy for accessing my intuition a few years ago? Something you do with your fingers?"

"Yeah, muscle testing," I reply. "But this feels like it's too big of a decision for that. What if I'm wrong? You know I was wrong in June when my intuition said I had to go to Florida because my dad was going to die. And he didn't die then. And I left Susan right after her mother's funeral to go to the airport. I felt so bad leaving her. But I trusted my intuition and went. And I was wrong."

"But didn't it turn out to be a good thing you went right when you did?" Liz questions. "Didn't you drive your mom to the hospital after the ambulance took your dad there?"

"Yes," I answer. "And I went to battle with the insurance company to get them to pay what they were supposed to pay with my dad transitioning from in-home care to the memory care facility. That ended up saving my mom almost forty thousand dollars. So, it was definitely a good thing I went. But I felt so bad leaving Susan right then when her mom had just died."

"Didn't you go because you thought your mother would need you?" Liz asks.

"I did."

"And didn't she?"

"She did," I acknowledge.

"So then your intuition was right. You did need to go. And the only thing that would have taken you away from Susan at that time was something as huge as thinking your dad was about to die. I don't think you would have gone for any other reason. So the universe did know what was best. And Susan had support here and was okay."

"So how about it, Sonja," Liz continues. "Why not check in with your intuition now about this whole car thing? You know you'll feel better once you do. You usually do feel better after you've made a decision."

"Alright," I sigh. "I know you're right. After our walk, I'll go in and meditate and tap into my intuition. But I'm a little nervous about what the answer will be. But I do trust that the universe has got my back and knows more about what I need than my anxious brain does." I pause for just another moment and then say, "Thanks, Liz. I don't know what I'm going to do without you while I'm gone."

"We can always call each other."

"I know, but it won't be the same. How are we going to hug each other over Zoom?"

"Well, you can throw your right arm over your left shoulder and your left arm over your right shoulder, squeeze and pretend it's me."

"Or you could come to visit me, and we could go hiking." My eyes sparkle.

"Or we could meet up in the Galápagos Islands," Liz teases.

"Or go white water rafting through the Grand Canyon!"

"Or hike the Appalachian Trail!"

We continue our walk up the familiar road. Color has returned to the world, and there is now a lightness in my step. I have decided to access my intuition and go with whatever the result will be.

THE MEDICINE

Self-muscle testing requires just a few ingredients: two thumbs and two index fingers. Oh, and a willingness to believe we have access to information outside of our thinking mind, books, or the internet. I'm referring to trusting our subconscious mind, our gut instinct, tapping into universal energy, and, or accessing the Akashic records. Visit https://en.wikipedia.org/wiki/Akashic_records to learn more about the Akashic records.

How it works: When something is true, or the answer is *yes,* our muscles are strong. When something is false, or the answer is *no,* our muscles are weak.

Chiropractors and acupuncturists use this technique to test for allergies and see what supplements might benefit you. However, you don't need a chiropractor to tap into your intuition. You can access this information yourself. See https://www.truthorganicspa.com/post/muscle-testing for more on self-muscle testing.

This is *not* a tool for medical self-diagnosis. If you have a health concern, please consult with your medical practitioner.

SELF-MUSCLE TESTING TECHNIQUE

1. Make a circle with your left thumb and left index finger.

2. Do the same with your right thumb and index finger.

3. Now interlock the two circles like two links in a chain.

4. Test the links by trying to pull them apart. The two links of the chain should feel strong. If this is not the case, go to **step 11**.

5. Ask yourself a question or make a statement where you know the answer to be true. I always go with "Is my name Sonja?" or "My name is Sonja."

6. Try to pull your linked fingers apart. Notice if the fingers feel strong and how strong they feel. Did the chain break? If it didn't break, continue to **step 7**. If it did break, no worries, go to **step 10** before you continue.

7. Ask yourself a question where you know the answer is *no.* I like going with something crazy like, "Am I a dog?" You can also make a false statement: "I am a dog."

8. Try pulling your linked fingers apart. Did they separate, or did the grip become noticeably weaker? If they did come apart or weaken, your energy flow is calibrated correctly for this little piece of magic, and you can continue to the next step. If your fingers didn't come apart, or you didn't notice any difference in muscle tension, please go to **step 12** before you continue.

9. You are now ready to start using muscle testing to help you make decisions. Be clear and specific in your questions. The more you practice this, the easier it becomes. Visit https://www.healing-with-eft.com/self-muscle-testing.html for more information and different ways to self-muscle test.

10. If your *yes* isn't strong and your *no* isn't weak, it could mean several things. It could be as simple as you are dehydrated. So drink a glass of water and start over.

11. It could be that you have an energy block. To open up the flow of energy, try this tapping sequence. With two fingers, tap five to ten times on each of the following points: top of the head, between the eyebrows, besides the eye, below the eye, under the nose, middle of the chin, on the upper chest, and four inches under the armpit. This is the basic Emotional Freedom Technique tapping sequence. See https://www.medicalnewstoday.com/articles/326434 for in-depth information on EFT and a body diagram showing the tapping points. After completing this sequence several times, return to **step 4**.

12. If it still doesn't work, it could be that your *yes* is weak for you and your *no* is strong, so try several test questions to which you know the answer. If *yes* is consistently weak, use weak for *yes* and strong for *no*.

13. And sometimes, for some people, muscle testing doesn't work. If that's the case, you could seek answers through meditation, prayer, divination card reading, or other self-muscle testing methods. See https://www.healing-with-eft.com/self-muscle-testing.html for other ways to self muscle test.

Practice and play with muscle testing and watch your self-trust grow. When your thinking brain can't help you make a decision, this way of accessing your intuition can help your decision-making process.

Following are some personal examples of how I have used muscle testing:

a. *Hey body, I would love a chai tea this morning. Can you handle the caffeine today?* I love it when the answer is *yes,* but I usually drive by Grab-A-Java when the answer is *no.* To be honest here, sometimes I get the tea anyway, knowing the consequence will be that I won't be able to get to sleep 'til the wee hours of the morning, but hey, I enjoyed the heck out of that tea.

CHAPTER 10 | 97

b. *Hey universe, will this beautiful crystal be a good gift for Sue as she's going through this tough time?* If the answer is *yes,* I buy it. If the answer is *no,* I keep searching and muscle test each item.

c. Now, something a little harder. *Is it time to put Sam to sleep?* The answer was *yes,* but my wife wasn't ready yet, so we waited a few more months until she was ready to say goodbye to our almost 18-year-old beloved dog. I was at peace with his passing, knowing he had lived a very full and happy life.

d. Now, the really tough one on which I didn't want to follow through. At the end of September, I asked, *When should I close down my office?*

May?

"No."

April?

"No."

June?

"No."

So now I'm getting a little nervous because those were the months I thought I'd be winding down my private practice. I had planned to start my three-year sabbatical in Hawaii in June.

March?

"No."

July?

"No."

Panic starts setting in.

February?

"No."

The end of this year?

"Yes."

Oh, shit! I'm not ready! How do I tell all my clients I'm closing my practice in just a few months? Forget it. No way.

I took a few deep breaths and asked myself, *Am I going to walk my talk? Am I going to trust myself and my intuition? Do I trust the universe has got my back? Alright then, let's figure out how we're going to do this.*

Trusting that the universe/God/goddess/my gut knows more than my thinking mind and my worries, I figured it out. I stopped seeing clients in my office at the end of December. I'm taking January to move out of my office and seeing most of my clients via Telehealth, working with them as they transition to other therapists.

In May, as I begin my newest journey, I will only be seeing a few clients through a Telehealth platform on a self-pay basis. I feel this way of ending my successful private practice of 18 years is the most gentle, and I need gentle at this time of immense change.

Muscle testing has brought me to where I am, right this very second. I am sitting at a table outside my room at the Dreaming House in mystical Teotihuacan, Mexico. When my friend, Ruth, first told me about this opportunity, I immediately muscle tested, and the answer was *yes!*

Six months after hearing about the trip, I sit in this sacred space, writing about the medicine that has helped me tremendously. When faced with indecision and the stress and worry that comes with it, I use self-muscle testing to resolve the issue.

May this little bit of magical medicine help bring you peace.

(By the way, I will be shipping my car to Hawaii as I go off on this solo adventure, following the road less traveled, being guided by my intuition.)

Sonja Glad, DPsS, LCPC, has her own private practice, working as a Mental Health Counselor specializing in trauma recovery and mood disorders. She is shifting her focus to working more exclusively with people who are in the process of making life changes or are seeking personal/spiritual growth. Sonja recently earned her Doctorate in PsychoSpiritual Studies. She is a shamanic minister, a reiki master, a breathwork facilitator, and a soul collage facilitator.

Sonja recently published her first children's book, *WooHoo For Sensitive Somjay*. She is excited about having more time for writing and illustrating future children's books as she reprioritizes her life.

Sonja is happiest when she can be outdoors. She loves reading, being creative, working on personal growth, hiking, kayaking, whitewater rafting, and exploring the world. Of course, doing things outdoors with a good friend puts the cherry on top of fabulous.

Learn more about Sonja:

On her website:
www.sonjaglad.com

On youtube at:
https://www.youtube.com/watch?v=qtZHo0NkJ5o

Find her book at:
https://www.amazon.com/WooHoo-Sensitive-Somjay-Sonja-Glad/dp/1945567279/

CHAPTER 11

BELLA THE INTREPID

HOW A RESCUE PONY RESCUED ME

Iva Enright, MA

MY STORY

"I found your horse! We need to go over to Connecticut and see her right now. I'm hitching up my trailer. This is so exciting!" My neighbor shouted through the phone.

My neighbor made it her mission to find the perfect horse for me. She somehow understood it would be a horse that would finally turn me into a farmer. I had just turned 50, and my world felt frayed and precarious. Six years before, I'd agreed to move with my husband and youngest son from Manhattan to a farm in the Hudson Valley. I loved living in Manhattan. I loved it when I was involved in a theater project and living in Greenwich Village. I loved wandering from Three Lives Books to a coffee shop and writing in the morning. It was a dreaming time, chatting with the butcher on Minetta Lane, imagining the trout stream that still ran underneath the pavement. I walked to pick the kids up from school. Manhattan was a symphony of art and words and stories. It seemed to be the perfect life for me, but for my husband and youngest son—not so much.

"So, let's move to the country then. I can just come to the city any time on the train. I can do that," I said blithely. Always the caretaker.

And so that's what we did, and at first, it was bucolic. I was enchanted. There was a gorgeous Dutch barn where we created a dwelling in the hayloft and moved in. *This was as cool as the village, but in a different way,* I said to myself. But this consolation quickly faded; for me, it wasn't home. It was cold and dirty. There were so many flies, and I was not a farmer. Never had been, didn't sign up to be one, and most likely never was going to be one. At the same time, my husband unilaterally decided we were going to be livestock farmers. This meant we would raise cows, pigs, and chickens for meat—humanely raised, pasture-fed, animals for slaughter so humans could eat them.

I didn't even know where to put myself on this one. Was it possible to be a farmer's wife who had no interest in farming or eating meat? But I didn't protest. I people pleased instead, rolled up my sleeves, and dug in. The problem was, as each season came and went, I heard more clearly the voices of these other species who were destined for the dinner plate. On chicken slaughter day, all the neighboring farmers brought their chickens, stuffed into flat yellow crates, to be slaughtered at our farm. The first head that was chopped started all the crated chickens screaming. They screamed all day until the last one was gone. Wednesdays became the days filled with the stench of blood, boiling feathers, and chickens screaming.

I stopped eating them. I stopped eating all the animal people, and I became a vegetarian wife of a livestock farmer. My husband grew more distant.

I created my own section of the farm across the street from the big barn. Everyone called this Iva's World and snickered a little that nothing died in my world. I grew medicinal plants and raised my own flock of hens that clucked and scratched about and were a world away from the business across the street.

Still, somehow, I was so lonely my teeth ached.

"I am so lonely here. I am lonely!" I cried out to my husband. He didn't know what to do or say, so he said and did nothing.

Finally, I shouted out to the bleak beauty of the drowned land swamp.

"I don't know how to do this! Help me. Please, I need help." I stood, tears streaming down my face. "I'm sorry to be such a baby. Sorry, I can't figure this out. There are so many real problems in the world. But I can't feel my heart. I don't know what I'm supposed to be doing. I have no purpose here. I am not a farmer."

A small wind rose out of the swamp. Something, a sound, a feeling, I don't know what, but something caught my attention. I remembered myself as a child wandering barefoot and free in the marsh in Charleston, South Carolina. I remembered that everything was alive and singing and innocent then.

I looked out over the frozen swamp. That innocence sailed right into me. A high-pitched sound like bird calls and wind and water bubbling beneath the ice, blending into a gorgeous chorus. It was the land. The land was singing.

Stop, look, listen. Feel the summer, feel the winter. I will teach you how to dream with me.

I spent hours photographing with my pinhole camera—the herons and the deer and the cattails shooting up from the edge of the boggy ground. However, the loneliness lingered. When I was outside in the swamp or in my garden, I remembered the dreaming language, and I felt better but still felt empty in my big barn home. The distance between my husband and me grew wider every day. It felt like there was a chasm of cold air and ice between us.

And then my friend called, "I found your horse!"

As we drove along towards the farm in Connecticut, my friend chattered on about the horse. "She is a rescue pony. She was headed to become dog food, but these people snapped her up. She was a cart-horse, and so she is very well trained, very sweet."

I conjured a story for my horse. *This horse will be the answer. She is mysterious and kind, athletic, and we will be admired together far and wide, and I will be taken seriously.*

We pulled into the farmyard. Several horses milled about in small paddocks. Over in a corner stood a tiny blonde pony.

"There she is! Her name is Bella."

What kind of horse is that? She's tiny and blonde like me. I sagged into the seat; *no one would take this pony or me seriously. She is not Black Beauty.*

"She's perfect for you!"

I started to say, "No, this is not my horse," but as we climbed out of the truck, I heard a snatch of music like the music that rose out of the swamp. I stopped. Bella looked at me and then went on grazing.

"Oh," I said. "Hmm."

And the next thing I knew, we were on our way home with Bella in the trailer.

When we arrived back at my farm, we quickly learned that she would not agree to be caught again once released from the halter. She would run as far from a human and a halter as possible.

"Well, you have to figure out how to catch her. You can't care for her if you can't put a halter on her. Let me show you what to do." She began to chase Bella by whirling a rope and trying to corral her into a corner of the paddock. Bella's eyes were wild and white in the sockets. Memories and the sick childhood terror of my stepfather raging and throwing things around the room iced up my veins. I stepped back. Bella and I were one being wrapped in fear.

"I don't get how chasing and terrifying her is going to persuade her to accept a halter."

"You have to show her who is boss. Make her respect you. This is how horses talk to each other."

Is all of life about this illusion that dominion over others was the only way in life?

Something snapped in me. I stepped up in defense of this horse. "Just leave her alone. She and I will figure it out."

"Suit yourself," she shrugged.

So, Bella and I were going to figure it out. She had to agree to accept a halter, and I didn't care what anybody knew or said. We were going to become friends and trust each other. This was how we were going to get this done.

Bella stood in the corner shaking. I stood by the little barn shaking. We eyed each other suspiciously. Neither of us understood anything about trust.

All that long, lonely winter, I sat on the cold ground in Bella's paddock, waiting for her to come to me. I knew this place by heart now. I knew where it got muddy in the rain. I learned how Bella preferred being out in the larger pasture if given a chance. I had plenty of time to think about how life in the big barn was unraveling. How all my life, I internalized the message that I was an interloper, unimportant, and needed to be good, nice, and quiet. *Hush. Don't make a fuss. What you want does not matter as much as what he wants. Learn to be invisible and take care of yourself.* I was a master people pleaser.

I'm so tired of being a people pleaser. I shook my head. Ugh. My butt was freezing. I stood up and walked defiantly over to Bella. She looked at me. I looked back at her then out to the place where she's been gazing. As if I heard her say the words, "Stop staring at me like you are a big cat ready to pounce and just stand near me and try to experience the world through my eyes. Try to be a horse."

Whoa!

I dropped my whole agenda and began to observe. I noticed all the random thoughts constantly looping through my mind, followed by gusts of emotion. When I was caught in these thoughts, I noticed she moved away. I tried to stop thinking, and I followed. I saw movement down in the trees. Bella lifted her head and cocked an ear towards the trees. A herd of deer moved silently as shadows in and out of the little forest. I stepped forward. Bella cocked one ear towards me and kept one in the direction of the deer. I let out a long breath.

I didn't even realize I was holding my breath.

Bella let out a long breath and relaxed her neck. She moved closer to me.

This is her language. I have been expecting her to fit into my perspective all this time without even considering her language, her way in the world.

The song I'd heard on the first day floated up around her. It was in harmony with the song the drowned land swamp had been trying to teach me. This was not a man-made kind of song. There were no words and no notes. The song was made of the rustle of spring leaves. It smelled like honeysuckle—warm and sweet. I loved this song. The song was Bella. The song was me. "We are all one spirit," Bella sang in a language that my heart understood, even if my mind couldn't.

The heron people, the owl people, and the babble of the river joined in a stream of light and formed the chorus. There were days when all my edges blurred, and I just was. The sun streamed through my molecules, and the earth began to warm up. Sometimes Bella stood right beside me, and other times she moved away. I learned that when the song was strong in my heart, she would come to me and stand peacefully beside me in total trust, but when I was caught up in the anger, sadness, and loneliness I brought with me from the big barn, she moved away. If I pretended or denied these feelings, Bella would turn and run.

She only trusted me when I was standing authentically in my real feelings, no matter how unpleasant they were. She demanded emotional congruency, was utterly trustworthy, and she never lied.

Life in the paddock with Bella was often peaceful and sometimes transcendent. Life in the big barn was heavy and dense. My husband and I didn't fight. We were just deadly polite or silent. In the big barn, it was clear that the foundation was deeply damaged. One warm day in late spring, I opened the lid to the dumpster and found a dead fox floating amongst putrid chicken guts and dirty ropes of plastic. Flies buzzed around his eyes. His red and gray tail, once magnificent, was caked in chicken blood. I gagged. I marched out to the pasture where my husband was feeding chickens. The song was strong in me, and it had the red-hot rhythm of rage.

"Why is there a dead fox in the dumpster?"

"The fox killed the meat chickens, so I shot him."

I closed my eyes. *This is the icy loneliness, right here.* I sucked in a breath.

"So, the fox was just a fox. Your job, as the human farmer, is to protect your chickens from the fox with a fence."

He looked at me, his lips tight. He was tired of this, tired of me. He stood for a minute, then turned his back and walked away, dismissing me with a wave of his hands as he went.

A silence fell over the world. No music. *This is over. I can't live here doing this, and he won't stop doing this.*

I couldn't breathe.

Almost 30 years ago, my husband and I had found each other, and in a flash, we knew, and we climbed into each other's bones and married each other. We made children and adventures and love, so much love. We laughed and fought and slept holding hands. And now it was broken. I have never before or since loved anyone like I loved that man. But, I'd brought all the broken, damaged parts of me into the heart of our life and expected him to love me through them, not understanding that I was unconsciously asking him to fix me. And I think he was asking me to do the same. Instead of coming together to heal, we slowly began to pick each other out of our bones and fill the holes with loneliness. I told myself it was a fox in a dumpster. It was chickens screaming from crates. It was a winter so cold it could leach the sunshine from my bones. But the truth was that my husband couldn't or wouldn't hear my song, and I needed, for my very life, to be heard.

I needed to be sung.

I stumbled to Bella, trying hard to suck in a breath. I fell. All the sadness in all the world fell out of me. My song was low and moaning. My song was a wail of loss. A warmth pressed against my back. A warm breath circled my head. Bella stood quietly, leaning against my back. So still, so solid. I never felt such acceptance and love without judgment. She rested her chin on my head as if I were another horse. The world expanded. A murder of crows fell across the sky, and then a gust of starlings chased them off. In Iva's world, the hens chortled and clucked. We stayed like that for an eternity. The sweet grassy horse smell filled me up, and we looked out at the drowned land swamp. A horse being and a human being bound together and filled up by the light of the sun.

We are dreaming here—the human beings and the other than human beings. We are dreaming with our hearts and our minds. We are dreaming here. We are collections of molecules formed into bodies, and we are spirit. We are separate, and we are one, all at the same time. The song was strong and clear now.

"The marriage over in the big barn shows me all the incomplete places in myself," I said to Bella. "The marriage isn't a strong enough container for the healing that needs to occur. I am going to Hawaii. I am going to live near my deep soul friend, Beth. I will find a way to bring you with me. I promise. I will find the money."

The song rose out of Bella and wove through my cells until we sang together. Bella is my song horse. She is the horse song of me. And we rode on the song together away from that place and began to heal.

Bella proves to be an intrepid companion, not only accepting a halter but traveling across continents and oceans with me. She came to Hawaii, and now she has returned with me to the mainland. She is strong and steadfast, even when I falter. She is easy to underestimate. She is cute, small, blonde, wise, and very serious about her mission. Every day I honor her. Every day she reminds me not to underestimate the power of the secret intrepid ones, the ones which might have been passed over and discarded—the ones who hold great wisdom.

Every day she asks me to step into my own authenticity.

When we walk with our hearts and our minds together, we become extraordinary.

We are all light. We are all love.

With all my love and no fear, thank you.

THE MEDICINE

It's possible to find this song of authenticity without the magical Bella or a horse companion. It is a simple exercise I learned from my friend in Peru, Jorge Luis Delgado.

Stand with your face towards the sunrise. Feel the sun or imagine the sun warming your face, belly, and heart. At the same time, notice any tension or gnarled-up feelings or thoughts held in your body and your heart. Begin to imagine that heavy energy draining down through your feet into the earth and let the golden light of the sun enter your body and fill you with golden molten light through the crown of your head. Soon Pacha Mama, Mother Earth, will be eating that heavy energy, and you will begin remembering that you are not only filled with light, but you are also the light.

You emanate your song, and the song is light.

Put your right hand on your heart and your left hand on your solar plexus.

Say out loud, "With all my love and no fear, I greet this day. Thank you."

Iva Enright is a filmmaker, photographer, writer, equine guided learning facilitator, and farmer. Iva, Bella, and the rest of the herd live together on Dreaming Horse Ranch in North Carolina and combine creativity and connection to the natural world to guide people on the heroic journey to their most authentic selves.

Iva also co-facilitates Book of Dreams retreats with fellow author Emily K. Grieves. The Book of Dreams is a powerful process of creative journaling to explore dreaming practices and intuitive development.

Iva has been initiated into the Andean Q'ero, Paqo tradition as an earth-based healer and is also a Reiki Master. Iva received a BFA degree in theater from Emerson College, and a MA degree in Equine Assisted Learning from Prescott College.

Iva particularly loves the human beings in her life, above all her three children and two grandchildren.

Connect with her on the following sites:

www.dreaminghorseranch.com

Facebook: https://www.facebook.com/IvaMargaretDundas

Instagram: https://www.instagram.com/Dreaminghorseranch

Iva and her son Jack Peele were invited to film never-before-seen ceremonies of reconnection by the Q'ero people of Peru. The film is out in the world and can be watched here: https://vimeo.com/picaflorproductions/roadtoqero.

Iva's TEDx about the film, including a demo of the medicine exercise, can be watched here: https://youtu.be/N1MeTUTZ-78

CHAPTER 12

BEYOND RELIGIOUS WOUNDS

HOW TO AWAKEN TO YOUR PERSONAL CONNECTION WITH THE DIVINE SOURCE

Rev. Dr. Ahriana Platten

My fingers wrapped around the cool metal railing as I pulled myself up more than a dozen broad steps leading to the church. The skeleton key turned in the lock with a perfect thunk, allowing the towering doors to swing open along ornate hinges. It seemed my heart would burst with excitement. After reaching up to dip little-girl-fingers in the half-moon-shaped basin of holy water, I made a hasty sign of the cross and began walking so fast I was nearly running down the red-carpeted aisle that led to the altar. *This is it! It's finally happening!*

MY STORY

"I want to be an altar boy. . .um. . .well. . .altar girl. . ."

I fumbled for the words, barely able to look into the piercing eyes behind the round-framed glasses. Though I had never seen a girl assist on the altar during Mass, it hadn't occurred to me that they couldn't. I assumed they didn't want to. I, on the other hand, wanted to be an altar girl with all my heart. I loved watching the altar boys ringing the four-toned bells softly at just the right moment in the prayer, creating a joyful noise to give thanks for the miracle taking place at the hands of the priest. I often imagined myself humbly carrying the cross and leading the recession after Mass was over. I could even feel the crisp fabric of the cassock swoosh as I walked, a worthy servant of the Holy. Each Sunday, from the pew where I sat with my family, I felt the loving eyes of a crucified savior looking down at me from the cross and beckoning me to take my place in service.

I finally mustered the courage to ask.

"Come with me," Father Patrick said coarsely. He stood up from the table and, without hesitation, I followed him across the street to the church. I heard every step of his black leather shoes as he hurried across the sidewalk, climbed the stairs, turned the rust-colored key, and pushed open one of the giant doors. He clicked his way across the marble lobby until his steps fell silent on the plush carpet that led to the altar. Tears of joy began to well up in my eyes. *This is it! It's finally happening!* I rushed ahead, reaching the altar before he did.

"Stop! Not another step."

Startled, I felt myself halt abruptly.

"Turn around and look at me. I want you to hear every word I'm saying to you."

Following his command, I turned. His voice was firm. His eyes were cold and hard. I'd never seen Father Patrick look so fierce.

"You are never. . .never. . .to step up on the altar unless you're here to clean the church, you're getting married, or I call you up there. Do you understand?"

No. . .no, I don't understand.

"As a daughter of Eve, it's too easy for you to be tempted. You remember the story of Eve and the serpent, don't you? Women can't help themselves. It's not your fault. It's just how you're made. We all have a cross to bear, and yours is being a woman. Women destroy everything good. They have no self-control."

Wait, can't you see he's calling me from up there, on the cross?

The words screamed in my head, but no sound came out of my mouth. Gravity lost its hold on me. I felt my soul float out of my body, an astronaut swimming in the weightless void of outer space. I had no roots to hold me down. On the outside, I was nodding and listening to the priest, but on the inside, my heart was torn to shreds. I was undone. I couldn't look at him. Instead, my gaze lifted to look into the iconic eyes of the man-god hanging, bigger than life, on the cross above me—the one I'd been taught gave his life for me—for me. The once soft and loving eyes seemed concrete and unfeeling. The living presence I had always felt was gone.

What's wrong with me? I'm at least as good as my brother, and he's an altar boy! I hardly ever get in trouble! What did I do wrong? I'm not Eve!

Had I imagined the beckoning? At that moment, I was confused and felt utterly lost. Was it me, or was it God who had made a mistake? I'd led the prayer group for my catechism class. I'd loved every moment of being in church, from the pungent fragrance of myrrh and frankincense wafting from the censor to the scarlet votives flickering for benediction. The soul's search for divine connection was the most important part of life to me. Even confession and the penance that followed felt like stepping into the comforting waters of a sacred well. I saw my life reflected in the scriptures and admired the priests and nuns who were committed to serving the God whose sacrificial lamb was suspended above the altar.

I loved it all, and I had done everything I could think to do, only to be rejected for the one thing I couldn't change—being a woman.

"Girls can't be altar boys," my mom said matter-of-factly when I returned home and told her why I wasn't Catholic anymore. "You're Catholic as long as you live in my house," she said in a kind but clear voice that reflected the long-time commitment of my Italian ancestry. "After that, you can do what you want." It was a statement I knew I couldn't challenge. I slouched to my room, shoulders rolled forward to shelter my broken heart, desperately wanting to erase the painful words ringing in my ears. "Women destroy everything good."

It took years to find my way back from that moment. The church I'd loved with all my heart became dark and empty for me. I no longer found the Holy there, though I often stood in front of the blue-veiled Virgin Mother, beseeching her to help me understand. She was my only solace. Over the years, I went to church with friends of different denominations, but the story of Eve and the judgment that women are unworthy followed me into each sanctuary. In many of them, women were clearly second-class citizens destined to obey their husbands, who presumably had to keep them from exercising their destructive ways.

When I moved out of my parent's house, I stopped going to church altogether, but I never stopped searching for the wonder of the Holy I'd once known. In my heart of hearts, I always believed there was something more, a loving and compassionate Source that was the undercurrent of all life. In quiet moments of reflection, I could feel it inviting me into service, just like it had when I was young. As the years passed, I came to understand that the concept of God—and of Woman—has been unforgivably distorted by the church.

As painful and life-impacting as this experience was for me, it was the catalyst for my spiritual journey. Not long after leaving my mother's home, I set out on this quest in earnest. I knew there was universal wisdom waiting just beyond my field of awareness. "Ask, and you shall receive," I'd been taught. Ask I did, and before I knew it, a series of newspaper articles about Earth-based religions led me to the many faces of the goddess. I spent a couple of decades traveling to sacred sites, delving deep into ancient practices, and immersing myself in communities whose foundational beliefs preceded Christianity.

"You are she, who is blessed to bring forth life, the Creatrix, and the Wise-woman, Maiden, Mother, and Crone."

My first initiation into the circle of the goddess opened floodwaters of emotion roaring down my cheeks, dripping onto the white robe I hand made, especially for the occasion. There would be many more tests before I wore the mantle of High Priestess, and with each one, the rip in my heart stitched firmer and firmer together. The journey became more important than the destination as my intuition led me to understand the goddess manifest in my every sensory experience, even finding her embodied in me through practices of visionary meditation, contemplation, and ecstatic movement. Discovering the divine feminine and exploring her qualities allowed me to slowly find my way back into the female body I vacated at the foot of the cross. As I regained access to my senses, my connection to the Holy became stronger.

Over time, it was clear that not only had the church caused great harm to women but in causing that harm, the sacred masculine was thrown out of balance, equally distorted and damaged. Power-over rather than power-within became the sacral masculine aspiration. Control superseded collaboration as the only measure of success, and, as a result, individual ownership continues to overshadow community well-being in many parts of the world. When the feminine was diminished, her relationship to the masculine could no longer be one of equality and mutual respect.

Recovering the sacred feminine led me to seek a healthy face for the divine masculine. In India, I met the elephant-headed Ganesh, who clears all obstacles. In South Korea, a visit to a 4,000-year-old temple brought me to my knees at the foot of the Buddha. The mythos of Herne, Cernunnos, and Pan provided me a picture of the wild and noble protector god of the forest, in whose presence I felt safe enough to explore my own untamed desires.

Nearly 30 years after the incident with Father Patrick, I found my way back to the man-god through the lens of metaphysical Christology at a Unity Spiritual Center, where I was invited to speak about earth-based religions and shamanism. Wondering if lightning would strike when I entered the sanctuary, I was pleasantly surprised to find myself at home in this community. The people who attended were welcoming, accepting, and kind. Moreover, they welcomed women ministers.

A few years later, I was called to take my position as a spiritual leader for the same community through a series of small miracles that included the loss and recovery of a medicine bag, a trip to teach eco-spirituality to the chaplains at a Catholic university (that's a story I'll save for another day), and the resignation of a dear minister friend. After completing the required studies, I was ordained as a Unity minister, finally answering the calling that had come to me before my twelfth year of life.

I knew I was in the right place. The Holy was ever-present, showing up to inspire me on a regular basis. Whether arriving as a butterfly messenger, a vision of a wise lion-headed she-cat, an angelic being, or Christ Consciousness, the many faces and expressions of the Holy guided me in my stewardship and support for this community. It's remarkable to realize it all began when I was 12 at the base of the cross when rejection thrust me forward to pick up my burden and begin a pilgrimage that started at the gates of a broken heart. That immensely painful first step over the threshold delivered me, in the end, to the inner sanctum of my soul.

THE MEDICINE

Whatever you were taught, know this: *the Holy is within you.*

Whether woman, man, or non-binary, no matter who you love or how you express yourself, regardless of the color of your skin, the home you have or don't have, the language you speak, or where you're from, *the Holy is within you.* Despite the religion you were raised in or the face or faces that show up when you pray—*the Holy is within you.* You are the living hands and heart of the Holy, here to bless the world. The Holy is never, ever, farther away than your own breath.

Also, know there is no greater authority than the Holy in your own heart. No Priest, Priestess, or person of the cloth has a closer connection to the sacred Source than you do. There are tools you can use to help you access your indwelling Divine. Learn them. You'll find many in this book. Please read each chapter.

Begin with silence. When we're quiet, we become sensitive in a special way. Our biology implores our senses to be more aware. We notice movements, sounds, colors, and textures when we stop speaking. Listen. Look. Touch. Taste. Open your awareness. The whole universe is waiting to connect with you. Everything is alive and infused with love.

Let the wind kiss your cheek and imagine its wispy voice. What message is it bringing you? Feel the cold surface of a statute in the garden and let it awaken your flesh. What if the entire universe is trying to communicate with you? That's what I've experienced. The Holy can be found in the eyes of those who offer you compassion, in the warm embrace of a loved one, in the soft, silky petals of a flower, and in the beating wings of a hummingbird. Most especially, the Holy can be found inside your heart, in the whispers of wisdom that come to you at times you need an answer you don't have, and then suddenly, as if by magic, the answer arrives.

Let me be clear, if you've chosen a religion to follow, I honor your path. Religion is a place to learn. There are many tools available through religious practice. My only caution is that you maintain your sovereignty. You are a divine expression, the only you we have in the world. Your unique perspective is needed. Let no one define you as anything less than your holy self.

I've come to understand, on this long and sometimes arduous journey, that there is one consciousness, a Divine Mind, and that we live within it, not separate from it. It moves through us and as us in real and tangible ways. Gratitude opens the door to deeper understanding. The more I express my thanks for the many ways my life is blessed, the more I notice the large and small miracles that happen every day, so many miracles that I'm repeatedly assured there is a Holy hand at work in every moment of my life.

As I reflect on the amazing quest that's taken me from feeling rejected by God to finding the Holy as close as my own breath, I'm without enough words to explain the wonder I feel. It's not religion that brought me to God, but the Holy who used both the good and the bad in religion to show me that I've never been separated from God, and neither have you.

To find your way home to your sacred center, widen your study and explore all the ways people experience the Holy. Entertain the possibility that the whole universe is simply waiting to be welcomed into your awareness, and remember that the *Holy is within you.*

If you've been harmed by religion, know that I care deeply about your wounding. My heart beats with yours as you seek healing. It's human-designed religion and not a divine edict that caused you harm. *The Holy is within you.* You are inseparably connected. Begin living as though that's true. Be the hands and heart of the Holy in all you do. In this way, over time, you'll experience a deep and personal spiritual connection to all that is.

Rev. Dr. Ahriana Platten, Priestess, Pastor, Peacemaker. As the founder of asoulfullworld.com, Ahriana leads a global wisdom community offering tools and teachings for transformation and personal growth.

Have you ever wondered how to find a spiritual teacher just right for you? At asoulfullworld.com, you can sample classes from a curated selection of experienced spiritual educators who provide beginners to master-level programs.

Ahriana teaches educators and practitioners in the intuitive and healing arts how to revitalize their business, emphasizing how relational leadership will generate higher profit and achieve a higher purpose. She leads an initiate's journey for those interested in ancient teachings and the mysteries of life, and you'll often find her speaking, through her newspaper column, podcast, and on conference stages, about what's happening at the crossroads of spirituality and cutting-edge science. Holding credentials in several religious traditions, Ahriana believes every path has value. She teaches from an interfaith perspective, welcoming people of all walks of life who are willing to accept that our differences are a gift in the world.

Ahriana shares her life with her deep-hearted husband, Mark, with whom she travels the inner and outer worlds, and with her children and grandchildren, who are her greatest treasure.

You can connect with Ahriana,

On her website: https://www.asoulfullworld.com

On her Facebook page:
https://www.facebook.com/ahriana.platten/

In the Soul-Full Community on Facebook:
https://www.facebook.com/groups/soulfully

And on Instagram: https://www.instagram.com/ahriana_platten/

You'll find free podcasts, articles, and other gifts at:
https://www.asoulfullworld.com/gifts-from-faculty

CHAPTER 13

DISCOVERING UNSEEN LOVE

CONNECTING WITH LOVE THROUGH NATURE AND SOUL REMEMBERING

Julianne Santini, BSN, RN, PHN

MY STORY

Like bees returning to the hive, a frenzy grew. The entrance to Omega's Main Hall teemed with activity. Our shamanic group was asked to go out onto the land and find a meaningful stone, a touchstone of our time spent there. We must have looked like a swarm of scout bees communicating through ecstatic dance—the sacred journeys completed to find our stones.

Near the door, I swooped in next to Girard. I could always pick him out in a crowd due to his towering height, and if I weren't looking upward, his infamous giraffe socks gave him away on the other end. They always made me smile.

"Did you find your stone, Girard?" I asked excitedly.

His grin stretched across his face like a Cheshire cat. He ceremonially bowed and, with the utmost reverence, pulled around his 80s style fanny-pack. He reached inside, carefully pulling out a bright, red satchel bound with leather strips.

What in God's name? I thought we were just supposed to bring back a rock.

With the skill of an entertainer, Girard flamboyantly opened his satchel. Inside there was indeed a rock, covered with what looked like tobacco, sage, and fragrant purple flowers.

"This stone has come to us from other lands," he began.

I blanked out. Truly, I don't recall the rest of his recitation. I can't even remember the color or size of his rock, but Girard's reverence for his stone still lives with me.

From the moment Girard lifted the satchel under my nose to smell the fragrant medicines bathing his stone, I felt sick. That feeling must have been written all over my face. He gently touched my arm and peered into my eyes.

"What's wrong?"

"I don't think I have the right rock."

Girard pulled a timepiece out of his fanny-pack. Looking at it quickly, he said, "Go! Hurry, you only have ten minutes to find it."

I took off running down the path like a wild cheetah after spotting her prey, but I had no clear destination. It felt like I was running into the void. I felt dizzy and desperate. Tears streamed down my face, and I was internally screaming.

Where is my fricking stone? Why the hell am I here? Maybe I can't hear Spirit. Maybe this isn't my path?

I ran, first past Omega's historic Ram Dass Library. On any other day, I'd have stopped, nestled into one of the overstuffed chairs draped in a swatch of sunshine, and poured over a handful of books, letting me taste, if only for a moment, the wisdom tales of the world. Panting, I made my way past Omega's overgrown, central garden with no time to meander its tanbark trails and smell the cornucopia of year-end vegetables. As I ran past the bustling café, I caught darting glances from an array of seasoned travelers. I must have been quite a sight, tears rolling down both cheeks, runny nose with no tissue to be found. There was no turning back. I continued to fly down the path, clinging to my bag containing all my shamanic claptrap.

Maybe I should leave it all here. Maybe I should just resign myself to the fact that I can't see through the heart of a shaman. What was I thinking?

Then a sound came out of me like a wounded animal, pain from the deepest part of my being. At the time, I didn't recognize it, but felt it. Every inch of me ached. It was a desperate cry to know and feel Spirit. This longing was recently triggered by my father's death, a man with an intense love for the Divine. I wondered why he died so young. He didn't have time to explain his faith to me. I saw it in his actions, though, from the way he tended the garden to his generous spirit as a mortician. He tended the hearts and souls of those who lost a loved one, but now I had lost him. I was lost.

Come to me. Come to the tree.

The words came quietly at first and then louder, so I couldn't miss them.

Come to me. Come to the tree!

I was on a sprawling 190-acre wooden oasis looking for one tree. The lush surroundings created a tranquil bed of safety. My first instinct upon arrival at Omega was always to exhale, and yet today, my heart raced. I sucked air with the intensity of a yogi's fire breath. My focus sharpened. The tears stopped.

I hear you, but where are you? What tree?

Before my father died, I asked him a question that had me barreling down this path. I was an oncology nurse, and I knew his pancreatic cancer was fast-growing. Most patients died within six weeks of their initial diagnosis, but my father lived almost four years. He was able to buy and remodel a home for my mom, send my sister off to college, see my brother graduate from high school, go on a trip to Lourdes, and meet three new grand-babies. I wondered what made his journey so different and what he attributed to his longevity.

"One percent medical intervention and 99% spirituality, faith," I can still hear Dad saying.

I was shocked by his response, for my father received every medical intervention offered to him: radiation, chemotherapy, and even a nine-hour

Whipple surgery. If his medical treatment only accounted for one percent of his longevity, I was certainly in the wrong profession. I began delving into all forms of healing and spirituality, searching for what my father discovered but did not have the time to teach me. It felt like I was standing in the middle of a raging river with my mouth wide open, drinking in every possibility. Shamanism was my godsend, and it offered me a marriage between two worlds. A shaman was known as both healer and priest for a community. Passionately, I dove into this training. My logical, medical mind questioned my new path continuously, but when I opened my heart and dared to feel it, magic happened.

What tree? I hear you and even feel you, but where are you?

I'm here. Come to me. I greet you every time you arrive. I show you a reflection of yourself in the growth and changes of my leaves. Come to me. Come to the tree.

Like a projector showing me every frame upon the reel, I saw my entire dance with this tree. I saw how I lovingly called out to it over the 218-mile drive to campus. I saw my elation each time I pulled into the parking lot and spied her new coat. Sometimes she wore chartreuse and seemed bursting with life. Other times she wore vibrant yellow, orange, and red, carrying the creative intensity of any master artist, and other times I found her bare willing to be naked with me. I saw my gratitude for our long afternoon talks. She always received me with compassion no matter my mood, my thoughts, or endless questions, as well as the times I did not need words at all. I loved to see and be with her, and as strange as it may sound, I felt loved by the tree.

Yes, of course, the tree! The tree! I'm coming, but I don't think you can help me. I am looking for a stone that will fit into the palm of my hand. I know you well, and there is only a perimeter wall around you with stones easily weighing 30 pounds.

Do you trust me?

What?

Do you trust me? If so, come to me. Run to me with all the faith you can muster.

As I ran, the hair on the back of my neck was on end. It felt like a burst of lighting moved through me, through what is called the mouth of God, where the head meets the neck and through which every nerve of the body passes. As my tree came into focus, I felt electric.

Run to me and when you reach my rock wall, place your hand inside.

I was coming in fast and hard. Without hesitating, I threw my hand out and into the first crevice I saw. I felt something. It was a smooth stone wedged into a crack. My breathing slowed until I was holding my breath.

Go ahead; she is yours. I have been waiting to gift her.

I audibly sighed as I pulled out a pale pink, polished stone—a piece of rose quartz two inches in diameter. It nestled perfectly into my hand. It was one of the most beautiful things I had ever seen. I clutched it to my chest.

"Oh, how is this possible?" I blurted out through soft, angel tears.

A strong wind whipped around my face. I could smell something familiar—my father's hair tonic. I then felt my dad place his arms around me. From the love of the unseen realms, I heard the answer.

Faith!

I was standing by my father and my beloved tree, both doorways to the unseen realms. I felt a connection to nature, the duality of being here and there, yet experiencing the energy of it all, the whole of life. I was not lost; I was home. The tree laughed from her roots to the tips of her branches. I saw her shudder, and each leaf began to wave. At that moment, I felt held and yet completely free.

With the exuberance of a preschooler, I waved and called out to the tree, "Thank you, thank you, thank you. With my whole being, thank you!"

I ran as quickly as I could, retracing my steps back up to Main Hall. The doors were still open, and the last practitioners were taking their seats. I skirted around one of the back jacks and fell onto a cushion.

"Let's see your stone," said a classmate opening my hand. "Did you bring that from home?"

"No," chimed another, "she bought it at the gift shop."

As I heard their laughter, the heat started to creep across my face. I could feel myself shrinking. I no longer wanted to share my story, and maybe I never would.

"Place your stones in the center of the room for a closing blessing," came the direction of the facilitator.

I had a decision to make. My instinct was to hide, to want to protect it, but the heart stone began to speak.

Julianne, only you can allow another to take away the magic of the moment. Let your stone sit proudly among all the other stones. Every stone is needed, and this is the time to claim your gift. You are the keeper of your faith!

Finding my feet, I stood up and added the pink stone to the sea of earthen colors. It is an image that I still ponder. Thankfully, the gift of that day remained. Faith was ever by my side, just like the little, pink piece of quartz. I often felt faith as warmth during times of darkness. It ushered me through periods of grief and transition—the loss of loved ones, locations, jobs, friends, and even a marriage.

Each death, move, and change brought a new depth of faith. I learned to rebirth myself time and time again. Each storm caused my roots to go deeper to seek out spiritual nourishment; the words of others taught me to go inward to find and know my truth; each longing brought me higher into an alignment with the Divine.

That tree I so loved continued to call out to me despite the miles like a whisper in the wind. Months went by.

Come to me. Come to the tree. Do you remember me?

Yes! Yes, of course, I do!

Do you still have your shaman heart stone?

Nodding, I touched the medicine bundle made with red fabric and leather lacings in honor of Girard. I was forever grateful for his soulful urging and the grace of having a friend upon the path.

Do you still carry your gift?

In response, I opened the satchel slowly and carefully so as not to spill the medicines covering the sweet, pink stone—tobacco and cornmeal (a mixture of masculine and feminine medicines) and rose petals from my father's garden (representing the love of my parents and the beauty of my ancestors).

It is not yet a gift unless it is shared.

I touched the side of my face and turned my head, straining to hear more.

A shaman's medicine is carried, but for it to be considered a gift, it must be given. That is why a shaman's medicine is found within the heart. As a shaman's heart shines, the gift is freely given.

I touched my heart, knowing faith resided there.

All you need to do is shine!

Guided by Spirit, I gave the stone to another and discovered a renewed passion for serving just as the tree had served me. What a tremendous gift to be with others in times of doubt and loss, offering faith until they found their own. Still, my greatest joy was seeing their shaman hearts shine and sharing their gifts with the world.

Author's Story Link: https://www.profoundlifewellness.com/book#js

THE MEDICINE

Enter the story and make it your own!

Imagine you hear a knocking. To your surprise, someone is standing at your front door wearing a t-shirt that reads: *Shaman Guide.*

Do you recognize this person? Go ahead, use your imagination. Is this a relative or an ancestor, or someone entirely new? Be curious. There is no mistake as to who has arrived. Allow yourself to greet this guide in whatever way is right for you.

Your guide touches your shoulder, and with the snap of two fingers, there are two. Out walks a little you, your inner child.

Winking, your Shaman Guide says, "I always love bringing children on a journey. They're so adventurous, and they still believe in magic!"

Your inner child looks up at you and takes your hand.

Notice your age. Are you six or seven, maybe younger? What style is your hair, and what are you wearing? Have you brought along a toy?

"I'm happy to answer questions," offers your Shaman Guide, "but know that this little one remembers the ways of the hidden world and can cross any veil."

Right on cue, a large velvet curtain falls from the sky, masking a grand stage. You rub your eyes, wondering if you're dreaming. Your Shaman Guide and little child both chuckle.

Then, from behind the curtain, you hear something. The words are faint at first, "Come to me. Come to the tree."

You walk so close to the curtain that the plush fabric brushes against your cheek. With increasing urgency, you hear the refrain: "Come to me. Come to the tree!"

"If the curtain were open," asks your Shaman Guide, "what would this tree of yours look like?"

What would you see? A tree from your childhood or your current backyard? Maybe it's a grand redwood that has lived upon the Earth for 2,000 years, or even the World Tree—the axis Mundi connecting Heaven, Earth, and the underworld. What does it look like?

Your Shaman Guide slowly pulls back the heavy drapes, and your inner child runs into the scene and right to the tree.

Take it all in, the landscape, the colors, the scents, and the sounds.

"Welcome to your tree," says your guide with an outstretched arm. "Do you see the tree roots going into the ground and the size of its trunk, the shape and color of the leaves, and the width of the canopy?"

The guide's words begin to drift off as you notice the sheer exquisiteness of the tree.

What catches your attention most about the tree?

As you take time to notice, the light around the tree becomes brighter. You feel a stirring within your heart.

"When you notice beauty," explains your Shaman Guide, "the heart opens. When you are grateful, the heart remains open."

You go over and warmly touch the tree. Your inner child hugs it, saying, "Thank you, thank you!"

The little one begins setting up a picnic at its base and excitedly explains, "I'll leave this here for when we return. The tree has great stories that carry us into the hidden realms."

A shower of leaves falls onto your heads, perhaps as a gentle reminder.

The little one jumps up, and before long, small arms wrap around your neck. The child looks seriously into your eyes, saying: "It's time to wake up. Please, remember who you are! Do you remember your gift?"

The child reaches into a pocket and pulls out a stone.

What type of stone do you see? A gem or a mineral, or something so uniquely-your-own?

The child places the stone into your palm, saying, "I have been keeping this for you to help you remember—the gift that you carry to share with the world."

It's your medicine.

Your Shaman Guide instructs, "The medicine can be anything: strength, compassion, creativity. . ."

With little hands making a megaphone, the child leans into your ear. With resounding clarity, you hear your gift. The child says it again.

What do you hear?

A smile creeps across your face. You embrace this little one while holding the touchstone to your heart.

"And so it is!" says your Shaman Guide with a great clap of the hands. Two become one, and your adult self is back at the door, peering out at your guest.

Your hand is still on your chest. You feel your heart and its rhythmic message: "Wake up! Wake up! Wake up! Thank you, thank you, thank you!"

Author's Medicine Link: https://www.profoundlifewellness.com/book#js

Julianne Santini, BSN, RN, PHN, Heart-Healer, Shaman Guide, Master-Level Energy Practitioner and Teacher, Energy Psychology Cycles Expert, and Sacred Site Travel Facilitator. When not offering sacred travel, workshops, or private sessions, she can be found visiting family, kayaking through the Everglades, and firewalking!

Julianne is a compassionate guide, meeting clients where they are. She listens to their language, determining where there is pain and suffering. Through practical tools and energy work, she brings awareness, relief, and a new way of being.

Julianne often asks, "If I had a magic wand and could give you anything, what would it be?" She teaches clients how to dream and make those dreams a reality. She uses an expert blend of healing arts, sciences, and energy psychology.

A certified trainer with decades of learning, she uses a combination of angelic and violet flame modalities, esoteric healing science, energy psychology, indigenous wisdom practices, and meditation. She reflects a rich tapestry of training from teachers around the globe—a Philippine master, a Buddhist teacher, an Indian saint, and wisdom keepers of North, Central, and South America. She's a graduate of the Foundation of Shamanic Studies and a founding member of the Society for Shamanic Practice.

Julianne recognizes mind, body, and spirit as integral parts of the healing process. She began her career as a registered nurse in 1992. She worked as an oncology nurse in California, nursing instructor in Colorado, owner of a wellness center in New Hampshire, manager of an urgent care in Massachusetts, and an energy practitioner for complimentary care centers in Colorado. She continues her life's work in Naples, Florida as co-founder of Profound Life Wellness.

Ready to collaborate and play? Connect with Julianne:

Website: https://www.profoundlifewellness.com

Book Resources: https://www.profoundlifewellness.com/book

Facebook: https://www.facebook.com/julianne.w.santini

Email: Julianne@ProfoundLifeWellness.com

CHAPTER 14

ROOTED IN PRAYER

UNIQUE, POWERFUL MEDICINE FOR SURVIVING DEPRESSION

Angela Bard M.S.

MY STORY

I look at my reflection and see a shell of a person staring back at me.

I hate you, everything about you.

I feel a waterfall of emotions—once again drowning out life, any and every thought or feeling.

Hidden from the world, I want to disappear altogether.

I'm locked in my bathroom, a place where I can safely escape from life.

This time would be the time.

Sliding down the wall, watching myself disappear from the mirror, I pray out loud.

"Why did you create a life like this? Why do you let people feel this way?"

The cold porcelain bathtub presses against my arm, the smell of lavender soap fills my lungs.

I hate the smell of lavender. I'm not sure why tonight is the night.

The devastating depression was no stronger tonight than any other night. Thoughts are running—about the daily paralyzing anxiety I live with, the time I was choked and assaulted, my eating disorder, my destructive inner critic, and my countless imperfections.

My mind and body can't take anymore. I'm tired of being uncomfortable in my skin. I'm tired of wearing a mask. I'm tired of life. I'm tired of it all.

Setting the stage in this tiny bathroom, I had my trusted friend, a glass of dry oaky chardonnay. She used to be the one that made everything better. She helped me forget and numb out from reality. I'm reminded of such sweetness and goodness from my childhood as I hold the black bowl I use every October 31st for handing out candy to trick or treaters. I used to love seeing this bowl on the table by the front door. Tonight, it holds a concoction of pink, white, and blue pills. Slowly I empty the bottles into the bowl. It sounds like a slot machine in a casino.

I'll hit the jackpot tonight. No more hurting. No more feeling pain. Just no more.

"Please don't let me wake up. I don't know how to do life. I don't want to do life."

I feel so lost in this world, not knowing who or what I'm praying to. Growing up Southern Baptist and attending church several times a week, I had a strong, supportive community. I enjoyed going to church and connecting with others. What I don't enjoy, nor can I relate to, is the immense fear of burning in Hell. I am told same-sex attraction is forbidden, that your body is a temple, and that eating disorders are not acknowledged, nor has anyone discussed a harmful inner critic. I'm fearful of saying and doing the wrong thing. I've tried to be perfect by looking and acting a certain way. Pleasing others to be accepted has proven to be a lost cause, and I've lost myself in trying.

I no longer recognize who I am. What do I like to do for fun? I don't even know what music I like.

Constantly going against myself, I'm abandoning and betraying myself.

Mixing the deadly cocktail in my stomach, I take one pill at a time and chase it with a crisp sip of my best friend. I feel loneliness, relief, and despair to a level I didn't know existed. Feeling numb, I lay down on the cold bathroom floor. I imagine my body merging with the beige linoleum. I feel as though my soul is leaking out of my chest, and I lie in a puddle on the floor that looks like liquid mercury.

Who's going to pick that up? How are they going to pick that up?

At that moment I decided to call someone to tell them goodbye. I contacted a friend of mine I used to work with. I hadn't seen or talked with her in over a year. Dialing Sherry's number, I waited for what seemed like hours for her to answer. "Hi, Sherry. It's been a long time. I wanted to tell you I just can't do life anymore. I am tired. I just took a bunch of pills." Going in and out of consciousness, Sherry called the police and Mike, my then-partner, to tell them what I said.

Being jolted back into consciousness with a constant banging on the door, I saw the sporadic yellow and red lights through the white curtains. I always knew I would be in the spotlight. I just thought I'd be on a stage in my best attire giving a leadership speech, not taking an unconscious, expensive free ride in my T-shirt and shorts to the hospital. I opened the door, stumbled to the ambulance, and collapsed onto the stretcher.

The following day, I woke up in the intensive care unit at the local hospital. Opening my eyes was a challenge. The dryness and scratchy feeling of my eyelids remind me of wiper blades on an icy windshield. I scanned the room, trying to make out anything or anyone. I feel raw. My throat is raw, my heart is raw, and my stomach is raw. The overwhelming smell of antiseptics and body odor stings my nostrils with each inhale.

Why am I waking up? It didn't work. I can't even kill myself correctly. I'm such a failure.

My thoughts are interrupted by the alarm sounding on the monitor. My heart rate is extremely high. The wires connected to my body let out the cries and screams I harbored in my head for decades. As I stand up on the bed to silence the alarm I lose my balance and crumble back into bed.

I feel a heaviness in my heart and stomach as I cautiously open my eyes the next afternoon. My body aches, and I feel like it's trying to move through thick marshes. Everything feels heavy and numb at the same time.

Okay, God, what now?

As I turn my aching head and look up, I see my mom. There is devastating fear in her eyes and sadness in her heart. I look at her and Mike.

"I'm going to die if I don't get help."

I check myself in a residential treatment program. I worked with a nutritionist, attended 12-step meetings, and dove into experiential trauma therapy. I became open and willing to connect with something greater than me as I reconnected with my inner child and my growing adult self.

Connection with a higher power is the most vital piece for me to live life. In the beginning, I didn't know how to connect, or if I even wanted to. I remember sitting outside on the ground in front of a tree at the treatment center, admiring it and relating to it.

I have always admired trees, but this tree had the perfect balance of strength and gentleness, characteristics I strive to embody. It would sway with a small amount of wind as if it were slow-dancing with a beloved. Looking at the grey bark covering its trunk and limbs, I was reminded of viewing life as grey and dull. When I continued to admire this tree, I saw the brightest green growth budding from each limb and reaching out. By going into treatment, I was reaching out. The roots were strong, and I could see them expand across the green grass. There was the most comfortable spot to nestle between the roots and the base of the trunk on the grass. The roots curved around as if to hold me.

A lady that worked as a residential assistant in the house I stayed in sat outside with me one morning and said, "Give yourself permission to say anything like a prayer. Try saying something to this tree."

Can I say anything like a prayer? Could it really be this simple? I feel silly.

I began to pray to this tree, "I don't know what to believe, but I do know I don't want to feel this sad. I am so angry at myself, with life, and with God. I want the vicious inner critic to stop running the show. I just want to feel okay."

For over four months, I prayed to that tree to find peace and direction and learn how to like myself. Incorporating my love of nature, my desire to move through paralyzing depression, and quieting the inner critic were the beginning of accepting and loving life.

"I want to be comfortable with the uncomfortable."

Many people have shared the power of prayer with me, but until I could stop disassociating and become present in the moment, I wasn't able to experience the calmness of the mind, body, and spirit that prayer can bring. I created a spiritual practice that helps me with my depression, keeps my overwhelming inner critic at bay, and helps me to feel connected to the great mystery of life.

THE MEDICINE

I have implemented a daily practice that includes clearing, connecting, grounding, somatic breathwork, and prayer. This practice can be any length it needs to be, from five minutes to more than an hour. I encourage you to explore what is the best timeframe for you.

CLEARING

I like to burn a little sage, incense, palo santo, or light a candle. If you're doing this inside, it's a good idea to open a window or door to allow the energy to move. You can use the smoke to clear your energy field and the energy around you. Or you can have the scent burning in the background. If you're sensitive to smoke, you can designate a stone or crystal each time and have it out during this practice.

CONNECTING

Stand up and shake your body. This is a way to shake off any stuck energy inside or outside the body. All traumas, including our thoughts, are stuck energy in the body.

Next, begin to massage your body gently. This is a way to wake up the meridians and ground yourself. Starting at the top of your head, massage your scalp, down your face, and your eyelids. Our lids are often neglected. Spend extra time on your ears. During this practice, think of reasons why you're grateful for these parts of your body. For example, I have gratitude for my eyelids because they keep dirt and debris out of my eyes. Working your way down your body from the back of your neck to the front of your throat chakra, say out loud something you wanted to say in a conversation that you didn't say at the time. Or say something you want to let go of and something you want to bring in today—rubbing down both arms one at a time and taking time with each finger.

On one hand, state five things you want to transform. On the other hand, state five things you love or like about yourself. Then, moving to your armpits, across to your heart, and down the rib cage, give extra sweetness to your kidneys, stomach, digestive tract, and womb. Think about what you'd like to create today—moving to each hip and down each leg. Conclude with massaging your feet and giving gratitude for the strength they have to carry you each day.

GROUNDING

I encourage you to find what you can relate to for this grounding exercise. Some examples you can relate to are a cross, an animal, feeling your feet on the ground, etc. It can be anything or anyone. For me, I relate my physical and spiritual body to trees. Think of your feet as the roots and imagine them spreading out just underneath the surface of the earth. They are supportive. Who or what supports you? Begin breathing that support up through your body. What are the strengths that create your trunk? Can you feel and connect with that strength within? Continue breathing up through your body and out of your crown chakra. Imagine that energy infinitely flowing gently out into the universe. Identify what you want to let flow in your life. For example, do you want to feel more connected to a community? Do you want to share your medicine with more clients? It can be anything.

SOMATIC BREATHWORK

Find a comfortable place to sit. Typically, I like to sit with the back of my heart against a tree if I'm outside or a door frame if I'm inside. I encourage you to be comfortable. This is not a practice to force your body or your breath to be a certain way. We're working with your natural breath, allowing it to explore your physical and emotional body.

Just allow your breath to inhale and exhale naturally. Allow any thoughts or feelings to come up. If the inner critic becomes loud, thank that voice and focus back on your natural breath. Checking inside, where do you notice your breath entering and exiting the body? Are you breathing in and out of your nose? Are you breathing in and out of your mouth? Is it a combination of both? Just notice. Notice any sensations you may be feeling. Is the air cold? Do you feel the warmth of the sun on your skin? Do you feel grass or carpet underneath you? Next, follow your breath as you inhale. Does your breath feel fluid, choppy, deep, or shallow? Where does your breath go? Can you feel your breath in your head, throat, chest, belly, or feet? Just notice, there is no right or wrong. There is only your natural breath.

If you notice an emotion, see if you can find where that energy is in the body and put a hand there. Does this emotion want to say something? Does this emotion want to cry, laugh, or move? Staying with your natural breath and allow this emotion. Does this emotion have a story? What does this emotion need? Again, stay with your natural breath, feel the back of your heart and allow.

If you do not notice an emotion, is there a place where you notice the breath is not flowing in your body? Without judgment, put a hand there and allow your natural breath to go to your hand. Does this place have a story? What does this place need? Stay with your breath and just breathe.

There are several different somatic breathwork tools that can be implemented with a trained practitioner. These tools can be helpful to move through and work with trauma, depression, anxiety, or grief.

PRAYER

I want to recognize that prayer can be a loaded word for many people as it once was for me. Different words I've used for prayer include: surrender, intention, and focused energy. I always remind myself and others that I can't do prayer wrong, just like I can't do life wrong.

Your prayer can be any words and any feeling. You can pray to anything and nothing. I would pray to the Great Mystery, the Universe, Mother Earth, or the Divine when I began praying. Many of my prayers today begin with Creator.

I found such freedom when I was given permission to pray to whomever or whatever. Often, I'm asked to lead a group in prayer during ceremonies, and it's an honor to say yes. I always say yes when asked because I realize it's not me. I do my personal work to keep my vessel clear so that Creator can speak through me.

Sometimes, the prayers are as simple as "Help me feel okay." Or, "Please help me. I don't know what I need." I still pray to be comfortable with the uncomfortable.

An important teaching from several elders, while I was pouring out my thoughts in the sweat lodge, was to surrender to the expectations of the prayers, meaning I had to let go of the way life is unfolding. Through prayer, I can see life's obstacles as gifts of growth.

I've never practiced nor rehearsed a prayer. For me, it's about connecting and allowing the words to come through for others to hear. I offer you this prayer I recorded as I spoke it after writing this chapter.

Oh Creator, Divine Mother,

I come to you with gratitude for this life. This ability to feel the despair of grief, the intense anger, along with the aching belly laughs and joy felt in my bones, remind me what it is to be truly alive. I ask that you continue to help me to see the different colors in the sunrises and sunsets. Please help me to really feel the beauty of the rain on my cheeks, to bathe in the healing waters, to connect with the spirit of the fire within, and to breathe life in each day. Please help me to embrace these so-called obstacles on my path and choose growth instead of defeat when they arise. I ask for strength and guidance to have those hard conversations, to share the truth of who I am, and trust this path I have chosen. Support me in continuing to be open and see the world from the innocence of a child, to incorporate play as an adult, to love myself unconditionally and others. To forgive without reason, accept and quiet my inner critic, and embrace all of me, including what I have once perceived as dark, unlovable, and unlikeable. I ask you to help me embody my duality into oneness and live every moment to the fullest, understanding that as a human, I will be uncomfortable. I pray to move with the fear and allow vulnerability to take the lead on this journey. I am forever grateful for this body, this mind, spirit, life, my tribe, and you.

Angela Bard, M.S. Trauma recovery coach, spiritual mentor, energy healer, firewalking instructor trainer, and empowerment leader guiding people to awaken to the gifts of who they are.

With a master's degree in management and leadership and over 20 years of experience working in the mental health, eating disorder, addictions, and trauma recovery field, Angela harmonizes:

- challenge course therapy
- firewalking
- somatic breath coaching
- transformational breathwork
- water rebirthing breathwork
- spiritual ceremonies
- Mexica (Meh-She-Ka) healings

These modalities work well for people who feel limited or constricted, transforming their routines to create the life they desire.

She apprenticed for many years with different healers, elders, medicine people, teachers, and trainers from around the world.

In addition to providing individual sessions, groups, workshops, healings, journeys abroad, and spiritual connecting, Angela rejuvenates by spending time in nature, hiking, swimming, and spending time with her four-legged family members. Angela balances life by incorporating self-care, play, and empowering others on their journey.

You can connect with Angela:
Website: https://www.breathingempowerment.com
Facebook: https://www.facebook.com/BreathingEmpowerment
Instagram: https://www.instagram.com/breathingempowerment_be
Email: breathingempowerment@gmail.com

CHAPTER 15

HARNESSING THE POWER OF ANGER

USING CREATIVE EXPRESSION TO RELEASE AND RESTORE BALANCE

Christine Falcon-Daigle, MFA, RYT-200

MY STORY

I stood in the middle of our quiet, suburban street with my five-year-old daughter. She was learning to ride her bike. It was summer, and we could hear the ice cream truck a few blocks away.

"If you give it one more try, I'll get you an ice cream," I bribed. It was late afternoon, with no breeze in sight. Smoke from a nearby wildfire hung heavy in the air. A demonic red pupil burned through the haze overhead in place of the sun.

A couple of houses up, a silver car came speeding around the corner. I did that mom-thing with my arm, shielding my daughter behind me. The female driver careened past without paying us any regard. *What the hell?*

Less than a minute later, the same car came speeding around the corner again, even faster.

This time I yelled, "Slow the fuck down!" as loud as I could. My entire body was shaking. She stopped her car in front of a house down the street, unleashed a string of profanities from her car window, and peeled out, leaving a cloud of burnt rubber in her wake.

A minute later, when she came flying around the corner a third time, apparently doing laps, I was ready. What may have been a lovers' quarrel for her was, for me, an all-out assault on the safety of our neighborhood.

Oh, hell no!

"Stay here!" I ordered my daughter, whose tiny hands gripped the handlebars of her bike even tighter.

I marched my mountain bike out from where it rested under the shade of a Monterey Pine and stood directly in the center of the street. When the driver realized I wasn't moving, it became a game of chicken. Straddling my bike, I stood my ground.

Seconds before impact, she slammed on the brakes. With a terrible crunching sound, her car ran over the front end of my bike while I jumped to the side.

"What the fuck do you think you're doing, you crazy bitch! You could've killed someone!" I gestured to my mangled bike frame underneath her front end.

I'd completely left my body, overtaken by a primal rage. I slammed my hands on the driver's side window, feeling no pain whatsoever, and tried to open her car door just as she hit the lock button.

I pounded and screamed, "Open the *fucking* door!"

She screamed back at me through the closed window, then grinding the gear shift and gunning the engine, backed off my mangled bike, reversing all the way to the corner.

High on adrenalin, I screamed, "And don't come back!" Blood pumped in my ears. A few concerned neighbors came outside.

Then I saw my daughter, who looked like she'd just seen a ten-foot cobra.

"Mommy," she said, "you said some scary things."

I realized she wasn't just scared. She was scared of *me.* "Oh, sweetheart, I'm so sorry. Mommy was really angry."

"You said some really bad words, Mommy." She made an awkward attempt to smile, her enormous eyes searching my face for any sign of the formerly fun, safe mother she knew and loved.

Shame rushed over me. "Yes, yes I did. Mommy didn't mean to get so upset."

At that moment, I traveled back in time to when I was a little girl. I watched my father, in one of his many fits of fury, jump out of his car at an intersection and try to instigate a fight with the man in front of us. "You son-of-a-bitch! You cut me off!"

Then I saw myself, hiding in my closet, wrapped in a blanket on the floor, having peed my pants out of fright. I saw myself frozen in fear in our hallway as his steel-toed boots stomped closer, knowing it was no use to try and run. I could feel his gold ring as it struck my head, the welts it left on my scalp for days afterward. I remembered how that little girl left her body as he dragged her down the street by her hair, watched from above as she was kicked, slapped, and punched for disobeying him.

Then I was back, standing in the street: a 37-year-old mother, lost and unhappy in a marriage I knew was ending. I was scared by my own uncontrolled rage. Although I'd never gotten physical with my daughter, I knew that potential existed. I'd been in more fistfights as a kid and young adult than I cared to admit and had enough therapy to know *hurt people hurt people*.

Fear of inflicting physical harm to my daughter caused me to seek help. What I learned about raising children from *my* parents nearly resulted in me taking my own life–something I'd contemplated more than once. With the support of my first husband, I went back into therapy. A few years later, I found my way to the intensive, weeklong Hoffman Process.

It took seeing myself through the eyes of a child–my own daughter–to realize this pattern of violence and aggression lived in me and was not something I wanted to perpetuate. I knew how this kind of behavior was hardwired into my nervous system, a result of what I'd lived with and learned as a child. And I knew I needed professional help.

Two weeks after completing my Hoffman Process, I knew three things for certain: 1.) The love for my daughter had led me to find unconditional love for myself. 2.) I had to face what my first husband and I already knew:

our marriage was over. 3.) I had to see my father, a man I hadn't seen in 20 years, face-to-face.

It was a sunny day, and when I pulled into the carport, my eyes took a few seconds to adjust. Then I saw a man, his back to me, standing at the other end of the driveway. I recognized the spider web tattoos on his elbows; the right one permanently cocked from the time he broke it falling off the horse at my older brother's fifth birthday party. At almost 70, he had a lot less hair, and what he had left was completely gray. He seemed smaller, more stooped, certainly not the same terrifying figure that tormented me in my childhood memories. He was crushing empty beer cans with a sledgehammer, something I'd seen him do a thousand times.

I took a deep breath and got out of the car. He turned to face me.

"Hello, Toots."

"Hi, Dad." I smiled.

He smiled back, "Long time, no see." His glasses had thicker lenses now, making his different colored eyes more visible. I always favored the brown eye over the blue one for its slightly softer energy when I was growing up.

"Must be important, whatever it is you came to say," he scanned me up and down.

Do I look different to you, too?

The last time we'd seen each other, I was 19 years old and six-months sober. I'd had many close calls with death by then—the kind you look back on and wonder how on earth you survived. Now, almost 40, I'd been married 14 years to a man he didn't know, and I was mother to his seven-year-old granddaughter he'd never met. The weight of all the time we'd never get back hit me then, a tsunami of grief.

Wow, it's been 20 years.

"Come on in." I followed him up the steps, covered in fake grass. He used the wobbly railing to help pull himself up. I could hear his labored breathing as he climbed. I knew he'd quit smoking when he was diagnosed with asbestosis from all those years in the Navy, but that didn't reverse the lung damage, only slowed it down.

Pink flamingos and garden gnomes dotted the neighboring yards of the other mobile homes in the trailer park. Colorful windsocks spun in circles and changed direction with the gentle breeze. Dad had a stone garden statue of a long-eared dog holding a basket of flowers in its mouth. To my amazement, a gentle-looking Jesus presided over the lava rock, spread out between two sprawling cypress bushes.

I entered behind him through the glass slider with its faded butterfly decals. The last time I'd been there was during the drama of our unexpected family reunion in 1990, an event featured on Oprah and, to my horror, splattered across the front page of our local newspaper, *The Vallejo Times-Herald.*

That long-ago summer was tough. Not only did I learn about my dad's other family for the first time––the one he'd had before ours and kept secret from my brother and me, but my beloved grandmother died, followed a month later by the devastation of my first heartbreak. Without drugs or alcohol, I felt it all. I cried for six months straight. I was certain I'd never survive what felt like an all-consuming, relentless agony. I considered, not for the first or the last time, taking my own life. But I didn't pick up a drink or use drugs, and by some miracle, I didn't die. This was the beginning of my lifelong journey home.

The week spent at the Hoffman Process in Saint Helena in 2010 was a quantum leap on that path of healing. I saw how, in my own attempt not to marry a man like my father, I did the opposite; however, that was a decision made more from the head than the heart. Being able to forgive myself for that and all the pain it caused was huge.

I found such forgiveness, compassion, and emotional freedom, not only for myself but also for my parents, who'd been divorced for over 20 years by this time. The all-too-familiar blame and resentment I carried around since I could remember were, much to my relief, replaced by genuine gratitude. Through the experiential learning of the week, I came to see they'd done their best with what they'd been given. This work also allowed me to begin an ongoing practice of self-compassion for all the mistakes I had yet to make as a parent. No one is perfect, and we do our best, or, as they say at Hoffman: "Everyone's guilty, but no one's to blame."

When my dad and I came together that spring afternoon in the dimly lit dining room of his mobile home, there was no fight left in me. For years, I'd channeled it into journals, poetry, and fictional characters, poured it out to therapists and sponsors, and exorcised it from my body through physical exercise. But the tipping point for me was Hoffman, where I could once-and-for-all lay down my battle-ax and surrender to love.

My dad and I looked at each other, face-to-face, across the table. He gulped his vodka over ice; I drank my diet 7-Up, grateful for the tingle of its cool spray on my nose. I let out a small belch and felt the silence between us thicken. Then I reached over and took both his hands in mine. I took a deep breath and squeezed. He squeezed back, and my eyes filled with tenderness.

"Dad, I just wanted to tell you, I love you." He swallowed hard. Hot tears fell from my eyes, but I didn't let go of his hands. "I'm so sorry I cut you out of my life all these years."

My father, a man I'd never seen shed a tear in my entire life, choked back sobs. I got up and put my arms around him. "Shhh…Dad. It's okay."

An ocean of healing waves broke over us both.

That day in my father's trailer, the miracle of love and the miracle of forgiveness took over. The miracles haven't stopped since, for either of us.

THE MEDICINE

"Anger without purpose is useless and even harmful." – Isabel Allende, *The Soul of a Woman.*

Anger is one of those emotions I was raised to believe was unacceptable as a nice Catholic girl. This was a big problem for me since I grew up being angry at the world.

On the path of my own healing journey, I have since discovered the value of anger, a powerful human emotion. By channeling it into creative expression, it becomes a vehicle for healing and transformation. It also keeps the energy flowing, necessary for overall health and well-being.

It's appropriate to feel angry about any number of things happening today. In addition to the limitations of the current global pandemic and all the uncertainty it's brought, there's: racial injustice, abuses of power, loss of habitat and species due to climate change, poor leadership, exploitation of the natural world, and lack of access to resources for those in need.

Without our *holy anger,* many of the most important movements for social change would've been impossible. Think of Women's Lib, Civil Rights, or various environmental movements, to name a few.

A few years ago, I attended a conference where I heard a former Catholic priest Matthew Fox in conversation with David Korten. He claimed the number one obstacle to solving the problems facing humanity wasn't ignorance but apathy. "Why are we sitting on our anger?" He cried, outraged.

I've got to believe it's because we're conditioned to *behave,* to *be good* little boys and girls. But complicity in systems that destroy the planet and create pain and suffering for all but a select minority is a problem we must address.

PERMISSION

Give yourself permission to feel angry. There's no such thing as a good or bad emotion. Anger is just one of many human emotions such as joy or sadness and has an important job. It's how the body tells us *something needs to change.*

Admitting we're angry is empowering and takes courage. Look yourself in the eyes in a mirror and *own* it. Then, sit with your eyes closed and tune into your body. Where does it live inside you: your stomach, face, neck, or chest? Engage with it to find out what, if anything, needs to be done. Sometimes, our anger just needs us to *feel it.*

AWARENESS

It's important to understand how unexpressed anger gets stuck and takes up residence in the body. Without awareness, anger can be like a band of squatters in an abandoned house. I had to live with the ravages of my own rage long enough to know the devastating toll it could take. Mine showed up as ulcers, heartburn, canker sores, skin inflammation, agitation, and headaches.

If you try to deny or block anger, it always comes out sideways. Often this results in unintentional and unfortunate collateral damage. If you notice yourself engaging in self-sabotaging behaviors—things that make you feel bad or hurt you like overeating, consuming too much alcohol, overly relying on prescription drugs that calm and numb, smoking cigarettes, driving recklessly, or picking fights with those around you, then ask yourself, what's really going on? It might be internalized anger.

EXPRESSION

Once you've identified your anger, try expressing it so it can move through you. These are some examples of channeling anger into action that worked for me:

- Journaling.
- Writing an angry letter and not sending it.
- Drawing or painting your rage.
- Giving voice to it in a song. This can even be fun and helps to diffuse the anger.
- Writing an imaginary dialogue between my anger and me.
- Creative fiction writing.
- Movement (Dancing, hiking, kickboxing, power walking, cycling, etc.)

COMMUNICATE

Call a friend or family member. Always ask if it's a good time to vent. Get permission before launching into a rant. Emotional dumping can become a dynamic you want to steer clear of; this can have a negative effect on a relationship if one person is always the dumper and the other is always the dumpee. Endeavor to create clear boundaries, safe containers, and self-awareness. Allow yourself 20 minutes. Set a timer. Although you might be angry, understand you are not your anger.

When it's appropriate to express your anger directly to the person who has harmed you, do so in a safe way. This could be in person, or it might be in a letter. Familiarize yourself with the basics of nonviolent communication (www.nonviolentcommunication.com) and put them to practice. Let go of the outcome. Just because you've expressed your hurt and anger, even rage over something someone has done, don't expect an apology. Your anger might trigger blame, shame, defensiveness, or denial.

Understand that one of the main stages a person moves through with grief is anger. Help people in your life understand when you are grieving, you will need time alone to express your anger safely. Since it can be scary or triggering for some people, before expressing anger, always ask permission if you share space. If you must, wait until you are alone and then have at it! Punch, kick and scream at a punching bag. Use a stick to beat a log. Whatever works, just get it moving.

NATURE

Get into nature. The earth has many excellent balms to soothe the burning heat of anger. An hour spent power walking barefoot on a sandy beach or hiking through a lush green forest can do wonders. If possible, get in saltwater. If nothing else, soak in a tub of hot water with Dead Sea salts.

GRATITUDE AND FORGIVENESS

Write yourself a love letter. Express your gratitude to your own body for allowing you to feel! Even if it isn't particularly pleasant, it's part of being alive. Know it will pass.

If you're angry at yourself, make amends as soon as you can. Write a letter of apology and don't hold back. Forgiving yourself is an act of radical self-love.

California Native **Christine Falcon-Daigle** has traveled a healing path for 30 years. She holds a BA in Psychology from Dominican University and an MFA in Writing and Consciousness from the California Institute of Integral Studies. Since 2011, she's supported adults committed to their personal growth and transformation through work with the Hoffman Institute, a non-profit that hosts the weeklong Hoffman Process on a 196-acre property, recently acquired from the Institute of Noetic Sciences, where she and her husband lived while raising their daughter, from 2012-2017.

Her award-winning poetry and fiction have appeared in print, online, and on stage; she's worked in radio and film, serving as associate producer for The Last Stand, an award-winning documentary that aired nationally on public television and internationally at film festivals.

In 2021, she completed Thomas Hubl's Collective Trauma Integration Process (CTIP) training and became a Women's Circle Facilitator with Global Sisterhood. She and her husband completed a two-year program with the Horticultural Therapy Institute (HTI) and together they've designed and installed labyrinths, beehives, flower gardens, and food forests.

She's a certified ski guide with Discovery Blind Sports and instructor of Baptiste Power of Yoga who's guided and taught since 1993. She craves adventure and has assisted with international yoga and meditation retreats in Cambodia, Thailand, Haiti, and Mexico.

Along with her love of physical fitness and creative expression, she's a passionate advocate for the natural world and enjoys rock climbing, kayaking, mountain biking, and hiking. You may find her forest bathing in the woods, watching a sunset at the beach, dancing at JazzFest in New Orleans, or expressing one of her alter egos at an all-night rave.

Contact info:

www.christinefalcondaigle.com

LinkedIn: Christine Falcon-Daigle

Instagram: @cfalconmoon @transformanity

Email: cfalcondaigle@gmail.com

Facebook: Christine Falcon-Daigle

Links/Resources: www.hoffmaninstitute.org

www.globalsisterhood.org

CHAPTER 16

TRAUMA HAPPENS

WRITE A FORGIVENESS LETTER TO FIND PEACE

Karen Ann Scott, RYT-200

MY STORY

Trigger warning: graphic content

Laying down in the single bed on the soupy wet cotton sheets, covered with Snow White and the Seven Dwarfs images, I could see that the dwarves' peach-colored faces were turning various shades of pink, red, and orange as the blood dried. I felt the blood and skin dripping down my thighs, onto my calves, and the bottom of my feet staining them. My father, George, had just finished his rounds of ripping out my insides with the bang of his penis against what seemed to be the pit of my stomach. I remembered as he moaned that in the blur of the tears of my eyes, I could see his face turning red as a tomato. The vein on his neck pumped, vibrating blood into every exertion of his penis into my body cavity.

I remember imagining all the parts of me trying to squeeze back together again. I could feel all the parts of my mind, heart, and soul crushed to pieces. My mind questioned, *what did I do to deserve this?* I thought that my voice was screaming, but my spirit, soul, and heart were yelling, and no sound was coming out of my mouth. I realized my soul, body, and mind kept themselves quiet so the little girl within me could store herself away somewhere deep inside her body.

I would know when to cry out later when it was safe.

My eyes, nose, and body were deceiving me. I could still smell the vanilla flavor, cinnamon spice, and lemon scent of the Old Spice cologne my father wore as he had rocked me to sleep just a few hours ago. Now my father was knocking me awake with the gyrations of pain in my body shooting up and down my spine while the whirls of his pleasure were making sounds of incredulous lust. As I was feeling the pain, I saw the head of a stuffed animal, Snoopy, fall from the bed and onto the floor.

In the meantime, the room began to spin. I felt a disconnect, and my spirit-self flew up to the ceiling. From up there, I saw everything he was doing to me without feeling any more pain. First, I was lying on the bed; next, my body was looking down at my father, George, hovering over my body as his hips moved up and down and the wires of the cot bed screeched as it etched pieces of my soul into the wood floors. I could feel a slimy, gooey liquid spray across my belly, and my father, George's weight lifted off from my belly. I slid out from under his weight, and my trembling, rubbery feeling legs allowed my feet to ground momentarily on the hardwood floor.

I felt my spirit-self float down to meet my physical body, and we landed feet first on the freezing wood floor. I could feel myself come down from the ceiling. I walked with a hobble to the room across the hall where my mother was sleeping. While I was hobbling, I remember the feeling of my hair standing up on the edge of my skin, feeling fear and boldness at the same time. I heard a little voice in my head say, *You wait till I tell Momma Karen what you did to me!*

I found the strength to walk to the next room and crawl into the bed where I thought my mother was. She would rescue me.

Exhausted and in pain, my consciousness went in and out. I pulled on her leg, using my right foot to push myself up. I climbed onto her bed by climbing up her leg like a fire pole and sat next to her big belly. I was scream-whispering, "Momma, look what he did to me!"

She was not listening.

She did not awaken as she rotated her body. As she turned over on her side, I saw the purple, blue, and green bruises on her belly and legs as the wrinkled flowered sheets moved away from her.

I yelled, "Momma, what happened to you? Did daddy do this to you, too?" Then she seemed to snore louder than before. I saw red colors in my eyes, and the room turned blood red. I tried to soothe myself. "Momma, why aren't you listening to me?" I began to pull open her eyes from the eyelashes. "Momma, wake up! I am hurt! I am bleeding!"

When she would not respond, I began to slap her lightly on the cheek repeating, "Mama, wake up. I am bleeding!" I half yelled, half wailed, half cried out in pain as I let out this yelp—a sound like a mother bear setting off an alarm that her cubs were in danger to a strange animal. The only thing was that I was not the mother. I sounded off that my siblings and I were in danger, and my mother was completely unable to wake up as I kept yelling, "Look at what Daddy did to me!" and, in surprise to myself, kept yelling, "Did Daddy, do that to you?" My legs hurt, my tummy hurt, and my heart lay shattered.

I just knew there was no way for me to get my mother up. And then my mother, turned over and said in a deep sleep-like voice, "What are you doing? Can't you see I am trying to sleep?"

Exasperated, I yelled, "Momma. Look! Look what Daddy did to me. I am bleeding. I am hurt."

My mother's eyes darted from side to side as she tried to focus. Then I remember her black and blue marks on her body, and I whisper-yell, "Did Daddy do that to you?" I touched my mother's bruises.

She flinched, winced and grumbled, "What did you say?"

I said, "Look. At. What Daddy. Did. To. Me!" I pointed to stains between my legs and on my thigh filled with blood and some skin hanging.

My mother, unnervingly, shouted out loud, "That is impossible. Your father loves you. Why are you lying about your father, George, like that?" For a quick minute, I thought I was imagining my mother speaking when she called me a liar in no uncertain terms. As I looked directly in her hazel eyes, and I pointed at bruised legs, "Daddy did that to you!"

She turned away and began to whimper. The voice in my head kept saying, *Why aren't you listening to me? I told you what daddy did to me. And you did not believe me.*

I thought *I'd have to protect my twin sister, Michelle. Daddy is not going to get her.* I remember crying myself asleep as the collar of my Lucy and Snoopy nightgown became puddled with tears of rage and shame. I think I remained quiet, calm, and in fear. My voice did not work. But the next day in school, my pencils and my crayons did.

The next day, Monday after the Christmas holiday, Ms. Friedman, my kindergarten teacher, listened to me. Ms. Friedman asked us to draw pictures of what we did over the Christmas vacation. We were to write the names of the people in the picture. I used my crayons to draw as best as I could and keep straight the facts of what I could remember happening over the holiday. I remembered my observance of the bruises on my Momma Karen's legs and belly, and I remember the pain in between my legs and thighs. I remember drawing a picture of me floating in the sky as I was lying on the bed and my father George raping me.

When we were done drawing, Ms. Friedman came around to each of us individually. She asked what I had drawn in the picture and who the people were. I explained, "This is a picture of my bed, where my father lay on me. He put something in my vagina while he was lying on me. He was making funny noises. I flew up to the ceiling as he squirted some liquid onto my belly after he put his private part into my private part."

The teacher asked me, as she put her hand on my shoulder, to calm me down, "Where was your mother when this was happening in the picture?

I said, "Mrs. Friedman, my mother was in the room across the hall! I went in to tell her what my father did to me."

Mrs. Friedman asked, "And what did your mother do? What did she say?" I told Ms. Friedman the truth that my mother said that I was lying about my daddy and that he loved me."

I remember waiting in the principal's office for a very long time.

I remembered, later as an adult, that a call was made to the police to do a rape kit. My mother was called. My father was called. And a school counselor was called. When my mother came into school, I met her in the principal's office. The principal asked my mother who we went to see for the Christmas holiday and she responded, "We stayed home. We did not see anyone. My husband, the two kids, and I stayed home together."

Ms. Salvatore, the principal, asked my mother about the pictures. The principal asked me to explain what I drew in the pictures. When I proceeded to describe what my father George did and that I saw bruises on my mother's body too, my mother, Karen Helen, flinched and sucked her teeth hard as she pulled her long coat and thin jacket around her legs.

She said, "My husband and I have our problems, but he loves my children. She made this whole story up about her father doing those bad things to her to get attention." I looked at the school principal's face as it turned to disgust. She got on her walkie-talkie radio and said, "Bring them in."

Two police, a man and a woman, came in. One took my mother in handcuffs and led her out of the room. Ms. Salvatore said, "Get her out of here."

For the first time in the five years, I'd been alive, I felt seen, listened to, and heard by the adults in my life.

As you can imagine, I've been working on healing my entire life. I found forgiveness was the only pathway to peace, and it took a number of forgiveness letters to heal. I've learned that forgiveness does not absolve me or someone else of our wrongdoing. However, taking responsibility for my own actions and making amends to the people I've harmed restores relationships, rebuilds trust, and reintegrates all parties back into the community.

Forgiveness is a process of finding peace and calm within my highest self. When I practice forgiveness, I let go of my anger, resentment and hate towards myself and others regardless of whether the pain stems from personal flaws, honest mistakes, or purposeful harm. My hope for you is that writing a forgiveness letter helps you release the story of any particular event that has hurt you and that overtime you find peace and calm. My personal practice of writing a forgiveness letter to myself and others has cleared a path to my physical and mental release of guilt, shame, anger and fear. Furthermore, it has opened me to giving, receiving, and accepting love, abundance and generosity without judgement or expectation. Remember, forgiveness is a gift to yourself.

THE MEDICINE

FORGIVENESS LETTERS

Remember that we are one with God, and God acts through us—living without judgment of good or evil and accepting what has happened to us. When we forgive, we set our hearts free and minds free. Forgiveness is an actionable choice that leads to peace.

Be true to your feelings. Acknowledge your experiences of pain, hurt, resentment, fears, or doubts that have arisen from your experience. Accept responsibility.

Identify any part you had in the event, using self-compassion to acknowledge any learning or insights.

Look for the blessing: Notice what in the situation is for you to do or what the situation is energetically and spiritually calling from you. Be exacting about the freedom and goodness you want to experience. Then release and let go.

PART 1

Look in the mirror.

Look at your life as a timeline of events.

Remember three people, dead or alive, you have not been able to forgive due to some hurt you experienced with them.

List these three people. Name the event or circumstances you associated with them.

Identify your feelings and judgments at the time of the events.

Take time to write down and name the hurt, pain, anger, resentment, fear, or doubts this has brought up for you.

NAME	EVENT	JUDGEMENT
1.		
2.		
3.		

PART 2

Choose one of the names or events from your list to heal and work through the forgiveness process with.

Write a letter to the chosen person, follow the pattern below:

1. Describe the event.
   What happened?
   What was painful?
   What were your feelings at the time?
   How is the event still affecting you today?
   Identify the part you played, attempting to understand some of their feelings and motivating factors around the event. View the person who hurt you as a human being rather than viewing them as a monster. Remember that they have their own unique histories, insecurities, and flaws.

2. Name and describe any part you had in the situation and any learnings or insights you may have had from the experience.

3. Tell the person what you want to happen. Write about what you would have liked to have experienced, how it is true for you now, and how it affects your life and desires.

4. Let it go. Write the release of the hurt and the erasure of all the feelings and pain from your mind.

5. I am grateful now. Acknowledge the contribution this experience gave to your life through what you understand now or what you have learned.

6. Complete and release. Write statements of completion and let go of the event or the other person.

Karen Ann Scott, RYT-200, is the CEO of Be More Here and Now Wellness. She is an expert in teaching yoga, mindfulness, and meditation to young people ages 12-24, in before and after school programs and community centers.

She has ten years of experience as an English to Speakers of Other Languages Teacher in Maryland and New York. Some of her hobbies are practicing Bikram and Yin Yoga and singing with the Charm City Labor Chorus.

Connect with her below:

Website: https://bemoreherenow.com
bemoreherenow@gmail.com

CHAPTER 17

EMBODYING THE INTUITIVE SELF

COLLECTING THE PIECES OF THE PSYCHE THROUGH GUIDED IMAGERY AND EXPRESSIVE ART

Tiffany McBride, MAC, LCPC, RMT, ORDM

MY STORY

Oh, Wow! I feel like shit, I thought to myself after waking up dizzy, trying to get to the bathroom. I could barely stand, let alone walk.

What happened last night?

I was sick to my stomach, and it took me a while to collect my thoughts and remember through the fog and haze. I quickly called one of my mentors.

"Hey Ruth, so sorry to bother you this morning, but I thought I needed to call someone."

"It's totally okay. What's going on?"

"Well, I'm just gonna be straight up and honest. Uh, I got blackout drunk last night. I mean, I haven't had that much to drink in over a year, and I can't believe I did that!"

"Oh, no! Are you okay?"

"I am so fucking hungover. I feel jittery and anxious. I just can't believe I did that," I said with shame.

"Can I ask you?" Ruth paused, "Was there anything in particular that triggered you to drink so much?"

I took a deep breath and tried to gather the pieces of the night before, realizing I had drunk—a lot! *What led me to numb myself so much?* Then I remembered my dream earlier that morning, a reminder of my real-life nightmare seven years ago.

I sighed heavily. "Oh man, I don't know why I try to forget. I had a dream about it last night." I paused and choked on the words, "It's been seven years today."

Ruth knew what I was referring to as I'd opened up about it in a group a few years ago. "That's very hard. Do you want to tell me about your dream?"

My head and heart were both pounding in sequence. I didn't want to talk about anything since I couldn't even stand the sound of my own voice. But the memories came back, and I knew isolating wouldn't be best for my recovery.

"The dream starts in the house I used to live in." I paused and felt the grief well up in my chest. "I really loved that old house. I dream about her all the time."

I began reminiscing. That beautiful three-story, 150-year-old house resided on an old road in an older part of town. It was right across the entrance to a park and zoo with a magnificent lake and walking pathways. I loved how I could walk over for my daily workouts and enjoy the holiday parades and fireworks. Within this house were three separate spaces for apartments. When I moved in, I opened up the whole house and enjoyed having the extra room.

The basement was an unfinished mystery with extra toilets and a water well that I always felt was a portal to another world. The house had a beautiful front porch where I enjoyed swinging during my lunch breaks. In the vast living room, I hosted classes and parties. The spacious kitchen allowed me to cook my favorite dishes for my friends and was the center of my home. The room off the kitchen was my recording studio with a full bath. The back studio was my office, where I practiced psychotherapy and energy healing. Up the stairs were my quarters where I slept and had space for myself.

A meadow was located just outside my backdoor. I enjoyed sitting under a big tree and soaking up the sun. I hosted drum circles there, and people used to call it the Healing House because it was a place people came for community.

Purple morning glories surrounded the house and invaded the bushes. Every spring and summer, new flowers would reemerge and die again once late fall came. I had a small garden where I grew herbs and vegetables. She was my sanctuary. And I was in the prime of my life.

I was in full recovery from alcohol and disordered eating. I lost 120 pounds in my first three years of sobriety. I began a new job I enjoyed, left an unhealthy codependent relationship, and bought my first home. I learned how to be independent and to love myself. Writing music and singing was a fantastic recovery tool, and my friends were terrific supports of my art. I was happy, but I was also very naive and a big people pleaser. Unfortunately, people took advantage of that. I wasn't used to the attention I got from men, especially since I had lost so much weight.

On New Year's Eve, I went to a party with some friends, and a guy named Rogan was very generous with repeatedly handing me alcoholic beverages. I ended up getting very drunk and briefly remembered dancing seductively on the pool table. I wanted to impress him. I vaguely remember my friends driving Rogan and me back to my house. Though, I do remember his arms wrapping around my waist, and then, just blackness.

I woke up on New Year's Day, now seven years ago, sick, vagina torn, and in pain. I thought I was so drunk that I had really rough sex. I believed the pain was my fault for allowing him into my home. A few days later, I went to see my gynecologist due to the pain. She looked at me with unease and asked, "What happened?"

"Oh, I just had rough sex, is all," I said as I laid there on the table with my legs spread apart. The doctor looked at me with concern and asked her nurse to run some tests. I ended up having a nasty bladder infection, urinary tract infection, and pain from the torn skin in my lady parts and anal opening.

It wasn't until a year later at a meditation retreat when the memories of that night came rushing back to me. As I sat there in the silence, meditating, my body ached, and I heard a scream within, *I was raped!* I left the meditation retreat six days early, distraught and unable to process this newfound truth. I went back home to medicate myself, to get away from this painful actuality.

My mental health went into a dark abyss for the next few years, and I dove deeply into hardcore addiction. I used weed to forget, drank to numb, and overate to suppress my emotions. I had a lot of sex with different men because that's all I thought I was suitable for. I was spiraling out of control.

I ran with unhealthy influences, allowing them to take advantage of me. I was raped again by a friend and drugged and date-raped by another man I met online. I was wild and impulsive. I allowed men to pressure me into sex and was re-traumatized repeatedly. I eventually burnt out, and my life became unmanageable.

I quit my agency job and began to work on my recovery part-time while also trying to start a new independent business. Unfortunately, I ended up losing that beautiful house and went bankrupt. I had no help, and all my friends and family had abandoned me at this point. For a year I was homeless, struggling to find places to stay. This was me hitting rock bottom.

After a year, I finally got on my feet and embraced stability. I started a full-time independent contracting job, got my apartment, and a new, used car. However, I struggled mentally, and my addictions were still eating me alive. That's when I met Ruth and other teachers who could help me on my recovery path.

"In this morning's dream, there were beer cans scattered all over my house, like pieces of my soul shattered that night. After all this work I've done, I still have all these pieces I have left to find."

"But I also want to encourage you," Ruth reminded me, "you've been doing the work. Look at the progress you've made."

"I know. I feel like there are more pieces to uncover. When will it end! I just don't know when something will come back to haunt me," I said, feeling defeated and angry with myself.

"I mean, I guess, I've decreased, if not stopped, my drinking and smoking. I'm much more aware of the codependent behaviors that used to lead me to people please or overwork." I paused, then continued, "I stopped seeking sex and love and practiced celibacy for a bit. I was also finally diagnosed with ADHD, which has helped manage my addictive impulses. But I feel like I have so much more work to do because of my compulsive eating and depression."

"You know, Tiffany, the path to healing is a spiral one. Our old wounds always come back again, so we learn something new or see things differently. Healing is not linear, and you know that as a practitioner. So ask yourself, why is this coming up again? What is it showing you?"

I thought about her questions. Over the past few years, I've uncovered many of my maladaptive behaviors and patterns. I knew they stemmed from my childhood trauma and saw how they repeated in adulthood. I did the work, and my life reflected that in the success of my private practice and other unique projects I worked on.

"It comes in layers," I said, "like the peeling of an onion." I paused and realized my head had begun to hurt. "Okay, I may need to get some sleep and get back to your question when my head is a little clearer. Thanks for letting me chat and giving me something to think about, Ruth."

"Sure, no problem. Let me know if you need anything."

"Okay, will do." We ended the call.

I kept thinking of how I've been able to pick up the pieces over the years. I utilized psychotherapy, the 12 steps, safe community, and altered states of consciousness like shamanic breathwork, art, painting, dancing, meditation, guided imagery, drumming, chanting, energy healing, singing, plant medicine ceremonies, hypnosis, bodily movement, and dream analysis. Each step and modality has been a key to becoming whole again.

I was starting to feel dizzy and lightheaded, so I closed my eyes and drifted off to sleep into another dream.

THE MEDICINE

Let me take you on a journey, through a guided meditation, to help find the pieces of your shattered self lost along the way. Come, follow me into the abyss of your soul through a dream to bring yourself back together again. Recovery is a spiral process; it's not linear. There is no timeline. Know that it's a dance to finding yourself when you begin this journey. Let's embark! (A recorded version of this meditation is available at www.tiffany-mcbride.org/embodyingtheintuitiveselfpt1)

Things you will need for this exercise:

- Paper
- Journal
- Pen/pencil
- Coloring utensils

Take a few deep breaths down into your body.

Breathing in. . .

Breathing out. . .

Feel free to keep your eyes open or allow them to close, whichever is more comfortable for you.

Breathing in. . .

Breathing out. . .

Imagine you're taking a beautiful walk on an easy trail up a mountain. As you walk, you can feel the soft earth beneath your feet, the quiet sounds with each step. There is so much greenery surrounding you, with trees, bushes, grasses, and birds singing and cawing. As you walk, you see the colors of the flowers, plants, and mushrooms along your path. You notice the clear, blue sky the warm sun and feel a soothing breeze kissing your cheek. With each step, you feel more and more relaxed and at peace. You continue to climb upward, but you stop when you notice a spot that looks like it has been carved out for you to sit. You take in the beauty of the wilderness all around.

You find yourself sitting comfortably in this spot. This spot can be a flat stone, a big rock, or the stump of a tree. As you sit and look out, you take in the vastness of the sky and the stillness of the earth. Then, slowly, as you look up into the sky, you begin to see a being. This being appears more and more clearly as it comes closer to you. This being may be in the form of a person, an animal, a nature element, or a spirit. It may be someone or something you know, or maybe something new.

You sense a feeling of safety, comfort, and wisdom from this being or energy. As you continue sitting, you feel this wise being come to sit with you. The being comes with a gift. You sense yourself opening your hands in a gesture of receiving. If there is hesitancy, know this is okay. The being only comes to bring a message for your healing path, a piece for your shattered soul. Know as you receive a new gift, you must let go of something old.

The wise being places the gift in your hands. What this gift is, is specifically for you. Your heart feels soft and open as you receive this gift. The wise being lets you know it is for you to take up your mountain journey. They also let you know you can revisit each other at any moment and all you need to do is bring your awareness back to this moment.

You hold this gift close as you ascend the mountain once more. The path becomes a little harder to walk as you climb and struggle to breathe from the high altitude. You know the way isn't easy, but you also sense that it will be worth it. Before you get to the top of the mountain, you notice smoke blowing up into the sky and the sound of faint drumming. As you reach the pinnacle, you see a significant fire burning and a Being drumming and singing. Singing:

I am La Huesera, Bone Woman,
waiting for the lost and wandering seekers of the broken.
Come to the fire, release, or request.
In exchange, you'll receive a bone for your quest.

La Huesera continues to drum and sing to you as you walk towards the fire.

What is your request? What is the reason for your seeking? What do you want to release into the fiery flames so that healing can begin? Is it to remove self-doubt or the darkness that haunts you within? Or do you have a request for lost joy, wanting it to be returned? Pause and see what comes to you.

Imagine you are standing before the fire, picking up the dirt at your feet, and throwing it into the fire as a potion or prayer. Whisper out loud what you wish to release or request.

"I wish to request/release _____."

As you whisper your statement, the fire sparks, and a flame spits out a bone. You pick up the bone, observe it, study it. What part of the body does this bone belong to? What piece of your weary soul is this? La Huesera continues to drum and sing a new song.

What is the gift you bring
from your inner being?
Release what you will
So, you can be refilled.
The bone chooses you.
This is your first clue.

She gestures you to the other side of the mountain, and you begin to descend. The path down is an easy and safe walk. As you reach the bottom of the hill, you take a few moments to take in the whole experience. You reflect on your gift, what you have released into the fire, and the new bone clue.

Notice your breath once again.

Breathing in. . .

Breathing out. . .

As you breathe, follow your breath into your body. Notice how it feels inside after taking this walk up the mountain, where you met your Inner Advisor receiving the gift of yourself.

Then the walk to the fire while being sung over by your Wild Self.

And let go of something that has held you down.

Now you have received a piece of your psyche. A bone. A specific bone to your embodied self.

Can you identify this bone? Where do you feel it belongs in your body? Is it from your leg, your pelvis, your arm, your torso, your back, your upper chest, or your face? Do a body scan and feel where this specific bone belongs in your body.

See if you can be friendly to whatever comes up for you (pause), see if colors, shapes, and images match these inner findings.

What does the gift feel or look like?

What did you release or request, and what does that feel or look like?

What part of the body does the bone come from?

When you're ready, open your eyes and be aware of where you are sitting. Notice the things in your space and stretch if you'd like. Then express your felt senses and images from your experience and put them on paper through art or by writing about it.

If you would like an example of this exercise, please visit www.tiffany-mcbride.org/embodyingtheintuitiveselfpt1. A Bone List link is provided below. This leads to a list of the parts of the bones in the body and ways to explore healing in those areas. If you would like to continue on this journey to find more pieces of yourself, please sign up with your email and put 2MOREPLZ in the message box so you can receive two free guided meditations.

You can also access more information on how to complete the series to embody your intuitive self by going to www.tiffany-mcbride.org/embodyingtheintuitiveselfseries.

If you are interested in exploring deeper into this exercise and working with a practitioner one-on-one, please contact Tiffany at www.tiffany-mcbride.org/contact.

Tiffany McBride (She, Her, They, Them) is an LCPC, Reiki Master Teacher, Birth Doula, and expressive artist. They run their private practice named Holistic Vibrations, LLC. They use holistic remedies and altered states of consciousness for those who struggle with trauma, addictions, and those seeking a deeper spiritual connection. Tiffany is currently working on their Doctorate in Shamanic Psycho-Spiritual Studies and is training to be a yoga teacher, a somatic practitioner, a clinical hypnotherapist, and a shamanic minister and breathwork facilitator.

Their holistic and altered states of consciousness modalities include emotional release therapies utilizing energy, positive psychology such as EMDR, EFT, MBSR, etc., expressive arts therapies, energy healing with a foundation in Reiki, womb healing, Doula services, sexual health education and empowerment, attachment trauma recovery, codependency recovery, motivational interviewing, transitional life coaching, spirituality, breathwork, hypnosis, somatic psychotherapy, and psychoeducation.

Tiffany hopes to eventually grow a community healing arts studio to help more people learn to express themselves and heal from their traumas and addictions. In Tiffany's downtime, they love to write, blog, paint, draw, play the ukulele and guitar, sing, be in nature, kayak, take photographs, read, go to concerts, hang with friends, and be a scholar.

Tiffany has been a recovering addict and complex trauma survivor for 19 years. They not only have many tools and modalities to help, but they also come with personal experience and wisdom gained from their own recovery process.

Connect with them on the following sites:

Website: https://www.tiffany-mcbride.org/

Facebook Group for Women/Non-Binary: SHEE: ReWilding The Sacred Yoni @ https://www.facebook.com/groups/1057289361484274

Instagram: https://www.instagram.com/witchycrowwmn83/

CHAPTER 18

EXPOSING THE ROOTS OF BODY SHAME

CARVING A PATH TO SELF-LOVE, ACCEPTANCE, AND FREEDOM

Tina Green

MY STORY

When is Mommy coming back?

I was a little girl with a round face, rosy cheeks, full lips, blue eyes, and a few wisps of blonde hair on my head. I was taking an evening bath. My tiny, curious hands were exploring my warm, smooth body, and they found a place that felt different. For a moment, I was lost in this place.

Suddenly, Mommy burst through the door and immediately noticed my exploring hand. Her face turned red, her blue eyes squinted, her thin lips tightened, and in a disgusted tone, she snapped, "Don't touch that! It's dirty! I don't ever want to see you do that again!"

I opened my mouth in shock, and my body tensed up, then I withdrew my hand as if I touched a hot burner on the stove. A warm sensation overtook my body.

"Why?"

She snapped, "It's dirty!"

This was the very first time I remember feeling body shame.

I went through my childhood having a seemingly wholesome childhood in the countryside of Pennsylvania. Something was missing, though, something that I wouldn't recognize as missing until I was an adult. There was almost no intimacy. I don't remember my parents telling me they loved me, hugging me, or even cuddling with me. Even beyond touch, there were no intimate conversations about how I felt, how things were going, or what I wanted. No one noticed when I was struggling. I had to figure it out for myself and know when to ask for help.

When I moved into my pre-teen years and hit puberty, things started to get a bit sketchy. This isn't about blame. I know my parents were doing the best they could with the tools they were given. This is my story.

I had a Catholic upbringing, so I was trained at a young age to put males before females and unconsciously took in all the ways that the church oppressed females. My parents provided no teaching about the changes in my body, only the insufficient, clinical Sex Ed classes in 1970s public school. I had no understanding of what sex was. I was completely innocent.

Then it happened: When I was 12 years old, with no parents home, in my living room, he said to me, "Tina will you take off your pants? I want to see what it looks like down there."

I obediently took off my pants.

"Now lay on the couch and open your legs as wide as you can, and I'll make you feel good."

I did what he asked. I loved and trusted this relative very much and looked up to him. I had no reason to think he was doing something wrong. He then proceeded to perform oral sex on me. It felt good to this child who had no intimacy in her life.

Why would he want to put his mouth on that dirty part of my body? Ew!

"How does that feel?" he asked.

"It feels good." He did it longer while I laid there totally still, taking in the sensation.

How could he possibly be enjoying this?

Then he said, "Okay, that's enough. Put your pants back on. You can't tell anyone about this, okay?"

I said, "Okay," and I meant it.

It happened one more time, then never again. Years later, I came into my own incomplete knowledge about sex and my body. It was enough to understand that what we did was wrong.

He knew it was wrong, and he took advantage of me. Oh well, it felt good at the time, he didn't hurt me, so it's not that big of a deal.

We never spoke of it, and I never told anyone until 40 years later when I discovered it was considered incest and sexual abuse, and it was a huge deal.

My twelfth year around the sun was monumental in establishing body shame.

I was at a girlfriend's house, changing my clothes in her bedroom after swimming. I took off my wet bathing suit, dried off my pubescent body, and stepped into my underwear, and suddenly I heard her little brother exclaim, "Wow! She is fat!"

He peeked through the door and watched me get dressed. I scrambled to put my t-shirt on to cover my newly budded breasts as fast as I could, so he couldn't see me. I heard him running away laughing.

I stood there frozen in shock. I was hot all over, and I felt the shame pour over me. *Me fat? Am I fat?*

I slowly finished dressing and walked out of my friend's room, cheeks flushed, shrouded with humiliation. A group of my friends was sitting on the couch right outside the room I was in, and I knew they heard what had happened. I couldn't even make eye contact with them.

I received absolute confirmation a few days later when my mom took me to the mall shopping for new clothes. As we entered the department store, we went straight to the Juniors section, where all the cool teen clothes were.

She said to me very matter-of-fact, "Oh no, Tina, we need to shop in the husky section because you are husky." We changed directions towards that small section of clothes.

Am I husky? Again, that familiar warmth in my body happened, and I felt shame. From that point on, shopping for clothes was something I hated, and would only do by myself.

In those first 12 years of my life, I made unconscious agreements with myself that became the deep roots of my body shame.

I am dirty. I can't trust men. Men don't respect me. I am fat. I am ashamed of my body. Boys think I am unattractive. I am husky. I don't like clothes. Cool clothes don't fit me.

Ironically, when I look back on photos of myself at that time, I was not fat. I was hitting puberty a bit earlier than my friends, but the words of others became my inner voice and then my reality. As the years went into adulthood, I gained weight, lost weight, gained it back, lost it again, and gained it back again.

Shame was a dominant, heavy force in my life. I was convinced that anytime someone looked at me, they always saw my deeply flawed, overweight, dirty body first. I dealt with it by avoiding it and focusing on my career at a powerhouse financial services firm in New York City.

I had great success at rapidly climbing the corporate ladder to the executive level. I married my career and conveniently wore the corporate suit. I put no energy into having intimate relationships, except for a tiny circle of close friends. My pain and shame were unacknowledged and buried deep in my body, unconsciously dictating how I moved through the world.

In this fast-moving, male-dominated financial industry, I often went out drinking after work with the men. I was sitting at a bar with a co-worker who I liked. We were buzzed, and he flirted with me.

"Do you want to come home with me and have some fun?"

I responded, "Why would anyone want to hook up with me? I'm fat."

He gave me his sexiest smile and whispered in my ear, "You've got all the right things in all the right places."

We didn't leave together that night. I went home alone. Again. I thought about what he said, "You've got all the right things in all the right places."

He really thought so. He complimented me. He told me he was attracted to me. Could this be true?

I don't believe it. He was just buzzed and wanted some action.

Here I was pro-actively self-rejecting. He didn't have a chance! Self-rejection was a consistent pattern for me. When I did allow someone to get close to me, it was always a man who was emotionally unavailable, married, or had no intention of entering a deep relationship.

Fast forward a few years. I'm on my daily walk along the San Francisco Bay in Sausalito, where I had recently relocated.

I live in this gorgeous place, have a beautiful home, lots of money, and I am still alone. I am still fat, and I am still ashamed. I've had so much success at so many things; why can't I seem to conquer this?

This is the question I continued to ask myself for the next 20 years.

One day a friend shared with me that several other friends were doing breathwork and taking these shamanic sacred healing journeys led by Stephanie Urbina Jones and Jeremy Pajer (authors in this book). I wasn't sure what any of that was, but these friends all had tremendous struggles, like addiction and chronic depression resulting from childhood trauma, and they were able to begin healing by doing this work.

I decided it was time for me to give it a try. The idea was both scary and exciting. I spent a lot of energy avoiding being vulnerable in my life, and I would have to step into vulnerability in a big way. The idea of finally conquering this challenge was exciting enough that I dove off the cliff into an incredibly profound experience that was no less than a rebirth. I journeyed to Teotihuacan, Mexico, to immerse myself in the ancient indigenous wisdom. This ancient city in Mexico has been considered one of the most influential spiritual centers in the world for thousands of years.

This is where I achieved profoundly deep healing through a week of journeying through the ancient pyramids and temples of Teotihuacan, following the initiate's journey of the Ancient Toltecs. Each step of this journey had me deeply contemplating my life and uncovering the agreements that no longer serve me.

When I arrived in Teotihuacan, I anticipated the week's intensity, and I wanted to set an intention for the journey. I asked myself, *What do I want to walk away with? My intention for the week is to truly love myself.*

After Opening Circle, Jeremy led us to a roaring fire on a temple with the backdrop of a drum's steady, haunting beat. As I reverently walked up the steep, narrow steps to the top of the temple, I could feel the heat from the fire. *Wow, this is serious.* The teachers kicked off the ceremony by calling in the directions—north, south, east, west, above, and below—our ancestors, guides, and helpers.

I don't know what this all means, but it sounds powerful.

I offered my written intention to the fire to release it into being.

I want to love myself. Could it be possible? Could I walk away from here loving myself?

The next day, we went to the pyramids for the first time. We stopped first at the Plaza of Hell, which includes the Temple of Quetzalcoatl and the Island of Safety. Jeremy invited us to walk around the plaza and identify five hurdles or vices that we wanted to leave behind in the Plaza of Hell and pick up a stone for each of them. As I slowly and pensively walked around the plaza, I picked up a stone: *My body is ugly.* I picked up another stone: *My body is undesirable.* I picked up another stone: *I am ashamed of my body.* I picked up another stone: *I give my power to men.* I picked up another stone: *I am not enough.*

I took my stones and climbed to the top of the island of safety. We built a temple with our gathered rocks as we shared our hurdles. *Wow, this is the first time I said these things out loud!* I was witnessed, and I got these agreements out of my head.

As we walked along the Avenue of the Dead the next day, we contemplated what our ancestors had given us. *Shame.* A teacher asked me, "Are you ready to die and be reborn?" "Yes!" and he let me pass to the first plaza, the plaza of Earth. Jeremy invited us to think about any agreements we had around our body or age, find a rock representing this, and bury it. I found a rock, and I dug a hole to bury it. *I buried all the shame handed to me by my ancestors around all things that are beautiful and powerful about being a woman.*

That night, we had a breathwork session. While we lay on a comfortable mat covered by a blanket, our teachers first led us in a meditation/visualization and then played intense, loud music specifically curated to enhance our journey. We started the breathwork, a rhythm of fast, deep inhales and exhales with no pauses. Eventually, I dropped into a lucid dream during this breathwork: I was standing in front of a tribunal of ancestors and made the motion of throwing something back at them, saying defiantly, "I give you back all the shame you gave me. It's not my shame, it's yours, and I don't want it!" My ancestors all smiled at me and willingly took back the shame. My grandfather said, "It was wrong to give you all the shame, and I see it now, and I don't want you to have it." I sobbed. This breathwork was powerful!

I had many other opportunities that week to change my story about my body, and I took every chance I had. *I want to conquer this!* I knew I was healing myself, my teachers were holding space, but I would only get out of it what I put into it. I didn't hold back. There were a lot of tears and anger, and I remember thinking, *Right! I've never actually cried about this; I never fully felt the emotions. I just stuffed them down inside my body.*

By the end of the week, I was able to release my shame and experience freedom around my body that I never knew in my adult life. I felt a sense of freedom and zest for life unfamiliar to me.

THE MEDICINE

CREATING A LIFE INVENTORY

What you'll need: A notebook, and a pen.

One of the most valuable exercises for me was to create an inventory of my life through the specific lens of body shame. It was an emotional process for me, so I always had privacy, a cup of tea, and comfort. I took a few deep breaths and set an intention: *I want to love myself.* I meditated on this intention and took it on as my top priority with no exceptions.

Step 1: Write at the top of the page: Birth through five, and list the significant events in your first five years through the lens of body shame.

Step 2: Start a new page, write at the top: Age six through ten, and list the significant events.

Step 3: Continue this same pattern in five-year increments until you reach the present day. Take a break when needed. This can be completed over multiple days.

Step 4: Set your life inventory aside for at least one full day.

Step 5: When you are ready, spend time with each event in your life inventory that might have created your body shame. Ask yourself: How did this create body shame? What story about or agreement with myself was created at that moment? Write the answers in your notebook. This can be very emotional. It is important to push yourself to tell the full truth and allow emotions to flow.

Step 6: If you have someone in your life like a spiritual teacher, therapist, life coach, or trusted friend, ask one of them if they would be willing to be your confidante and review your life inventory. When you walk through your life inventory with another person and fully tell the truth and allow the emotions to surface, you open the pathways to healing. Being witnessed is very potent medicine.

Step 7: Surrender! You set an intention, told the truth about your life events, identified the story or agreement that was created, and shared the inventory with a confidante. Now it is time to allow the healing to begin. Allow your confidante to share their wisdom and give you advice. Follow your intuition, and take action!

Tina Green, Life Coach—I have struggled with and overcome issues around self-love and body shame.

I see you. You are a kind, compassionate, and intelligent woman, and you are a loving daughter/mother/friend/sister. You are great at your job, care about your community, eat a lot of vegetables, try to exercise every day, and try to prioritize your self-care. Even given all this, you struggle to be committed to yourself, and you are hard on yourself. You are even ashamed. You do things to sabotage yourself, like emotional eating, putting up protective walls, or thinking negative things about yourself. Then, you feel more ashamed.

You've tried every diet imaginable, joined gyms, made resolutions, read countless self-help books, attended workshops, talked to a therapist, and still, you can't seem to love yourself. You ask yourself: I am successful at so many things: Why can't I love myself? Why can't I conquer this?

I've been there. I draw on decades of personal experience to help women achieve self-love and acceptance by exposing the roots of their body shame and low self-esteem. Once the roots are exposed, then healing can occur. I am a trained life coach, natural chef, and massage therapist. I am also training to be a minister, sacred journey breathwork facilitator, and transformational healing arts facilitator. I have had 20 years of experience as an executive in non-profit and financial services.

I live with my husband and two teenage daughters in Northern California, where I am a personal transformation enthusiast, foodie, outdoor adventurer, gardener, and cook.

Connect with Tina:

On her website: https://www.ExposingTheRoots.com

On Facebook: https://www.facebook.com/ExposingTheRoots/

On Twitter: @ExposingTheRoots

On Instagram: https://www.Instagram.com/ExposingTheRoots

Via Email: Tina@ExposingTheRoots.com

Via Phone: 707-872-7706

CHAPTER 19

RITUAL TO RECOVERY

A DAILY PRACTICE TO HEAL FROM TRAUMATIC LOSS

Sherrie L. Phillips, LMT

MY STORY

Wake up
your life is changing
Wake up
Your sister passed away
Wake up
her heartbeat extinguished
Wake up, don't breathe
Get up she lays dead
Get up the sandman waits for no one
Let's go, we have to leave her
Let's go, Nowhere
Where to? Nowhere
but I can't breathe

Wake up
You're not dreaming
Get up life is changing
Let's go
back to bed forever
So, when I wake up it isn't true

I sat up from my warm bed, startled awake by a call at 1:00 a.m. "Your sister has passed; get up; we have to go to the hospital." I heard the words slide from my wife's lips from some faraway land I could not identify. This would be my last few hours of peaceful slumber for many months to come. I slid into my shoes, but I could not feel my feet. Blood rushed like sharp needles under every inch of my skin. The unfathomable was being delivered to my soul like a semi-truck running a red light through a crowded intersection filled not with cars but my beating heart, my sense of safety, and my trust in life. I pulled cold cotton sweats over my shaking legs and wrapped my trembling body in something, anything.

"Quick, call someone to come and sit with the kids; we have to go," I said as I rushed downstairs, feeling the cold knob of the garage door.

NO, NO, NO! No, not Christie!

I slid onto the cold leather seat of the car. *Hurry!*

Racing through empty streets, I imagine if we go fast enough, we can bend time, and it won't be true. I feel a boiling tone rising, toes to knees, up my thighs, through my rapidly disintegrating chest, overflowing out of cracked lips, a primal scream over and over, unrecognizable. I'm a caged animal going mad. My hands grip the cold of the window, willing it to hold me upright as I fall away from myself, splintering, shattering.

Tires screech as we pull into the emergency room parking lot of Memorial Hospital, where just 30 years earlier, I held my mother's hand as she took her last breath.

"We are here," my wife says as she pulls me to her.

I can't do this. I can't do this! Silently staring into her eyes, pleading with her to tell me this is a vicious lie.

Not my sister! She is too young. Why?

I watch with resistance as my feet pull me up the walk toward my nieces, Christie's husband, and my beloved sister, Michelle. Automatic doors opened and closed with no person visible, as if the spirits of the dead are leaving out the front door while we circle up to mourn the impossible.

"We can only go in two at a time due to COVID."

Where is my sister? What is happening?

My niece falls into my arms. I recognize the hollow shake of the dismembered daughter who has just lost her mother. "Oh, baby, I'm so sorry, I am so sorry!"

"Who wants to go in next?"

I do; I mean, I will. I grasped my wife's hand and my sister's. We begin the walk of hell. *I'll be damned if they stop us from going in together.*

Crossing through thick glass doors, "Let me just check your temperatures, please put your masks... "

Fucking really? Let me see my sister!

"Right this way."

Walking to see her for the last time, each step closer, the smell of disinfectant, blood, and urine climbing up my nostrils. I felt strangers' eyes averting from us as if they would catch what we have. *If they look too long, they too will be cursed.*

The curtain pulls back—suddenly, I'm on *Let's Make a Deal,* and I'm being force-fed what's behind door number one. I'm in quicksand, sinking further away from my life with each step closer. Gasp, air filling my lungs, now seemingly lined with shards of broken glass.

I think I see her. But no, this is not my sweet sister, bruised and bloodied, tube in her mouth from the desperate attempts to restart her broken heart. Then I see her hands, her beautiful hands, and her recently manicured gel nails she had done just for my wedding, where she walked me down the aisle just two weeks prior.

She is still so warm. I reach across her broken ribs to my sister Michelle's hand. You see, it has always been just the three of us, no parents, orphaned for the last 30 years. We hold her hands and each other's as we attempt, for the last time, to absorb her essence and infuse into our cells her love, her mothering, her safe space to land. We understand our sisterhood has been broken—our connection, always the envy of others, fractured forever.

This moment in my life is the most recent in a long pattern of traumatic losses. I lost my mother when she was just 52. Several close friends died that same year as AIDS ravaged our community. I nursed my beloved grandmother until she drew her last breath and held my best friend's hand when at age 46, he walked defiantly out of his body from cancer. Several more friends died young, too many to name, and most recently, the call in the middle of the night.

"Your sister is gone. She is dead."

For me, these moments and so many more have been a labyrinth laced with breadcrumbs leading to the core of my very being and, miraculously, to the center of my purpose and passion in life: helping others heal. I was born to hold the place between the worlds, walk with people and show them unconditional love and safety so they can begin to heal and find a way back from the crippling effects of trauma and grief.

I know now that the only way out of the pain is through the pain. We must find a way to feel and witness our anger and sorrow, or we tuck it away in some dark place where it festers and causes dis-ease or, at the very least, a fractured and half-felt life.

No one taught me how to grieve. I was surrounded by wounded men and women who either lashed out or internalized their deepest wounds, leading to early death and disease. It is not only death that brings us to our knees but all the dreams that did not come true.

It's the parents who were hurt, so they hurt us, or the abusive grandmother or guardian, the spouse or partner who was not faithful. It could have been a career that never took off or a failed relationship. The sometimes senselessness of our humanity, and then the ultimate grief comes when we look in the mirror and face the truth of our choices.

It's about how we have stored these losses in our bodies and the truth of how we have hurt ourselves and others with this choice. A loss is a loss. A broken heart is something we as humans all have in common at one point or another in our lives. However, the ability to walk into our sorrow, heartbreak, and grief, and allow it to transform us, is still foreign and isolating for many of us.

We must begin to make friends with our bodies and recognize when we disassociate (feeling detached from your environment, the people around you, or your body). We must heed the warning signs when we start wanting to run away or numb out from our feelings. Storing regret, resentment, or shame in our bodies can lead us to act out in destructive ways.

This can look like overeating, over-investing in another person's drama, drinking too much, or sexual deviance, just to name a few. We will do just about anything to not connect with what we feel because we've not been shown how to honor the losses. When we numb out to not feel grief or anger, we also numb out to our joy and passion. This leaves us feeling hollow and afraid, which invites us into more addictive and harmful behaviors.

"This one is taking me out," I said to my therapist in a recent session.

"It isn't the actual grief taking you out; it's your story around your grief that's torturing you."

Oh my god. At that moment, I knew she was right. I had to save myself, get into my body, and allow the trauma story to leave so my heart would begin to heal.

"Sherrie, where is the pain? Put your hands on where it hurts."

I listened through the choking sobs and an unbearable sensation that the entire world would fall out from under me if I took one more breath.

"Where does your body call to you the most?"

I allowed myself to close my eyes and, without much thought, felt my hands begin to cradle my heart and lower abdomen.

"Send your breath to the places under your hands. When you exhale, see or imagine the pain leaving with your breath out your feet."

I am so sad; I have felt like this my whole life.

"Breathe, Sherrie. That's it, keep exhaling."

Warm waves seemed to pour over the fractured spaces inside of me; clenched fists began to uncurl, light began to fill in the dark cracks that had formed around my heart.

"Deepen and speed up your breath. Yes, that's it. You are safe here, Sherrie. What is the feeling?"

I am so tired. I can't do this again. "Everyone I love leaves me."

As soon as I heard the words come out of my mouth, I knew I had reached a core belief that was solidified by this latest traumatic death of my sister. **Everyone I love leaves me.**

I stayed with my breath and allowed the deepest sorrow to surface. I was not only experiencing the loss of my sister, but the story in my mind had, like a strip of Velcro, reached back to the beginning of my life to every other loss, starting with my father from the day I was born. At that moment, I wailed for all the losses and my sister. As the tsunami of tears began to subside, stillness began to come in place of panic; warmth replaced cold and frozen, wholeness began to replace fracture and disassociation.

There is so much in this world we cannot control. Bad things happen to good people; loved ones pass away, trauma comes and takes us to our knees. As I lived through these losses and traumas, I have learned that I must be my own healer. I must seek out support from others, and most importantly, the pain must be witnessed and honored, first and foremost by me, before it can transform into something that makes me more than I was before the loss.

What I would like to share with you is a ritual and a tool you can do at home for free if you've been through a traumatic loss or you're just noticing your current way of living isn't working anymore. I'll help you to become present in your body and from this place. If you feel called, reach out for support.

You never have to walk alone. Whatever you're walking through, I promise many have also been where you are, felt and thought what you're feeling and thinking.

I've spent my life stalking my pain so I could use it for my medicine in a positive way. My life reflects a life that has gone through great loss and heartache, suffered many things, and now I'm in service and thriving, joy-filled and sorrow-filled. I now can give all my feelings equal and appropriate expression, allowing me to show up whole, authentic, and living my passion and purpose.

I'm here to let you know there is a way to turn your deepest pain and darkest nights into your own medicine. You, too, can find your passion and your purpose through the lens of your losses. This is why we are here; there is nothing more important than healing your traumas and dysfunctions so that you can make your world a more loving place to be. We need you. We are the ones we have been waiting for.

THE MEDICINE

Do you know those days when you "wake up on the wrong side of the bed" feeling extra cranky or just weepy? This is the body's way of letting us know we need to take a moment to check in, not just keep checking out!

This is particularly important if we have recently gone through a traumatic loss of any kind. When we experience trauma, whether it was when we were younger or now as adults, we tend to separate from our bodies because often it is just too painful. This is called dissociation. This leaves us vulnerable to acting out, projecting onto others, or personal injury. I want to share a technique that allows us to come back in, identify the belief or feelings we are trying to avoid, and allow them to surface, move through, and be witnessed.

Find a quiet space. Privacy is key. This may be a walk-in closet, or a car, wherever you can be alone and undisturbed. Have a journal or phone close to take notes at the end of the experience to write down feelings that may come up.

Closing the eyes and placing one hand on the heart, place the other hand right below the belly button.

Begin breathing slowly, deeply, without pausing in between breaths.

Repeat these words: *"I am safe, I am supported, I am listening."*

Continue to breathe and notice how the body is feeling, noticing the thoughts and sensations that begin to arise.

Asking, *where is the pain today? What part of the body is holding this story?*

Let the hands go wherever the pain is. Keep witnessing any thoughts without judging them. Allowing everything to come up and through while continuing the mantra: *"I am safe, I am supported, I am listening."*

Use the breath as a river; the inhale is the flowing water pouring in from the top of the head. Exhaling, water flows down through the abdomen, down the legs, and out of the feet into the earth.

Continue to repeat the mantra while visualizing this beautiful water cleansing supporting you. Allowing the fear, grief, anger, or whatever it is to come to the surface and leave the body. Notice where the hands are being drawn.

Hold yourself as you would a small child. Make sounds, open your mouth, and allow an AHHHHH, AHHHHH, AHHHHHH, to flow from the body, low and deep or loud and expressive whatever feels right at this moment. Let the water, the energy from the hands, and the vibration of the voice be the vessel that begins to carry you through this moment.

Cry, scream, or just relax as you begin to come back together and witness the body's experience and any messages that have come through.

Stay with this process. . .

Breath/mantra/vocalizing/witnessing/breath/mantra/vocalizing/ witnessing for at least five minutes or continue for as long as you feel called. When you feel complete, and notice a sense of wholeness, gently open your eyes, come back into the space, and write any awareness or message in your journal or phone. Reflecting on these messages with a therapist or a minister is another way to continue deepening your healing experience.

This technique is just one channel of support when we experience post-traumatic loss or anytime life feels stressful or disconnected. This is a powerful tool to add to your journey as you become your own advocate and healer.

Another ritual is to have a space where you can have a small altar that is just for you. I like to imagine my altar as an anchor to my life. It can remind me to stay present, honor the losses, and acknowledge the energies, allies, and ancestors who support me in the unseen world.

An altar does not have to be in a cathedral or some big display; it can be a candle, a picture, or a rock, anything meaningful for you. Light the candle, hold the stone, say a prayer, or set an intention. All this means is that you let the universe or God know where your heart is today, what you need, i.e., asking for help, and what you are grateful for. This daily practice can help you remember you are not alone. Stating your intention to notice if you begin to disassociate and take a moment to tell yourself you are safe, you are supported, you are listening.

Breathwork and daily rituals are some of the most profound modalities I have found that allow me to connect back into my body when life is, feeling too painful and I want to run and numb out.

Transformative Breathwork is now the cornerstone of my healing practice. I found this modality because I had done so much to alleviate my pain, and while talk therapy was a wonderful tool, it did not shift the trauma stored in my body. Using your breath, your intent, and your deep love for your life is a way to begin to heal. I know this because I have been where you are. I have survived death, divorce, rape, miscarriage, and many other traumas in this life. There is a way through your grief and shame. It takes courage, love, and support.

Sherrie L. Phillips, LMT, Minister, Soul Tracker, Doula of Dreams
Sherrie was born to feel the fire coming from her hands and touch the spaces in your body where your secrets hide, to offer a door to your recovery and rebirth—holding you in a safe and sacred connection, so you never have to walk alone. She was born with an ability to translate unconditional love and reflect your potential and beauty. She offers her own heart on the altar and walks alongside you as you heal, not above, not separate from but as a fellow journeyer who longs for more love and more connection for all of us.

Sherrie is the CEO of Your Zen Matters, where they specialize in trauma recovery, ministerial counseling, and Transformative Breathwork experiences. She has spent 33 years in integrative bodywork, energy medicine, and life coaching. Most of those years have been in private practice. She has now expanded her offerings to focus on leading groups through transformational breathwork, retreats, weddings, rites of passage rituals, and weeklong adventures in Mexico, diving into the traditions and mythology of the indigenous peoples from many different cultures.

Sherrie is a master teacher and is passionate about helping people become empowered to heal themselves. She holds certifications in Jin Shin Jyutsu, Neuromuscular massage, Kinesiology, Therapeutic Touch, Reiki, and Breathwork facilitation. Sherrie is an ordained Shamanic Minister and life coach. She is also an accomplished musician and recording artist.

Her passions are creating and performing music with her original rock band, Hangman's Daughter, writing poetry, being a mom and a wife, and spending quality time with her family and friends as often as possible.

Connect with her on the following sites:
Website: www.yourzenmatters.com
Facebook: https://www.Facebook.com/yourzenmatters
Instagram: https://www.Instagram.com/your.zen.matters
Email: www.yourzenmatters@gmail.com
Facebook: https://Facebook.com/Hangmansdaughter2.0

CHAPTER 20

SACRED WITNESS

THE POWER OF HOLY BEHOLDING IN TIMES OF DARKNESS

Rev. Annie Mark, CSC, CCM

"The wings of transformation are born of patience and struggle."

Janet S. Dickens

MY STORY

My mother's family had what I call an invisible ***Book of Secrets:*** "Don't tell anyone." How often had I heard that growing up? It was like a mantra in my family.

As I write this, I can feel that urge to tell a different story, to shy away from the truth about my mother's family, my pain, the truth about my life.

Recovery programs teach that "we are only as sick as our secrets." It's time for me to tell more of mine.

Sometimes I think that I was possibly born depressed. Either that or spending almost a year in the womb of my mother who at the time was grieving both the death of her father and a recent miscarriage, I believe I began life swimming in a sea of sorrow.

At any rate I remember very early on feeling out of place in the world. Even though I had a big family (I am the seventh of nine children), and yes there was love and laughter, but oh the underbelly, the secret shadow, and the secrets; they were there too.

I think my mother created the family she would have liked to have had and what she thought was loving. It was, but like everything, there is more to the story.

My mother grew up with two alcoholic parents who could get violent and a mother who was insanely jealous of her three daughters and their relationship with their father, my grandfather.

My grandmother (Big Mama, is what we called her) lost her own mother early in life, not to death, but her mother was committed for a time by her father, as their marriage was ending, and he was already in a new relationship. By all accounts, it was a classic evil stepmother story.

Every picture of my Scots-born grandmother when she was young is of a big-eyed, sad, little girl lost. I think that lost little girl had no clue how to be a mother to her own children and so that trauma and lineage passed to my mother, and yes, then to me.

I so appreciate my mother for deciding to *do it differently* than her own upbringing and give us what she hadn't been given. But how can a mother who has not been mothered mother her own children without some pain and trauma passed down?

I was profoundly shy as a little girl, especially outside our home. I could barely say hello or speak my name aloud. I was scared of loud noises, scared of the dark, scared of people, just scared. All the while still having this longing to belong but feeling separate.

I was also a mama's girl. I loved my mother. She was smart, funny, sweet, pretty, kind, spiritual, and like me, a lifelong seeker. She could also be hyper critical, sarcastic, a perfectionist and prone to body shaming and sexism.

She was a writer, avid reader, and an artist. She was a high school drop out for which she held profound shame, and she never got her license for fear of failing the driver's test.

She was also depressed on and off throughout my childhood. As a child, I can remember feeling my mother *disappear,* not physically, but emotionally, and becoming energetically unreachable. It scared me and I'd do anything to bring her back.

An early unconscious inner agreement for me was, *don't make waves, be sweet, don't make Mom's already hard life harder.* I was a good girl.

We were, she and I, enmeshed. Lots of love there and lots of dysfunction, too. It was confusing. Many times, I didn't know who I was without her, where I began and she ended.

I had a lazy eye and had to wear an eye patch and because we were poor, I many times, had mismatched socks and unfashionable old clothes and hand me downs. This certainly amped up my already deep-seated feelings of being different and profoundly flawed and less-than.

I was terrified if I had to stand in front of the class to do an oral report. I often ate my lunch in a bathroom stall at school, hiding away, too scared to socialize. I always felt things deeply and from an early age, I did not want to be *here.* I just wanted out.

The three Ds (depression, despair, discouragement) were always nipping at my heels, my almost constant companions. And along with them, that pervasive feeling that I did not quite belong anywhere. I did not fit in, I was odd, out of place, and not good enough. No matter what I did or accomplished it was never ever enough.

The other truth is that I had a spiritual side early on. Even as a little girl I would pray and would feel a profound energy and knowing of something more, an intermittent connection to a *Divine Loving Presence.* It was as real as anything to me.

And I had music. Music was an integral part of my family. My grandmother (my father's mother) sang and played piano and lent us her piano. My older sister and brother both played. We all sang together. I learned to sing harmony at Catholic Mass. I picked up the guitar, learning to accompany myself when I sang. Listening to songs, writing songs, and playing songs, I discovered a whole world there that delivered and transported me and reached in and grabbed and cradled my heart. It still does.

Music got *me* and I got *it*. I've said it before and often that in very real ways music both gave me a life and saved my life. It's a gift that keeps on giving to this day.

I set out and about to discover what I hoped would cure and fix me and get me out of me enough to have a joyful life. My mission was to chip away and amputate those diseased parts of myself and finally feel normal.

Initially, I just yearned for relief and release from the pain living inside me. I picked up all sorts of distractions and dysfunctional ways to avoid going within and for a time those distractions worked. Sometimes they still do. Some of them nearly destroyed me. What a relief and release alcohol was! Until it wasn't.

On a shamanic spiritual journey-retreat hosted by Freedom Folk and Soul, with co-founder Stephanie Urbina Jones and guest facilitator Ruby Falconer to Teotihuacan Mexico in 2018, I experienced a whole new awareness and awakening within me.

What brought me to this retreat was yet another bout with my lifelong companion, depression. I felt hopeless again and discouraged to my core—half dead. Any dreams I had along the way were dead or dying and I was at a loss as to how to resurrect them or breathe life into them.

Failure to launch again and again and again. Like my grandmother, I felt like I too was a little girl lost.

All the trainings I'd been through, education, certifications, sobriety, years of recovery, seminary, ministry, spiritual counseling, breathwork, breakdowns, breakthroughs, music, and still once again, I felt like a loser and a failure. None of it saved or delivered me from me.

Who was I to hold space for anyone when I couldn't get out of my own way? Here I was again. I blamed myself for having failed yet again and felt a profound sense of shame about not being further along in my life.

I show up and breathe and go deep into journey. As I breathe, I feel myself giving birth to a dead baby, first one, and then another, and another. They keep coming in a seemingly endless loop and I know these babies are dreams in me that never quite came to life. A lineage of dead dreams.

I'd been holding their lifeless bodies inside of me for a good long while. No wonder I felt so heavy and stuck. Ruby comes to my side and with an obsidian blade cuts the cords, symbolically releasing the dead babies from my body.

Then I climbed to the top of the pyramid of the moon.

It was there, as I looked out across the land, that I had a visceral experience of feeling and seeing the power our bloodlines have on our lives, and was having on my life.

I could see my mother and her mother and her mother's mother and on and on and on. I knew the lineage of depression, discouragement, and hopelessness ran far, wide, and deep. Blame, shame, and pain swirled all around, passed down generation to generation.

Simultaneously, in the same scene, I could see strong, courageous, resilient women too, just like me, able to laugh and push through. But oh Lord I had gotten so tired of pushing through again and again and again.

I could see and feel the power these old agreements were having on my life. They were suffocating me. I needed air. I needed to breathe from a different, less toxic source and to further break the chains and free myself from my lineage of codependency, addiction, and dysfunctional ways of expressing love.

I needed to consciously open my family's **Book of Secrets,** because those secrets were killing the life force within me.

In those moments I could see clearly what I had been up against. *No Wonder I'd struggled so much.*

Right beside those visions and awareness's there was also the realization, an opening, an expansion and softening of my heart, with a deep feeling of compassion for myself, my mother, her mother, her mother's mother and so on and so on.

It was as if I'd stepped outside of myself and could be a sacred witness to my story and history, and to my mother's story. I knew I needed a new story and part of the key to that was going back so I could move forward.

My two main dreams when I was little were that I wanted to be a writer and I wanted to be an archeologist.

Today I can say in some very real ways I am fulfilling both those dreams.

I write. I write songs, stories, prayers, and poems, and I consider myself a kind of archeologist of my soul, being a sacred witness to my own patterns, digging away, excavating and uncovering truths and clearing ground for new visions and new ways of being to emerge.

In digging deep into my own past and that of my family's lineage I have found profound insight, understanding, and yes joy, and in turn the fulfillment in witnessing other people's unique paths as they too uncover, recover and discover their unique stories and tap into their unique gifts and dreams.

"It is Time." Very recently, I wake from another journey dream where Mary Magdalene is speaking these words to me.

In the journey, I find myself at a sacred burial ground where all those dead babies, those dead dreams I carried within me have been laid to rest. I am honoring them all in silent prayer.

I look around and instead of dead babies I am suddenly surrounded by the most beautiful, colorful and vibrant garden of wildflowers.

Deep in my cells I feel it and know it. It is time to embrace and accept and rejoice the me I am today.

Depression, alcoholism, grief, all of it, has sent me on the path to my own buried treasure. I took the road less travelled, clearing away and excavating for the gold within me.

In very real ways, depression has been my doorway to new dreams and passions.

I still have dark times and yes, some bouts with that old well-grooved pattern of depression. I'd like to say it's gone for good. But that's not how it's been for me. I am much less inclined to shame myself about it now. The difference is that I visit depression these days. Annie doesn't live there anymore.

What I do have is a vast and varied toolbox that I draw from when those dark times come.

I hold sacred witness for myself over and over.

Just as crucial is to reach out and partner up with a trusted friend, mentor, minister, counselor or teacher.

We are not meant to do it alone.

For more than twenty years I have had a prayer partner and dear friend where we have held sacred witness for each other.

We have prayed and listened as we raised our children, went to seminary, grieved losses, rejoiced in each other's triumphs, held each other through life's often messy challenges.

Again, and again, I breathe and call in that Divine Presence and ask for help, listen in a prayerful space to whatever arises, and I continue to expand my sacred witness circles.

I come from a lineage of empowerment born of pain.

I am who I am today because a little girl born in sorrow and depression set out on a journey for relief and release.

That same little girl who was too shy to say her name aloud now officiates and leads sacred ceremonies and journeys, teaches and sings and performs to large crowds all over. I have so much love in my life, rich soulful authentic friendships born from my darkness. What a truly miraculous path this has been and continues to be.

I am so very grateful for the many gifts I've received from following this sacred path to wholeness.

I am a dream doula; I am a sacred witness.

I am a writer, and I am an archeologist of the soul.

My mother's *Book of Secrets* and that mantra of *don't tell anyone* are losing steam and no longer have the hold on me that they once did.

I can feel and hear my beloved mother Faith Williams Mark and her mother and her mother 's mother whispering in my ear a new mantra:

Underneath the blame and the shame and the pain, is a flame, is a spark, through the dark, to your heart.

THE MEDICINE

SACRED WITNESS MIRROR MEDITATION

Materials needed:

- Candle and lighter
- A handheld mirror
- A timer
- Journal/Paper and pen /pencil

Set aside some time to be alone with no distractions.

Light your candle.

Invite your spirit guides, divine beings, ancestors, any four legged or two legged helpers to be with you on this journey of self-discovery.

Invoke a prayer.

This can be read silently or spoken aloud and can be as short or as long as you like. You can make it up or have a written prayer handy. Honor your own unique belief system and word it accordingly.

For example, for this exercise I might invoke this prayer:

Holy Presence of Love
I call on You to assist me in being sacred witness to myself. Help me to look at and into myself with the eyes of love. Help me to face with courage and compassion whatever might come up for me as I spend time being with myself with no distractions. Thank you-Aho.

Bring your attention to your breath, at first just witnessing it without changing it, noticing your in-breath/noticing your out breath.

Begin now to take at least three slow deep breaths in through your nose and out through your mouth.

Set timer for five minutes.

Pick up your mirror, holding it up to your face, looking at yourself, just witnessing and noticing what comes up for you over the five minutes:

Any discomfort? Judgement? Challenging Feelings? Grief? Sadness?

Negative self-talk? Positive self-talk?

Acceptance? Enjoyment? Peace? Disturbance? Impatience? Whatever comes up, just notice- keep breathing and looking.

Stay with yourself through the process. When the timer goes off, place your hand on your heart and take three slow deep breaths.

Write in your journal about the experience and how it was for you.

Place your hand on your heart again, thanking yourself for showing up for and with yourself.

Blow out candle.

Option: Repeat exercise regularly and witness and notice if anything changes for you over time.

Rev. Annie Mark, CSC, CCM, is a writer, an Interfaith and Shamanic Minister, a Certified Contemplative Musician, Shamanic Breathwork Master Practitioner, Singer Songwriter, Harpist, Guitarist and a performing and recording artist. She is the Co-Creator of Freedom Folk and Soul's Experiential Ministerial Training program with Stephanie Urbina Jones and Jeremy Pajer.

Annie has many years' experience in all aspects of ministry including planning, creating, and officiating ceremonies. She assists and walks with people through all phases and stages of life from birth to death, including weddings, baby blessings, baptisms, funerals, memorial services, grief and bereavement, and more. With a wealth of experience and training in many of the world's spiritual traditions, Annie brings her heartfelt reverence and expertise to each ceremony honoring all of life's passages.

She is the creator of Singing in the Sacred, Meet Me in the Mess support groups, Build a Song Build a Story Creativity Workshops and more.

Annie is especially passionate about inspiring others to uncover, recover and discover their unique and authentic voice and gifts, awaken their dreams, and offers Sacred Witness Sessions, Breathwork workshops, and retreats for individuals and groups.

Annie loves traveling, stand-up paddle boarding at her local beach, walking with friends, cuddling at home with her husband Chris and dog Einstein, and regular playdates with her adult son Zach.

Connect with her on the following sites:

https://www.RevAnnieMark.com
https://www.AnnieMarkmusic.com
Email contact: revannie@optonline.net

CHAPTER 21

FREE FROM PAIN

THE BRIDGE OF ACCEPTANCE

John Mercede

MY STORY

It's springtime, and I'm playing alone outside my house when I hear the familiar theme song from Rawhide on TV. I run into the house singing, "Rollin', rollin', rollin', keep them doggies rollin', Rawhide." The door slams, "Rawhide's on," I shout to my mom, who is working in the kitchen. I shake off my jacket, run down the hall, and jump onto the big chair to watch the show. I'm captivated by the action on the screen, where Gil and Rowdy are trying to keep a pack of wolves away from some cattle. I sense something approaching me, and at the edge of my vision, I notice motion coming toward the side of my head. I had not heard my mother come down the hall. Then, bam!

With the speed and intensity of a viper, my face absorbs a stinging strike. I move my arms up to cover my face, drop to the floor, and draw myself into a ball, knowing what's about to come. As I hit the floor, I feel a part of me falling deep within myself. My body is twisting, flipping, and flopping like a fish in the bottom of a boat, trying to get away from each strike that comes. My flesh collapses in surrender, and I travel deeper inside myself. My legs and back are raw and throbbing with pain. I summon my strength to tuck even tighter.

Why is this happening? What did I do this time? Inside my head, there's a whooshing sound, and an inner voice urges me: *run for your life!*

I can't get up from the floor, so I run deeper within. The whooshing sound changes to a primal scream, and I land in a place of inner stillness. *Nothing can touch me in here.* My body lays on the floor absorbing each strike, yet everything is happening around me, not to me. Despite all the noise, I hear only the sound of my body breathing steadily in and out. The hitting stops. I hear her footsteps leave the room. My eyes are closed, my thoughts racing. *I forgot to hang up my jacket. She's just in a bad mood. It'll be okay soon.* I lay on the floor listening to the sounds of a cattle drive on television.

I get up slowly and pick up the jacket I mistakenly left in the middle of the floor. I dutifully hang it in the closet and go into the bathroom to blow my nose. I hear typewriter keys clacking in the kitchen. *Maybe there's something to eat.* In silence, I walk on eggshells into the kitchen. A book of matches and a pack of L&M's are on the table. Her cigarette is burning in the ashtray, and the air is thick. The smoke swirls toward the ceiling, which has turned a dingy yellow from years of smoking. I politely ask, "May I have some bread and butter?" I get a nod and open the bag of bread, "Just one," I hear. I put the bread on a plate, open the drawer, get a knife, and spread a thick layer of butter on the bread. I look at her as she types, wondering why she hit me so much and so hard. I take my bread and butter toward the TV room. As I walk down the hallway, I hear, "We'll have supper when your father comes home." "Okay, Mom." I sit down with my two brothers, and we watch the Three Stooges. Soon we are laughing together.

We lived near the shore of Long Island Sound in an affluent town but on the other side of the tracks. I was one of four kids, with four years between each of us. My sister was born first, followed by my down-syndrome brother, then me, then my younger brother. Mom did a lot. She took care of us, did the housework, and worked from home typing manuscripts. She had mood swings and a fiery temper that could explode violently without warning. We did our best to be good kids, but we were never certain when the mood would strike her and then us. My father worked two jobs to afford to live in this town. It was important to him that we had the opportunity to grow up here. My dad was always working, but his example set a direction for me to follow. He worked for a swimming pool company building pools and installing filtration systems. He wasn't at home much, and I would often get up on Saturday mornings and go to work with him. We'd hop into his 1961 Greenbriar van that needed a muffler and rumble our way to Tony's diner.

No matter where we went, my dad knew somebody, and as we walked in, Tony shouted out, "Hey, Soupy boy! Ya' got Johnny with you today." I never liked being called Johnny, but it stuck with me through childhood. Soup was my dad's nickname from his time as a cook in the army. My dad had a second job as a chef and bartender at the local Italian-American club. Tony was talking over his shoulder with my dad while he cooked. He turned and handed me a hot chocolate and a bag with two egg sandwiches. "Let's go, Johnny," said my dad. He grabbed his coffee, and we headed out the door.

We drove toward the shore in the noisy old van. On the drive, we passed beautiful homes, stately mansions, and rolling estates with barns and open fields. Through the buzzing of the AM radio, I heard, "Ten-Ten Wins, All the News, All the Time." My dad turned up the radio and barked, "Listen to the news. You gotta know what's goin' on in the world so you can talk to people." My dad was a smart man who grew up during tough times. He never finished high school and was a bit of a gambler. He would often comment about life, saying, "You gotta play the cards in your hand." This subtle lesson supported me in tough times.

We pulled into a long driveway near the beach that led to a house built right on the edge of Long Island Sound. There were three cars in the driveway. A red one with a prancing horse on the grill looked like it was going fast just sitting there. "What kind of car is that?" I asked. "That's a Ferrari. It's from Italy." I stared at the car, wanting to ride away, and as if my dad read my mind, he blurted out, "It takes hard work to get what you want. C'mon, it's time to work."

I survived growing up in a home with violence. The violence began at such a young age that I didn't know it was violence. Violence was a normal part of my life—one part of everything else that happened. I went to school and church, did homework, played with friends, celebrated birthdays and holidays, went to work with my dad, and went to the beach. Those are all very normal things. I didn't like the violence. I learned that when it happened, all I had to do was dive deep inside myself and hide. My inner hiding place was so deep I was no longer a part of the world around me. I could hide and feel safe, but I was alone. Food became my friend. I ate to soothe myself, and I became a fat kid. My mother's Sicilian lineage gave me olive-brown skin, which tanned easily in the sun.

Many of the kids in school would call me "Fatty" and "Blackie" and sometimes beat on me. I was getting whacked at home and mocked and bullied at school, and, in the mirror, I saw a kid who was different and confused. Pain kept me continually inside my hiding place. One night, sobbing and staring at the ceiling, the pain of sadness, frustration, anger, and confusion coursed through me. I silently screamed; *You put yourself in here! Take yourself out! Make the choice: live or die, live or die, live or die.* I drifted off to sleep.

It was summer, and I would soon be eleven. I liked watching my dad work, and I easily understood how to use tools and machines. I asked him if he would show me how to start the lawnmower so I could mow the lawn. We went into the backyard, and he removed the cardboard box protecting the engine. "Simple," my dad said, "Check the gas, pull the choke out. Pull the rope hard, push the choke in before it stalls." I quickly learned the technique. The process of starting the engine connected me with my body and with the machine. The loudness of the engine drowned out all the noise in my head. Walking back and forth, measuring each pass, gave my mind a place to focus, which calmed me. Seeing the beauty of the freshly mowed lawn brought a smile to my face. It was me and machine, mowing the lawn—and I felt free!

Fascinating. Nothing really changed on that day, and, at the same time, my perception of everything changed. From that day forward, I would find ways to do something that got me moving. I asked the neighbors if I could take care of their yards. I played baseball and football with the neighborhood kids. Yup, sometimes I would get called "Fatty" and "Blackie," but on the plus side, I never got sunburned, and I learned that being fat got me some crazy strong legs. One day playing football with the kids in the neighborhood, I was just as surprised as they were to discover how fast I could run! And those skinny kids couldn't tackle me. The inner pain of being *not good enough* stopped mocking me. For one moment, I *was* good enough. That moment showed me it was time to stop hiding all of me just because some of me was afraid and ashamed. I made peace with my inner fatty. It took time for the body to change, but one moment of acceptance was all it took to bring my inner athlete out of hiding.

I wanted to feel free, like the feeling I had when I saw the red Ferrari. As an almost-eleven-year-old, a car was not yet on my wish list. However, I did see the bike of my dreams in the window of Jules' Cycle Shoppe downtown. It was the Schwinn Sting-Ray Fastback with 5-speed stick shift and sports car styling. It looked fast just sitting there. I had almost enough money from doing yard work to buy it. My friend George used his brand-new bike to deliver newspapers, so I went to see him. "George, how much do you make delivering newspapers?" George never made fun of me, and he methodically shared what he was making and how I could get my own paper route. Now, I had a plan to get my bike!

While we were talking, some friends showed up. We were all playing when George's dad opened the front door and yelled, "Who wants ice cream!?" We all started hooting and hollering, running toward his big blue machine. George's dad was very proud of his Pontiac Bonneville. Each time we got into the car, he would preach its specifications as though they were a prayer. He was on top of the world as he prattled on about his car. "Kids, this baby has a four-hundred-twenty-one-cubic-inch-tri-power-vee-eight-with-four-hundred-fifty-five-foot-pounds-of-torque-and-three-hundred-seventy-five-horse-power, and it will scare your mama—so don't tell her! Brah-ha-ha-ha."

We all laughed with him and climbed in for a ride down the Post Road to the Dairy Queen. For the ride home, George's dad always got on the highway for a fast, one-exit ride. Entering slowly, he shouted with a rowdy voice, "Time to blow the carbon outta' this thing." I had no idea what that meant, but with a huge grin, George yelled, "Hold on!" The engine sang its song of power, and a violent rush of acceleration pushed us back into the seat. George's dad shouted out our speed as we accelerated: "twenty-forty-sixty-eighty-ninety-one-hundred—'hundred-ten—'hundred-fifteen—'hundred-eighteeen." All of us were laughing as he exited onto the ramp – and then straining to stay in our seats as the brakes hauled the behemoth of a car to a stop. I felt free, happy, connected—and alive! The next day, I talked with my mom and dad about getting a paper route. Soon, I was happily on my way toward doing something I wanted to do. I stopped hiding. I took action toward experiences I enjoyed.

In the coming years, it took awareness and action to stay free from pain. I learned to "play the cards in my hands" without complaining or blaming. My mother joined a group advocating for children with developmental disabilities, and she seemed very happy doing this work. Seeing this allowed me to acknowledge and appreciate that she had always done the best she could. Her strict attitude taught me to do things correctly, and my dad showed me that I could get what I wanted with hard work. It was a moment of acceptance that led me to freedom. From that moment on, I began building the bridge to a new life.

THE MEDICINE

The *bridge of acceptance* is a medicine that will help you become free from pain. This medicine is effective with outer pain, inner pain, and the likely combination of inner and outer pain.

Take a moment to imagine these experiences:

- A situation where a stubbed toe is just a stubbed toe.
- A situation where emotional or mental pain leads to a stubbed toe.
- A situation where a stubbed toe leads to emotional or mental pain.
- A situation where you're just screwed, and you lose your toe.

You probably easily imagined one or more of those situations. Imagination is a powerful tool that is always available. Imagination has no rules, and you're free to create, explore, or heal any part of your life in any way you can imagine.

When you're lost in the woods and walking, stop. Become aware, then *decide* to move toward a new direction. Before walking, see a place you want to go to and *declare one word* that describes that destination. Your focus will take you there.

Similarly, when you're lost in pain and walking, stop. Become aware, then *decide* to move toward freedom. Before moving, *declare one word* that describes a specific feeling that you will *feel* at your destination. Your imagination will take you there.

This exercise will show you the way. As you build and travel *the bridge of acceptance,* you'll transform the inner pain of shame, heal a part of your past, and step into a new experience of life.

For an audio version of the exercise, go here: https://www.profoundlifewellness.com/book#jm

Smile and take a breath. As you smile and breathe, become aware of the breath moving in and out of your body. Let the breath find its rhythm and timing, as you allow your body to settle. Take your time.

Recall a time in your life when you experienced thoughts and feelings of shame. Someone may have done something to you. You may have felt, done, or said something that caused you to be embarrassed. Perhaps someone put "shame on you" with their words or deeds.

Imagine shame as a burden you're carrying. Imagine its size and weight and where you are carrying it on your body. Imagine this fully. Imagine the pain this burden represents. See yourself walking in nature, carrying this burden with you. As you walk, you approach a chasm. It's here that you'll build your bridge of acceptance.

Still holding this burden of shame, imagine you're digging a hole. You're free to imagine any way of digging. As you dig, ask the shame to show you all the ways it has affected your life and decisions. When the hole is big enough, put your burden into the hole. With reverence and gratitude, ask the earth to transmute the shame into the energy of support. Watch as the energy of shame becomes the energy of support. Then fill the hole and stand on top of this place. Feel the energy of support. Love that feeling.

Standing supported, look across the chasm. On the other side, a new beginning is available as the energy of pride. Imagine the energy of pride moving in and through you. Where is pride in your body? What emotions do you feel? What thoughts do you have? Imagine yourself filled with pride. How will you act in the world?

Now, begin to build a bridge from where you're standing to the new beginning on the other side. Stretch your mind, thoughts, and feelings across the chasm. Stretch your consciousness to a place above the chasm. Now, use your imagination and combine all you've brought to this moment to build the bridge of acceptance. Imagine the dense and solid nature of this bridge.

With full faith, step out onto the bridge. Begin walking to a new beginning. The energy of pride leads you to what is next. As you walk across the bridge, feel your feet taking each step. Listen to each sound. Look in all directions. Notice everything you see. Who, and how will you be? What will you create?

Now, move faster across the bridge. Move with joy. Move with enthusiasm. When you reach the other side, find something to eat or drink. Imagine its flavor and aroma. Absorb the nourishment.

Anchor this experience of pride. Be still. Be aware. Be Free.

Write or draw about what you feel.

John Mercede is a master-level energy healing practitioner and teacher, transformational coach, workshop leader, and sacred site travel facilitator. With 20 years of experience, he's an expert at transforming inner and outer pain and bringing people from the pain of their past to freedom.

John grew up playing and working outdoors with a love for machines and an innate knowledge of how things work. He harnessed his work ethic and passion for excellence to become a sponsored elite athlete and a black belt martial artist. A self-declared car nut, he raced Formula cars and restored three British sports cars.

John is a master craftsman who earned a degree in Mechanical Engineering at night while working full time as a fabricator, designer, inventor, engineering project manager, engineering VP; then an entrepreneur renovating houses and transforming lives.

John facilitates individual and group transformational sessions using a fusion of movement, breath, energy healing, practical examples, and meditation. He empowers people to free themselves from pain and raises their awareness. John will show you how to connect with your body, emotions, mind, and spirit to create a new experience of life.

John's passion for excellence in athletics led him to meditation. A sports injury caused him to seek the secrets of energy healing. For over 15 years, he studied energy healing and enlightenment with a master from the Philippines, a Mahayana Buddhist teacher, and a saint from India.

John is the co-founder of Profound Life Wellness, where they work as divine alchemists revealing the hidden teachings of life. Connect for a personal healing session, group experience, or travel to a sacred site.

When he's not working with clients or traveling, John enjoys working with his hands, playing in nature, fitness, coffee, chocolate, and visiting with family.

Connect with John:
Website: https://www.profoundlifewellness.com
Email: john@profoundlifewellness.com

CHAPTER 22

SOJOURNER

HOW TO TRAVEL WITH ROCKS IN YOUR POCKETS

Lisa A. Newton, M.Ed.

I survived growing up in a crazy house without protection, with repressed tools, and with a purpose I have only now come to know. I have wounds that bleed a thick resin that slowly binds to form a healing shell of amber. I glow in the sun and dazzle in the moon. I survived my arrival. Here I am. I grew out my clipped feathers and am soaring in a flight.

MY STORY

I found a way to make my low moments the foundation of my next soul journey through a practice common to shamanic breathwork, known as life story reframing, by utilizing various perspectives of a harmful past occurrence with a current perspective. A soul journey is a lesson one learns on their own to self-heal, thus allowing the soul to achieve a closer understanding about God's divine love, also known as earning your soul's ticket to God's mysteries of the universe answer session. My story documents the pathway I took to begin my next soul journey.

I came to this spiritual retreat at the most irrational time, the COVID epidemic, January 2022, because I was called to do so. This is not my first calling, that was to become an inner-city high school teacher, and the second was to adopt a child from an orphanage on the other side of the world. Yet this time, the calling said to go on a spiritual pilgrimage to Teotihuacan, Mexico, and be open to everything. It was that clear. On the second night of the retreat, I found myself in a mediation like no other I have experienced, called Toltec Sacred Journey Breathwork. This experience opens my memories with a whole new perspective of reviewing my childhood traumas with the clarity and the understanding of my current 53-year-old self. For about an hour, tears stream down my face, and my body reacts like I am being tasered, but I feel no physical pain. I am exhausted and weirded out. I had promised God that I would be open to everything, so I just went with the experience. If I had not made that promise to God, I know I would have stopped at the first review of painful memories, but because I did not stop this time, I found that I was being given a great gift of perspective. After the breathwork session is done, a small group debriefing is led by an experienced shamanic spiritual teacher. I have been trying to grasp the next chapter of my life by purposefully sojourning seeking God's message with no success. However, tonight during the sharing of my experience, our group leader listened to me explain my experience. She congratulated me on confronting my avoidance of dealing with my childhood traumas. She helps by clarifying for me that by me examining my traumatic events fully as an adult, I'm healing myself, and more importantly, I have set a foundation upon which to start my next soul journey. I know she was right, and I left the session very content.

Well, apparently, God has a sense of humor because the next morning, my eyes are swollen shut. It is time for me to purge some of the childhood trauma.

"I feel like I have propelled myself over the rocks of a class five rapids," I say, explaining my physical condition of swollen eyes and scratchy voice to the concerned faces in the spiritual retreat common room. As soon as I say it, I regret it. I head straight for the coffee mugs, knowing that caffeine has always been my friend at these times. It should open me up, reduce my swelling, and jazz my bloodstream.

What I'm feeling this morning is a visceral experience of pain in the sense I value more than any other, my sight. I have always valued my eyesight because I use it to meditate myself into a place I find peace. I often stare at a focal point and slip into a mediative stream of thought. I often got in trouble for it in elementary and middle school.

"Jeremy, I think I'm having an allergic reaction to something, maybe from the ragweed exposure yesterday in Mexico City? I think my left eye is going to swell shut. I didn't bring anything with me. Can you please find me an antihistamine of some kind?" Jeremy Pajer is one half of the Freedom, Folk, and Soul spiritual leadership team. Stephanie Urbina Jones is the other leader of the retreat and a person with whom I feel a strong, unexplainable bond of trust.

"Ya, of course. I carry a big medicine box of everything. I'll go see what I can find. If we need to go to the doctor, I'll take you," he replied with a quick turn on his heels and left out the closest door.

I don't think it will come to that. Honestly, this is no big deal. I think in my head.

Once again, I feel the painful memories of what resulted in my interrupting others to ask for something for myself. I fall back on my old ways, and I decide to go back to my room to hide. As I reached the door to escape, gentle touches of assurance rested on my shoulder, and medicated eye drops were pressed in my palm. I go to my room, pull the curtains, and administer the eye drops into the worst eye.

Holy fuck! I grasp the bathroom door jam with one hand and cover-up what I feel is an eye being consumed by acid with my other. My mind flashes back to all the times I have been scolded for not reading directions, taking people at their word, and most clearly not reading labels on medications. My rational mind kicks in, and I remember that I no longer have enough vision to see much of anything and follow the verbal directions as given. I lay down on my unmade bed and wait for something to change.

My eyes are getting worse at the moment. At least the drops are making my eyes tear, and I think that the worst must be over because I am crying out the acid feeling. It dawns on me that I am hiding from my problem again.

So, I put on my sunglasses walk back into the common room, and retake my seat. Jeremy has returned with enough antihistamine to administer a prescription dose. I pop them fast and try to calculate how much longer it will take for the antihistamine to take effect.

Lord, is this how you answer my prayers for help? I don't get it. Or maybe I do get it.

My traumas left me with an involuntary profanity tick; where my head jerks as if my cheek has been slapped and the words "no", "fuck", or "shit, shit, shit" blurt out. I often pray for a release from this tick. I was now ready to move on from the shackles of shit that are part of my history. I knew that meant I had to continue to face facts too difficult for me, in the past to deal with by now remembering clearly. I'm talking about shit that happened to me this round that my mind hid from me so I could still walk the planet. I believe God has directed me to shamanism and to show up at this spiritual retreat in Teotihuacan at The Dreaming House to face my traumas. I am contemplating all of this in the common room when a motherly voice blurs into a form on my left and then on my right. I can sense she is reading me and sizing me up.

Her voice is warm and soft, "You're not sick. Your body is purging the negative energy you scraped up to the surface and dealt with last night in the breathwork session. This will continue as you heal yourself." She asks permission to assist me in moving the energy out of my body.

What an odd question, to ask personal permission to offer help as if the offer would possibly burden me?

Well, my issues were that my body was spilling out the poison of my crazy life, out my eyeballs, so I accepted her offer to help me, "Yes, please."

Carly Mattimore places her healing hands on my face and head. She had been my group leader in the breathwork exercise the night before and had spent some extra time with me. It was my first experience with this type of experiential therapeutic process. Now, she is sending cool waves of light through my body. I no longer feel like I'm in the common room. I feel like I'm sitting in a chair outside in an open field of long grasses, a breeze is present, and I'm relaxing. I realize that I don't care if people are watching me because I am safe.

"This is to be expected." She says, as I feel her fingers lightly touch my face and hold the back of my head, "Let's move some energy."

I always wanted to try this again. I had a friend in college who worked on my shoulder, and it had worked. Immediately, this felt different from what I had expected. I had expected to feel the warmth of her hands, but instead, I felt a gentle, cool vibration underneath my skin. I felt my left sinus cavity drain completely, then my right. The pain in my forehead disappears, followed by the ceasing of cough, and finally, the pressure of my jaw clinching dissipates into nothing. The swelling around my eyes is completely gone. And no one in the room is surprised but for me. My vision returns. And I reach up and touch her hands.

"Thank you," I say with both my spoken and unspoken words. It's like she is giving me a battery jump inside my face. I knew at that moment I wanted to learn how to do what Carly is doing, bridging her energy into me so I can use it to heal faster than on my own. By the time the antihistamine kicks in, I'm already in the van heading out to a day of walking and climbing in the pyramids.

Apparently, I have just experienced a well-known healer's gifts, but I only knew her last night as a great listener with insightful advice. Carly is well known in shamanic circles as a master energetic healer. She has a traditional psychology background with a master's degree and certification as a licensed professional counselor.

While studying with the Toltec shaman, I was introduced to two new perspectives that solidified how I was going to create a solid foundation from my crazy childhood: first, I must head deep into the truths of my childhood traumas, and second, I must grow from those negative experiences—the positive growth. Fortunately, in the days to follow, the Toltec shaman taught me how to appreciate my scars and wounds and how to put my guts back inside my body.

My story of a childhood filled with trauma is not uncommon. The fact that I am common and could turn my pain into the foundation for a positive next chapter in life makes me sure that anyone could do the same. Years of picking myself up from self-constructed disappointments, failed marriages, and failed friendships all brought me into the years of reading self-help books, professional counseling, and drowning my feelings in obsessive-compulsive behaviors of trying to achieve an elusive something better than what I was capable of. I lived my life trying to better myself, but I mostly just squashed myself under my heavy baggage. For me, I lost my voice, my dancing feet, and caring about the health of my body. My life was not all that bad because I had achieved two of my soul callings. That's right; I believe that I had already fulfilled the deficits God had instructed me to improve about my soul. I was all good, right? No. It eventually became clear to me that I was stuck in my soul growth journey and had more I needed to work on. I did a Needs Assessment and put a checkmark next to it. Yep, I have all my needs met. I did a Happy Assessment and could not put a checkmark in the box. Why wasn't I happy? Why was I not keeping my body and mind healthy to live a long life? It was not the professional help nor the books I read that propelled me forward now to seek a longer, healthy lifestyle; it was my desire to be my best self as a parent and teacher.

I have perfect reasons to live, but now I need to learn how to live well and take care of myself. Prior to visiting The Dreaming House on the spiritual pilgrimage, I found that taking care of myself was impossible. For decades I had digested the negativity and dug in deep on the lies I told myself about what happened to me when I was powerless. I lied to myself and belittled myself in that process as an adult. But my experience with the Toltec Sacred Journey Breathwork has been transformational. I now feel empowered by childhood, and I have already moved beyond all negative ramifications. I feel worthy of my own self-care.

THE MEDICINE

If I was ever asked to empty out my pockets there would be healing rocks in the right-side pocket and protection rocks in the left-side pocket. In metaphysical circles, rocks hold magical powers and there are secrets on how to utilize them. So, let's talk rocks and some basics about how to utilize them as part of your daily affirmational meditation and protection from negative energy.

I have utilized rocks as part of my daily life for many years both in my home and in my affirmation meditation grids. I have found that they help me focus on projecting out healing energy and remind me to keep my guard up against negative energy. My personal energy level is affected by the people in my life, situations at work, or even what is happening in the world. If I am surrounded or near negativity, my energy is drained. If I stay away from the negativity then I find myself full of positive energy that I can share with others. I believe we all live and breathe from a collective energy community pool, and metaphysical rocks are little regulator knobs that help us adjust. My favorite metaphysical healing rocks help me promote my healing energy into my world, and my favorite protection rocks help me block the world from getting me down and draining my energy. For the purpose of this chapter, I will focus on using metaphysical protection rocks.

If you feel that you need a forcefield to protect you from negative people and events in your life, then I suggest you get some protection rocks. Metaphysical protection rocks are generally black in color and form shields that reflect off negativity. Protection rocks are also known as disseminators that dissolve negative energy and sometimes even trap and kill bad intentions that are trying to attach to our lives. Protection rocks are to be carried in the left-side pocket, because humans absorb energy from the left side of the body, and so that is the side that needs protection from negative people, negative intentions, and harmful energies. By placing a piece of black obsidian, shungite, or tourmaline on the left side a basic forcefield will form around the body to protect it. A common rock associated directly with protection rocks is called selenite. Selenite white energy rock acts as a purifier and battery to support the work of the protection rocks. When used together, selenite and protections rocks can be used in the four corners of a bedroom, house, or even property to form metaphysical safety walls that free the interior space from negativity.

Obsidian comes in many variations, but the most powerful are gold obsidian, rainbow obsidian, and green obsidian. Green obsidian, prized by indigenous ceremonial leaders, is very rare and found only in small geological pockets in Central America. Gold obsidian is exclusively found in the sacred land of Teotihuacan, Mexico. I usually keep gold obsidian in my left pocket or wear a bracelet that contains rainbow obsidian on my left wrist for protection.

Try Using Protection Rocks to Shield from Negativity:

- Place a protection rock in your left-side pocket, left wrist, or in ring form, when you are fearful of a negative person coming into your personal space.
- Place a protection rock with selenite in the four corners of your home to create walls of protection for all who dwell within the home.
- Place protection rocks on your meditation altar to hold a positive space to protect your positive metaphysical healing rocks.

To learn more about the qualities of obsidian and other metaphysical protection stones, please visit

https://earthaffirmations.com/product/obsidian-ancient-artifact/

Lisa A. Newton, M.Ed. is a lifelong special education, English as a second language educator, and lifelong learner. She is a contributing Amazon #1 Best Seller E-Books: Sacred Death, Ancestors Within Volumes 1 and 2, and has developed three virtual language arts curriculums. She uses her gifts as an intuitive and empath to fulfill her calling as a teacher. She believes that all people have gifts and spiritual powers and that they just need to learn how to tap into them. The key is positive affirmations, learning from elders, and meditation journeying.

Also known as The Intuitive Eye Jewelry Maker, she is the owner of Earth Affirmations. She selects her stones and crystals by feeling the vibrations. She creates her metaphysical jewelry in a meditative state and uses fine sterling silver to maximize the energetic connectivity. Her work is available at

The Black Crow Art Gallery in Sandwich, Massachusetts

Black Crow Gallery | Local Art & Funky Finds (wordpress.com)

EarthAffirmations.com https://earthaffirmations.com/

Facebook https://www.facebook.com/EarthAffirmationsLisa/

Etsy https://www.etsy.com/shop/EarthAffirmations

CHAPTER 23

DARK NIGHT OF THE SOUL

TURNING TRAGEDY INTO TRANSFORMATION

Mark J. Platten, MBA

MY STORY

Zero, zero, zero, zero. That's what the computer screen showed when I looked at the four stocks I owned. *Strange. There must be something wrong with this site.*

"Shit! Oh my god! What the fuck!?" I screamed throughout the house, raining down expletives in my desire for someone to witness my pain, to relieve the pressure which built with each new website I opened, hunting for one that would show me the stocks still had value.

"What are you yelling about?" My wife appeared with the concern I was hoping for, knowing I rarely swore.

"All of our stocks are at zero!"

"What do you mean?"

"Every-thing-is-at-zero," I emphasized, as though she didn't understand the language, and saying it slower and more loudly would get the point across.

"How could that be? I thought that wasn't possible."

"I don't know, but I've checked three different sites, and they're all showing zeros. I've called my broker a dozen times, but I can't get through. Fuck!"

Over the next few weeks, I found out the securities exchange commission had closed the brokerage firm due to illicit practices. This was straight out of *The Wolf of Wallstreet,* except I was the rabbit Leonardo DiCaprio's character captured and consumed. Not a bone or a hair left to witness the disappearance of my identity and almost $400K in stocks.

I played in the volatile world of penny stocks and initial public offerings. I was omnipotent, the former Air Force Officer with three undergraduate degrees and an MBA in Organizational Management. If I couldn't figure this out, who could? Sure, I knew it was a gamble, but that's true of everything in life.

August 6, 1996, sealed my doom. On that day, the all-knowing wizard board at the New York Stock Exchange revealed a gain of $101K! One of my stocks was acquired by another company, and the merger sent my stock soaring. The sweet lure of the sticky-tongued broker flicked in my ear, telling me all the indicators were pointing to it going up another eight-to-ten dollars a share. I was going to be a multi-millionaire! The poison seeped further into the crevices of my soul, exclaiming fortune, fame, and power.

A year later, I woke up like every other day, sure of myself, with a bit of superiority in my step, as I fired up the computer to check my gains. The profit required nothing of me other than saying "buy" or "sell." Maybe that was the true seduction, the ease of making money, which tied to my intelligence instead of hard, physical work. Yet the fates would have their due as they called me on my ruse, and my world collapsed. There was nothing I could do to prevent myself from swirling down the slimy drain of my creation.

The nightmare became real when I heard the *beep, beep, beep* of the tow truck, followed by chains dropping on its aluminum bed as it collected my prized Acura Integra. I knew what was happening even before I pulled back the curtain, just slightly, in case a neighbor might be watching in judgment. Over the following weeks, months, and years, I watched my kingdom dismantle, possession by possession and dream by dream, as the reaper claimed his due.

You might think it was the loss of the material items which haunted my days and stole my sleep, but it was the pain I brought on my family and friends, those who trusted and counted on me. My first child was born a few months after that fateful morning. *What sort of father was I? How could I have been so irresponsible? I had failed him even before he gasped his first breath. I had destroyed his legacy, the empire he would never rule over.*

The loathing continued as each day crept by. I didn't have any income because I was living off the stock gains and was planning on opening a restaurant in downtown Colorado Springs. The cold, heartless glare of the woman who handed me the paperwork for food stamps cut through me like a razor, as though I were an inconvenience. Filling out the tomes of paperwork for the pittance of food was demoralizing. I looked around at the forlorn expression on my new peers' faces, wondering what spate of foul luck had befallen them or what hand they were dealt that resulted in them waiting at the Department of Human Suffering (DHS).

At the supermarket, I leaned toward the cashier and whispered, "Can you run this for food stamps?" I felt her previously jovial disposition turn toward judgment as her facial expression spoke to me. *Oh great. Another one I need to support because he doesn't want to work. What a loser.*

"You can't purchase these items with food stamps. They aren't food," she exclaimed in a much louder voice than was necessary, ensuring everyone knew I was scamming the system.

"I'm sorry," I murmured as my cheeks flushed with anger and humiliation. I took out the sole debit card I had left, noticing the empty slots in my wallet that used to be filled with high-balance credit cards.

At the bankruptcy hearing, I was shocked to see former friends who were part of the restaurant planning team. I didn't know why they were there, but I could smell my searing flesh as their eyes cut through me. No one told me creditors could attend the hearing and were allowed to speak!

"You're a fucking, lowlife cheat! I can't believe you stole from me. What a piece of shit!" my former architect screamed.

"I lost *all* my money. I couldn't have paid you anyway because the bankruptcy court wouldn't let me. Can't you see I've lost everything?" I cried out in anguish, not knowing why they did this to me. It was one of the most difficult days of my life, cycling through a range of emotions, confused by how cruel people could be and how deeply I had affected their lives.

It was the venom that seeped through every cell of my being. I became the very thing I despised. I was no man at all. My ego was erased, and I entered the dark night of the soul, an existential crisis of faith and belief, where nothing had meaning. I drifted into the chasm of all-consuming darkness. I was the judge and jury. I wasn't lenient, nor did I offer a reduced sentence for good behavior. I was no longer capable of good because shame sunk its teeth into the marrow of my being.

According to St. John of the Cross, when you finally surrender to the dark night of the soul, three things happen: you *release* that which has held you captive, you have *relief* because you are no longer fighting for control of the situation, and finally, the feeling that you don't want the darkness to end too quickly because you want to drink every drop of the elixir of wisdom and growth it has to offer.

Several months into the onslaught, I was deep in meditation—one of the few places I could escape myself—when I heard it. "Mark. Windancer (my spirit name), we are still with you," just as clearly as if someone stepped in the room and started talking to me. I was startled out of my meditation, my eyes darting, willing themselves to see in the darkened room. *Where had that come from?*

It was the beginning of my staircase out of Hell. I grew up on a 120-acre farm, blessed with the darkest, richest soil in the world. I had a deep connection to the land and my pets, communicating with them constantly. I know what you're thinking. It's the same spell of denial I was under as I built my empire, thinking it was just my childhood imagination. Then I remembered the rich, musty scent of soil and the dust rising off the cornstalks as I walked through their sequoia-like heights when I was four years old. I remembered the land as my friend, companion, and guide. I remembered.

I knew I had to resurrect from the inside by rebuilding the truth of who I was. I sank my roots deep into the heart of nature and followed the thread back to the part of myself I surrendered all those years ago. I went to heal the sacred wound of my soul.

To do so, I needed to get closer to the land, so I found work with the US Forest Service. I consumed every book on connecting with nature and spiritual practices I could find and attended classes related to the Divine. Over time, my interior world began to soften, and I let go of the shame, recognizing the loss was the catalyst for revealing my sacred self. It was the gift the dark night of the soul promised.

The final loss occurred nearly two years after the fall—my marriage. If I were more truthful, I would say it had been over several years before the event, but I just kept believing if I gave it more time, trust, and patience, things would change. As I approached my 33rd birthday, in the fall of 1999, I separated from my wife and moved to the Manitou Experimental Forest into a small cabin where I would spend the next year of my life.

I was hurting from the separation. My heart was torn out when I found out she had been cheating on me for years and recently moved another man into our house and my bed! Finally, a line was crossed, which allowed me to let her go. She told our friends and family I was in a cult and involved in drugs, as though this were all my fault. My ego fought back, needing to tell everyone it wasn't true until I shared the story so many times, even I was tired of it.

Several months into the separation, Spirit awakened me, and urged me to meditate. It was 3 a.m., but I learned to listen when it beckoned. Approximately 45 minutes in, my wife's higher self appeared.

What are you doing here? How could you do this to me? To the family?

I know this has been hard for you, but I needed to get more abusive because you didn't leave when it was time.

So, you're saying it's my fault you cheated on me and turned our friends against me?

That's correct. We had a soul contract where I agreed to help get you back on your spiritual path, but we weren't supposed to stay together. The only way I could complete our agreement was to make things so bad you couldn't help but step away.

Why did I have to step away? Why couldn't you have done it?

Because your childhood wounds required you to act and claim yourself above everyone else, now you can fully step onto your path.

I hate that it had to go this way, and I understand the part I played. I wish I had been stronger and not so wounded. I see things so differently now.

This conversation was only possible because I was doing deep, spiritual work. As I stepped from my cabin each day, I welcomed life and stayed fully present to each moment. The more I practiced speaking and relating with nature, as though it were a friend and constant companion, the more attuned I became to the subtleties it had to offer. I was in a phase of growth and relationship with the sacred.

After being in the cabin for a year, it was time to exit the abyss and start a new chapter. One day, I heard nature's voice in a new way. *It's time for you to re-enter society. You have learned the skills and deep truths, and if you don't share them with the world, it will all be for naught. What purpose will it have served if you take all this information to the grave with you? It's not meant to be withheld, cloistered, or for you alone. Share what so many have forgotten, what so many need for their healing. Being connected to the Divine, sacred, holy mother is your birthright, and theirs too. It's what will fill the hallowed space inside their souls. Most have forgotten their relationship with nature and ache for that reunion but are unaware of how to lift the fog. Help them, Windancer. Share this gift you have reclaimed.*

When I left the cabin, I sat on the floor and wept deep rivers of gratitude and love for the sacred womb where I had been nurtured. It was time for me to be birthed, time for me to enter society and help others remember.

THE MEDICINE

It isn't a matter of *if* you'll experience a dark night of the soul; it's a matter of *when*. Whether it's a loss like mine, the passing of someone close, a health diagnosis, or any other number of dark night paths, no one escapes its grip. The process is the same, inviting you to resurrect yourself into a new version that won't look or feel anything like your previous self.

Two pitfalls await us when the dark night arrives. The first is spiritual bypass, where we avoid going into the abyss. We pretend we're above it because of our God or our spiritual abilities or training, and never surrender to the grief. You know you're in spiritual bypass when you can't experience the grief of the loss, and you find yourself saying things like, "There's a higher purpose," or "We all have to die sometime," or some iteration of the avoidance of *feeling* pain. If we stay here, we can't realize our full potential because the journey to the chasm is a requirement for rebirth and the growth the dark night promises. This is one of the immutable spiritual laws.

The second pitfall arises when we lean into the wound and allow it to consume us, and we become the pain and don't move past it, fail to learn the lesson, and are then unable to teach others how to move through their grief. It can be very intoxicating to share our wound with a world more than willing to sanctify our victimhood or villainhood. It may seem noble, but it doesn't serve you, or humanity, to stay stuck here.

If you don't move through this stage, you *become* the wound. But how do you transmute something that carries so much grief? The key is understanding what St. John of the Cross taught: to get everything it has to offer, meaning that once you surrender to the dark night, part of the process is to look for the gift(s) it presents. I'm talking about positive outcomes and staying open to growing through the wound. So, the transmutation occurs through the anticipation of change and looking for the gifts it has to offer.

It takes a tremendous amount of courage to recognize you are more than the injury. It's something that happened to you, or you caused, but it is not you. It is merely a chapter in the story with many before and after the incident.

When the dark night of the soul shows up, do everything to make it a holy, sacred experience. This is the key to the gift. How do you do that? Embrace it as your teacher and guide out of the abyss. Meditate as the sun rises, remembering your roots to the land, softening your interior world, and allowing yourself to be guided by the invisible pull of Spirit. Consider changing who you spent time with, filling the space with ceremony and deep-hearted people. Go into nature as often as possible and read about others who connect with it, drinking deeply from what they have to offer. For those who want to go deeper, I suggest participating in shamanic journeys, shamanic breathwork, sweat lodge, or even vision quests with those trained in such pursuits.

Your relationship with nature will mature as you dedicate time and become receptive to its gifts. My invitation is to find a spot that calls to you and go there a couple of times a week, open to communication, ask questions, and anticipate a response. This can be your backyard, a park, a meadow, or a forest. Enter with the wonder of a child, with deep curiosity and the sense that you are in a magical place. When possible, remove your shoes and socks and place your feet and hands directly on the earth. There is science on the benefits, but the journey through the abyss is one of the soul's, not the mind. This is how you ground to the earth. You should notice a shift happen when you surrender to your feelings. Notice the subtle things that capture your attention and move to it, asking what it wants to share with you, and listen for the response. As your relationship grows, you can ask deeper questions and even spend a night in the space, if possible. I suggest using a journal to capture all you have learned so you can reflect on what has transpired over time and see your pathway through the dark night.

This nature connection is the medicine I offer you. It provides riches beyond any material item and is the holy grail of your being, the direct link between you and the Divine. No intermediary. The holy dialog, when encountered, can never be taken away or diminished. It is a lighted pathway out of the abyss that guides you through the transition, always by your side on the journey, for you are integrally linked, and part of it.

Mark J. Platten's soul is rooted in nature, the holy and sacred communion with the earth and cosmos. His drive lies in helping people find their passion, purpose, and path through developing human potential and connecting them to nature. He integrates brain science, indigenous wisdom, rites/rituals/ceremonies, connection with nature, and the practical application in the physical realm to become the best version of ourselves.

He is the founder of Integral Man Institute and helps men align with their highest selves through Jungian archetypes, the four subtle bodies (physical, mental, emotional, and spiritual), and exploring the twelve dimensions of a man's life. He then guides men into the practical application of these tenets.

Mark's bestselling book, *The Art of Connecting With Nature,* is an anthology of 22 co-authors sharing how they connect with nature through various rites, rituals, ceremonies, and practices. You can find author interviews on his YouTube channel below and information about courses, rituals, and ceremonies on his website.

On the academic/professional side, Mark has an MBA in Organizational Management, served seven years as an Air Force Officer, taught natural resources at the collegiate level, traveled internationally for 16 years as the lead environmental specialist, and since 2008, has been Extension faculty at Colorado State University. These are part of bringing the sacred and spiritual into the corporate world—what Spirit has beseeched him to do.

You can connect with him on the following sites:

www.markjplatten.com
Integral Man Institute www.integralmaninstitute.com

Facebook pages:
https://www.facebook.com/TheArtofConnectingWithNature
https://www.facebook.com/whennaturespeaks
https://www.facebook.com/IntegralManInstitute

YouTube for The Art of Connecting With Nature author interviews:
https://www.youtube.com/channel/UCQVjtyoGFr25I8xrz2dGQ8A
YouTube for Integral Man Institute:
https://www.youtube.com/channel/UCZ-eLsxRb8wAQ2FqfRO7t4g

You can contact Mark via email at
markjplatten@gmail.com or Mark@integralmaninstitute.com

CHAPTER 24

AWAKENING THE SHAMAN WITHIN

STALKING THE DARKNESS, CHASING THE SUN

Dhela Griffith, Shamanic Minister,
Breathwork Facilitator, Reiki Master

MY STORY

Life. What a beautiful dream. Enter the Light Brother.

"What are you," I asked as I looked up from my crib at this beautiful auburn-headed boy with smiling green eyes.

"A brother," he replied.

"What is that?"

"A brother is your protector, a teacher who will always love you."

Wow, I didn't know what I'd been born into, but I like this brother idea. "Can we play," I asked?

He replied, "Forever."

My brother, Dhelas, was the firstborn child and much loved. He grew tall and lanky with dark red hair, green eyes, and fine features. He took to life at White Bluff Ranch like a fish to water, riding horses, roping, and exploring as if he was born to it, as indeed he was. He was an avid tree climber and lover of the natural world.

When I met him, he was dead.

Dhelas died of polio after a long bout of illness as a teenager. He spent several weeks inside an iron lung at a hospital in San Antonio, Texas, emerging a twisted and broken young boy.

My father climbed six floors on a brick wall just to peer in the window to see Dhelas' full head of red hair protruding from the metal monster pushing air into his tortured lungs. My mother patiently waited below.

It was eight months before he came home--a home that was sprayed and disinfected by people in hazmat suits and which no longer had his wolf-dog because someone poisoned him while Dhelas was away. He came home to our shuttered family movie theater, where he once sold popcorn and dreamed of a life riding the range. The small town retreated in fear of the polio contagion and, of that fear, stopped patronizing the family theater. Some horrible person even fed broken glass to Wolf out of that same fear.

Dhelas did not want to live, yet his spirit was strong. He went back to school and tried very hard to act normal with his twisted spine and broken body. On his 15th birthday, he told our mother he wanted to die because of the pain in his back, and the struggle to breathe was too great.

He wrote in his journal that his life was over, and so it was. He passed two days after his 15th birthday. His body had only one functioning lung, and he developed pneumonia. He left behind a younger, angry, and tormented brother and grieving parents who never recovered.

After the death of Dhelas, my mother grieved and dreamed me into being. She wanted a little girl to distract her from her pain and loss. She wanted a reason to live and laugh, someone who could bring the balance she needed. She dreamed a red-headed, green-eyed child into her womb, one that would wear lace and ruffles and patent leather shoes.

22 months after she laid one child in the ground, I was born. After laboring 72 hours with ever-tightening leather straps around her abdomen, forceps rudely pulled me into this world. Mother dropped the S from my brother's name and called me Dhela.

Poor Mother. After all that dreaming, she birthed a hoyden—a wild child who talked to dead people—dark brown eyes instead of green and brown hair instead of red. The ruffled dresses became jeans and pearl snap shirts. The patent leather shoes became scuffed cowboy boots. With uncombed hair and dirty knees, I rode my dead brother's saddle thrown over a gate, with his spirit at my side.

An appetite grew in me that could not be quenched by any adventure or thrill.

Enter the darkness: my older brother.

Eyes open in two-year-old disbelief, I felt my head crack the pavement. I had just been pushed from the backseat of the family Oldsmobile by my brother. The screeching brakes, the screams of my mother, and the smirk on my brother's face haunt me to this day.

Thus began the fear of this red-faced, popping-veined demon that populated the next few years of my childhood. I learned to climb high in the trees, sleep with my eyes open, hide in the dark, and run like the wind to evade him and the anger I had never understood.

"Brother, why do you hate me," I asked.

"You breathed," he responded.

Hiding from Dark Brother became a competition, and I learned to stalk him and beat him at his own game. The box of condoms I found in his car became a bouquet of balloons. The love notes and girl's underwear I found became wall art. The fudge I sweetly made for him was made with salt. I learned to be a warrior early, and I fought dirty. I can find traces of amusement in the actions of the frightened little girl I was and the fearless little girl I became.

The light and dark of the two brothers have permeated my life. The faces of good and evil—the shadow and the sunlight. The hidden secrets of both. The joy I felt as my Light Brother taught me to skip rocks, climb trees, and talk to the birds and the squirrels.

The fear, anguish, and nervousness my Dark Brother brought forth. Dhelas taught me to see through his living and dead eyes and fear neither. He was my constant companion until I started school at six, when he refused to come with me. I cried.

I could not wait to ride the bus home in the afternoons and begin my adventures with him. I loved Dhelas Wilbur Gamel then, and I love him now. I needed him. He was indeed my Light Brother and my protector. As I grew up, Dhelas began to go his own way, and I saw him for the last time when I was 16.

We called him into a seance where he sat beside me, leaned in, and whispered in my ear. "Sister, you like that boy sitting across from us?"

"Yes."

"He will die soon."

I had to leave the room and throw up. And yes, that boy I liked, who once wrote me the sweetest story, did die that very summer in a car accident.

Life, what a beautiful dream.

The Dark Brother taught me pain and fear: the pinches at the dinner table, the chewing gum in my hair, and tossing me into a river when I couldn't swim--Uncle had to rescue me. My Dark Brother threw me into a tree and cracked my arm. There were so many ways he punished me for breathing.

What was wrong with him, you might ask?

The anger, despair, and loneliness he experienced while Dhelas was ill? Did that push his young psyche over the edge? Grieving parents excused his every act and gave him everything he ever wanted—except his brother back. Those neglected years were never returned.

He died broken in the most horrible of ways, and I couldn't even cry. I still can't. The only thing left is for me to forgive him—and that one has been hard to do. Someday atop a mountain somewhere in the world, maybe I can cry for what could have been and let it fly away with the wind.

Before he died, Dark Brother married and became the father to a little pink-haired angel on Earth. She was beautifully perfect in every way. She was a bit fey and an innocent, magical being. Her home life was hard as both parents were too mired in the pain of their own existence to parent.

She never had enough healthy food or clothing and lived like a feral kitten in a tiny mobile home. As early as five, she began to tell us she wouldn't live long. Every summer, she would come to live with me for a month, and we had so many adventures. She had her bedroom and clean clothes.

I taught her to cook, and she would spend hours in the grocery store pouring over fresh fruits and vegetables. She shopped for whatever dish she discovered in a cookbook that she wanted to prepare. I taught her to sew and run and play. I bought her school clothes so she might fit in, yet she was bullied beyond belief back in that small, judging town she grew up in.

Her clothes were too colorful; her hair smelled like cigarettes, and her coat smelled like ferrets. The cruelty of the young surrounding this fey angel hurt me then and hurts me still. Her pain became a palpable thing. It was heartbreaking to watch. She died in a car wreck 20 days after her 18th birthday, fulfilling her self-prophecy.

She left behind a younger brother who has grown into a good yet broken man. I love him dearly and pray that the family cycle has come full circle. I loved Genora Gayle Gamel then, and I love her now and forever. She will always be a part of my heart.

Life is indeed a beautiful dream.

Dammit, I feel cheated. I should have had two brothers, two protectors, two teachers who would always be there for me, even if one was walking two worlds. Light and dark. Shadow and sunlight.

Balance.

In addition to being born a hoyden and wild child, I was born with scoliosis. Maybe from the forceps birth, but who knows? The family doctor recommended a brace, but my mother's grieving heart could not bear the thought of another twisted child, so she ignored it. Maybe it would go away.

My spine is in an S shape, and I walk with a strange gait. I never felt it affected me, but I did get laughed at a great deal as I grew up. My nickname was Miss Priss, and it seemed someone was always making lewd comments and whistling.

Did that hurt me? Au contraire. It angered me. I learned a way of walking despite one leg being shorter than the other. I stalk and throw my shoulders back and head held high. I am not a victim as I walk the world and hunt. I am a jaguar.

But then, I was raped at 19. After I recovered physically and got over the victim syndrome, I got angry again. Never again, I said. I built a wall around myself that shielded me, not just physically but emotionally. I continued to breathe, but I ceased to live.

I married poorly the first time. I chose a broken young man filled with ego and anger. He left me with a broken ankle, three cracked ribs, and a broken jaw. I was victimized again, and my walls got higher.

My second marriage was to yet another broken man who is still broken almost 50 years later. He will not be healed in this lifetime, yet he gave me an amazing daughter who is the light of my life.

The light and dark again. The balance.

Then the love of my life came shuffling in—another broken man pulling a trainload of baggage behind him. I didn't care and knew I couldn't fix him. I didn't even try. We spent a decade laughing, loving, and living.

Then he died of prostate cancer. The light was snuffed out again, and I began stalking death. Not just his, but my own. Alcohol anesthetizes the pain, and I partied away the loneliness.

Was this life? No! It was existing. It appeared the walls I built around my heart were unsurmountable.

One day I woke up and decided enough was enough. I began to question why I was put on this Earth. I knew in my soul I was not to continue fighting battles and abuse this amazingly twisted body I was given. Thus, I began to go back into nature and explore the places I once found refuge in as a child.

I climbed trees, explored the woods, stood on mountaintops, and danced with lightning. If nothing else, I just took a moment to breathe in deeply, to take a pause, to fill my lungs with our planet's healing oxygen.

It was good, but not enough.

My daughter met a Shaman from Argentina, and, like all connections meant to happen, she met a true Yatiri from Peru through him. Along with other healers and oracles who introduced us to a whole new way of viewing and living life. We went to Mexico with them on a forever-changing life experience. Our first stop was a Curandera in Monterrey who pulled a Chinese rat out of my body.

Truth or fiction?

I didn't care. This Curandera had the juice. I felt broken and ill in my body, but my mind was beginning to clear.

We then ventured to San Cristobal de las Casas and visited children in the orphanages. I began to reconnect, not just with the natural world but with the people that populated it. I was profoundly learning that it's about turning off the grid-life mentality and simply allowing myself to be present.

Then—the real purpose for our journey—the introduction to Grandmother Ayahuasca. She brought me back to the mother of creation, and it rocked my world. When I returned to the States and looked at the fake temples built and the phony lives so far removed from reality, I truly began to metamorphize into my shamanic life.

It took a couple more Grandmother Ceremonies to explore my ancestral lineage and past lives fully. I then began step-by-step, stone-by-stone, to learn to build the pyramid of my life.

I learned to pray to the natural world and express my gratitude for every breath. I learned to trust my gifts. I learned to walk the world in a shamanic way, releasing ego and just relearning the oneness Dhelas taught me long ago. Sometimes rebirthing yourself means remembering who you once were.

The medicine I found in the Pyramids of Teotihuacan, the Place of the Jaguars at Mont Alban, Teotitlan, the Tule tree, the Basilica where la Virgen de Guadalupe appeared to Juan Diego, the food and the people all nurture my soul.

I drink in the medicine. Sometimes I feel as if I am dancing between the two worlds as I lose my sure-footed jaguar stalk and seem to stumble.

A wise Azteca explained that when the Spaniards invaded and destroyed the temples to build their roads and churches, they used sacred stones, and I stumbled because I felt the energy of a stone from an altar.

Never have I felt more alive and at peace after learning these lessons. All I ever had to do was listen and breathe, to heal the doubt, the fear, and the pain that life gave me. I just had to be one with it all.

Light and dark. Balanced.

THE MEDICINE

Medicine is everywhere, but mostly it is within you, especially when you connect to the natural world.

Take the time to feel the energy in the stones. Pick up a rock, any rock, and feel its vibration. Lean on a large boulder and just let the medicine speak to you.

Listen to the trees. Touch them and let their wisdom seep into your bones. Smell the freshness of the leaves, and know the bark carries its own brand of medicine.

Let the wind blow around your body. Hear its song in your ears. Hear the mysteries offered to you through the air.

Breathe it all in like a starving beast and sense the magic that is offered.

Take as many quiet, meditative moments in nature as possible. Be mindful of the sounds and smells that surround you. Take them in and let them help heal your pain. Give your wounds to the natural world, to Earth, and let your energy shift.

Connect with humans at the most basic level of understanding: empathy, compassion, and the universal knowledge that everyone is the same. You have all the same wants and needs, physical and emotional, as everyone else.

And while languages are different, humans can speak to each other intuitively by trusting the messages received through spirit. At the very core of who you are—who you were thousands of years ago—is the wisdom and trust that navigated this entire universe.

Give yourself the gift of connecting to that universal truth.

As long as there is darkness to stalk as a jaguar and the sunlight to fly into as an eagle, there will be medicine to drink and magic to be explored. There are adventures to be experienced all over this world and an entire universe to discover.

Hurt, pain, torture behind all of the agreements we make with ourselves as children—not being good enough, not worthy of love, not smart enough, body shame—you can heal all these torments.

You can offer to heal to your ancestral lineage when you heal yourself.

And when they begin to heal the cycles of darkness, the pain we are born into will fade away, and our children and their children will no longer be born into that guilt and shame.

We are all born to live and dance and dream and love.

We cheat ourselves by dwelling in the darkness when we can stalk it and learn to grow from it. The light is right there in front of you.

In my experience, there are no step-by-step instructions on how to build the pyramid of your life. However, I learned to listen, feel, and believe in myself at my deepest core. I learned to love myself unconditionally.

I learned to see myself in my darkest moments by the illumination of my soul, the peace I made from years of pain, and the ancestral healing I restored from diligent and painstaking self-work. That's when the magic happens.

I offer you my medicine. It can be scary, but it's worth it. A'ho.

Life. What a beautiful dream.

 **Dhela Griffith** spent 26 years of leadership as a distinguished crop insurance agent of the Texas Hill Country, cultivating the trust and respect of farmers and ancestral descendants of the surrounding community. After a heartfelt farewell, Dhela sold her insurance business, retiring to pursue an enlightened path of shamanic healing. In 2018 she became an ordained shamanic minister, breathwork facilitator, and a shamanic, Usei, and Tibetan Reiki master.

Dhela's passion is to offer to heal to those in need around the world and promote holistic solutions and practices in her hometown. Native to Gillespie County, Dhela was born at Keidel Hospital in Fredericksburg and grew up in Harper. Her roots are deeply connected as her maternal and paternal lineage founded Harper and Mason, Texas, respectively.

Prior to insurance and shamanic endeavors, Dhela was notably one of Texas' first female drilling fluids engineers, maintaining solids control and well-planning for 11 years, and a personnel manager for a Fortune 500 company for five years.

While she's in the process of building a wellness center to offer healing, Dhela is traveling extensively to expand her knowledge of worldly shamanic applications and traditions. When she's not on an adventure, she enjoys spending time with family, animals, reading, and crafting. She can often be found wandering in the woods with her white, spirit-speaker dog, Diego

CHAPTER 25

BECOMING ONE OF "THE GROUP"

MANAGING PTSD AND LIVING IN TRAUMA RESPONSE THROUGH CHAKRA BALANCING

Pamila Johnson

MY STORY

My story is one that many healers have in common, a thing that happened to me that shifted my whole existence, and I am not the same person I was, nor will I ever be again. The trauma that I experienced led me to find healing for myself, and somewhere along the way, my life purpose of being a guide and healer was revealed to me. This is the story of how I became one of "The Group."

In May of 2004, I was a single mom and a MEd student at Xavier University in Cincinnati, Ohio, working on my teaching certification. I lived with my son Joshua, who was a junior in high school. I worked part-time as a bookkeeper and office manager for a manufacturing company that just offered a full-time position working around my school schedule until I finished. I was content with my life, as I was about to start making more money than I ever had while completing my degree. And for the first time in a long time, I felt like I was on the right track.

I just came back from San Diego the night before, where I was attending my best friend Crystal's graduation. Josh told me he was going to a graduation party that night with friends, and after being on vacation, I didn't feel like sitting home alone, so I decided to go to a birthday gathering. It was at the most popular club downtown, which I frequented. The last things I remember were standing at the bar sipping my drink, talking to my bartender, then walking out the door, looking up at the lights that lined the awning, and saying, "Wow, those lights are so pretty."

The next thing I knew, it was eleven in the morning, and I was in Eden Park (15 minutes north of downtown) at the condo of a guy I knew through a friend. I was really sick, but I felt an urgency to get home, and I asked him to give me a ride to my car. I was barely able to make the ten-minute drive home. I was so nauseous couldn't walk in, so I called Josh to help me. I slept most of the day, and when Jamie called to see if I was okay, I learned that I said I was at a party in a suburb in Kentucky. This was 20 minutes south of the city and over state lines, but I didn't remember any of it. It was eight p.m. when I finally woke up and got out of bed, and then I noticed my condition—my body was bruised, I had scratches on my upper legs and thighs from rivets on my jean skirt, which was torn in the seam, and my underwear was missing. I took a cursory shower in complete denial, changed into pajamas, ate a piece of pizza, and went back to bed.

The next day I went to work as usual, but then I started to have flashes of memory and remembered I had also called my friend Crystal from the party. I was walking around in a daze, and though I was doing my work, my female boss noticed something was off. Susan pulled me aside and asked if I was okay. I told her what happened Saturday night. She listened and then verbalized what had happened to me. She urged me to get a rape exam. Later I was glad she did because I met Sarrah—an advocate from Women Helping Women. Sarrah met me at the hospital and went through the entire degrading process of the exam.

I arrived at the ER lot and hesitated, contemplating if I should go in or not. After the longest ten minutes ever, I went in. The door whooshed open, and the smell of Lysol greeted me. The floors were gleaming and polished like glass as I followed the runners guiding me to the desk. I waited for the person to step away from the front desk so that no one would be in earshot. "How can I help you this evening," said the receptionist as she shuffled files away on the desk. The whole way there, I was fine, but my voice cracked as I said, "I'm here. . ." and I started to cry.

I closed my eyes as silent tears streamed down my face. She handed me a tissue and looked at me for the first time. As we locked eyes, I felt she knew what I was going to say. I took a breath and nearly whispered, "I'm here to get a rape exam." She said, "Okay, I have to call a female police officer to do the report, and if you would like Women Helping Women to have a service that provides an advocate to come and go through the process with you. Would you like me to call them?" I nodded silently, still crying, trying not to break down. She said, "We aren't that busy, so I am going to take you back right now." I was relieved. I wouldn't have to sit with others in the waiting area. I followed her into the exam area. She parted the curtains and directed me to the bed, and the tears kept flowing. She said, "Just relax until the advocate and police officer get here." I lay down, and the nurse came in and wrapped me in a warm blanket.

Soon I was greeted by a woman with blonde hair and a beautiful face. She came in and sat by me. "Hello, my name is Sarrah. Do you need anything? I said, "I'm okay." She nodded, and she explained the exam process. "Is there anyone you want to call to come to meet you here?" I replied, "My friends Deana and Jamie." She took my phone and called them, and I felt comfortable for the first time since I got to the ER.

The woman police officer arrived, and the exam started. I answered so many questions it seemed to go on for hours as I lay there with the bright lights shining in my eyes. I kept thinking, *is this really happening to me? How did I get here? What will people think of me now?* My mother's voice rang in my head. "You shouldn't have been there; this would have never happened if you hadn't been out!"

Sarrah held my hand as I lay there with hot tears streaming down my face, and she did not let go till my friends Deana and Jamie came. I don't think I would have made it if she had not come into my life that day. She was also the voice on the other end of the line many times after, for all the days I was in a bad place, as I navigated the legal morass and the stages of the healing process. One of the things that plague me is that I don't know who did this to me; I could be standing next to the person(s), and I would not know it. This is a tormenting feeling that caused me fear and debilitating shame. I only told a handful of people what happened to me. It was easy to deny since I was drugged and didn't remember most of it. But as we survivors know, "the body keeps the score," so after a year and a half of oscillating from denial to knowing something was really wrong in my life, I decided to get some help and joined a support group.

February 1, 2007, Journal Entry (the first time I ever told/wrote my story):

This journal entry has been a long time coming; in fact, it has been almost a year to date since I initially started coming to this support group. Ironically, this is the first time I have attempted to write about what happened to me, though writing had always been a way for me to express my feelings in the past. In this instance, I don't find the usual comfort in committing these thoughts to paper. This has been one step of many for me since May 23, 2004. But with you, my friends, I have found a place to be heard, understood, feel unconditional acceptance, and most importantly, feel like I am not alone with the cross that I had been carrying on my own. The road here has been a long and bumpy path, and I am glad to finally have the courage to add my words, my story, to those that have gone before. On May 23, 2004, my life changed completely and irrevocably, as I became part of "The Group". . .the one in four women who are sexually assaulted throughout their lifetime.

Ironic that since I wrote this journal entry, the stats have changed to "one in three," but of course, many moons have passed. The week after the rape, I lost my job. Since they didn't officially hire me yet, they could let me go, and I had no recourse. I was sent to these churches and agencies, and none could help. There was no help at all unless I went into a shelter. I was jobless for 13 weeks. Josh and I would have been destitute if a family member didn't help me. I applied to the Victims Compensation Fund 18 months later, and after a long, arduous process they denied me.

Journal Entry cont.

A year ago, I realized the point where my life had taken a turn and had never been the same—was that day in May. Sarrah never gave up on me; she kept sending me the new session startup letters for the WHW Support Group, though I did not come. The first week in February 2006, I came to my first Thursday night group meeting led by Sarrah and Sandra. I met some great people there, but one person, in particular, made me feel welcome. It was that special woman that made me feel I had to come back. Her honesty and open way of speaking floored me; I thought I needed to come to the group, but after listening to Tracey, I knew it. I left the first time with a sense of relief that would become a regular occurrence.

While in the support group sponsored by Women Helping Women, I met many wonderful women who helped me heal. There was a survivor sister named Sharon that I will be eternally grateful to for introducing me to Theta Healing. Sharon was getting healings done and shared with me about it as she thought I would benefit from it. In a short time, I saw her life transform. She went from being anxious, crying a lot, and being overwhelmed, to being calm, in control of her life, and balanced. I told her, "I don't know what you are doing, I don't know how much it costs, and I don't care; whatever you are doing, I need to be doing it." She laughed and said she would take me to a session with her. The next week, I met Donna Cannava at Healing Touch of Hyde Park. Theta Healing is a guided meditation which allows you to access the unconscious mind in order to change the beliefs and thoughts that are no longer useful. This very deep inner work is transformative and very healing.

Later that year, my son and I went to the local Holistic Healing, and Physic Fair called the Victory of Light. While there, Josh introduced me to Crystals. He put a stone in my hand, and I immediately felt the pull of the energy. He took me to a booth, and I met my first mentor. Six months later, I took a class on Crystal Healing. I was introduced to Chakra Balancing and basic Crystal Healing techniques in this class. After struggling for years living in trauma response mode and being overwhelmed for days, weeks, or months at a time, I learned how to shift myself out of it. It was so liberating. I didn't need to go to anyone, and I could heal myself!

Journal Entry cont.

In the last year, I have grown so much that it is hard for me to believe the way my life has changed. Though I still have things that are not resolved. I am in a much better place than I was then. I have made peace with my son, I went back to school last year, and I recently met someone I am willing to risk opening up myself with. Being in a relationship for the first time since I was raped is truly a milestone for me. I am rediscovering a part of myself that I didn't know if I would ever get back. Though it is terrifying, it's also exciting and wonderful all at the same time. Now I have something that I did not have a year ago, the knowledge that I am going to be all right. I will get through this, and when I stubble, one of you will help me get up, and I will begin again, if necessary— but in the end, I am going to live again and be okay with myself again someday soon. It's just going to take a bit more time. This is a gift that I credit to everyone I have met through this group over the last year. I thank each of you for all your support and for always knowing that no matter where life takes me, a piece of you will always be in my heart. All I can say for newcomers to the group is that you are in the right place. Just have the courage to open yourself to these beautiful people. You will not be judged in this space, you will not be told to "just get over it," and you will definitely never be alone again.

Much love to the WHW Thursday Night Group!

Recent studies in the US show that trauma is a public health crisis. As the shootings, suicide, and violent crime rates are increasing; it is apparent that the current mental health system is broken. The studies also revealed that the root cause of these issues—mental illness, addiction, violent crime, domestic violence, homelessness, and suicide, is unhealed trauma. Though newer treatments and holistic healing modalities are proven to be more effective, there is a lack of awareness and integration of these methods in the current healthcare system. Living the nightmare of having limited resources for Trauma Survivors, outside domestic violence situations, inspired me to want to help others. After I completed the Crystal Healing Training, I went on to be certified in various other modalities of holistic healing and shamanic practice. In 2014, the tenth anniversary year, I started volunteering on the Take Back the Night Committee, and my 15th anniversary year I started a nonprofit called "The Lotus Sanctuary" on May 23rd 2019.

I was called to this project to share what I have learned with others. If you are reading this, you are here to be a witness, and it is my greatest wish that this information is helpful to you or someone in your sphere. I know if I hadn't learned how to heal myself and manage my PTSD, I wouldn't be alive to share this or be in the place I am today of giving back to others who are walking this walk.

THE MEDICINE

All spiritual practice aims to reach a place of balance between mind, body, and spirit in nature with the earth and elements. Likewise, the key to keeping depression, anxiety, and PTSD in check is balancing and maintaining your chakras regularly.

The most common techniques used to clear and heal the chakras include:

- Chakra meditation - meditation that assists in bringing attention to a state of pure awareness and focus on each chakra

- Affirmations/Mantras – positive statements or sounds that strengthen and heal damaged parts of ourselves

- Crystal Healing – laying one or two crystals in each chakra area to balance

- Sound Healing – tones/music that produces frequencies that balance

- Essential oils – various scents and combinations of scents balance the chakras.

- Yoga – postures encourage the flow of vital energy back into the body and can release blockages

- Energy Work – Reiki or other forms of healing that manage energy

My favorite method is combining three of them – I use a guided meditation, a crystal layout on the body, and incorporate essential oils.

BASIC SELF-CHAKRA BALANCING TECHNIQUE:

1. Smudge the room and yourself with Palo Santo or a Sage blend of your choice.

2. Choose the crystals – at least one for each chakra in the corresponding color/frequency.

3. If using oils, place near or put on cotton pads to be used when needed for each chakra.

4. Cue meditation and put on earphones (best) or adjust the sound. Turn off your phone or other distractions.

5. Lay down and place each stone on the appropriate chakra.

6. When adjusted, take a couple of deep breaths and start the meditation.

7. Use the bottle or cotton pad with the oil to breathe in the oil that corresponds with each chakra as guided in the meditation.

Your frequency is the key to balancing your emotional state, and when you can keep yourself on a higher vibration with these tools, you can regain control of your life. Many thanks to all the teachers I have met on my path, and especially Donna Cannava, Barbara Jackson, Niasha Ashian, Vivian Schapera, Patricia Garry, Becky McCleary, Vickie Young, Dr. Steven Farmer, Linda Star Wolf, PH.D, Judy Redhawk, HeatherAsh Amara, Stephanie Urbina Jones and Jeremy Pajer.

Pamila Johnson is a licensed Esthetician/ Cosmetologist, certified Healing Practitioner and Workshop facilitator located in Newport, KY. She has certifications as a Melody trained Crysotolgist, Reiki Master, Munay Ki (9) Earth Keeper's Rites, Earth Magic Shamanic Practitioner, Shamanic Shakti Rising (Women's Group Facilitator), 1st Level Facilitator with Warrior Goddess Training Circle and will complete the 2nd Level Facilitator for Warrior Goddess Training and the Dragontree Life Coaching Program in 2022. Ms. Johnson also has a BFA in Theater Production & Design and has been a collaborator in the telling of stories since 1997, as a designer and in various roles in regional theaters such as the College Conservatory of Music Cincinnati, The Old Globe Theater (San Diego), the Taft Theater (Cincinnati) and local theaters.

In May of 2019, she founded and is the Executive Director of The Lotus Sanctuary, a nonprofit serving PTSD and Trauma Survivors in the northern Kentucky and Greater Cincinnati area, reopening services in May of 2022. She is the CEO of Emergence Wellness Oasis now offering private sessions and workshops, with future plans to open a brick-and-mortar healing center in 2023. There are future plans to open a brick-and-mortar healing center in 2023. Pamila is a certified first responder and advocate for Trauma survivors, served on the Cincy/NKY Take Back the Night Planning Committee since 2014 and was Co-Chair in 2016. She is also on the External Affairs Committee for the Tristate Trauma Network.

Pamila is a creative free spirit to the soul who enjoys trying new things and living life to the fullest. She prefers being in nature, going on an adventure exploring a new place or activity. Pastimes include travel to sacred sites, reading, writing, yoga, salsa dancing, gatherings with friends & family, and hanging out with her grandkids or her familiar/healing kitty Minx.

Connect with her on the following sites:

Website: https://www.EmergenceWellness.net
LinkedIn: https://www.linkedin.com/in/pamila-johnson-pjj/
Facebook: https://www.facebook.com/pamilajeanjohnson/
https://www.facebook.com/emergencewellnessoasis
https://www.facebook.com/thelotussanctuary
Facebook Survivor Support Group:
 www.facebook.com/groups/thegroupgenderinclusive/

CHAPTER 26

HERE ON EARTH

SAYING YES TO LIFE, RECLAIMING YOUR SACRED BODY

Maura A. Finn

"Whatever truth we feel compelled to withhold, no matter how unthinkable it is to imagine ourselves telling it, not to is a way of spiritually holding our breath. You can only do it for so long."

-Mark Nepo

Our bodies are living libraries: repositories of our dreams, hopes, memories, traumas, and experiences. There is a vast array of sensations we can feel through and with our physical bodies. It's because we are in a body that we experience life. The miracle of existence begins in the form of a heart within the womb. From that heart, we grow into our sacred bodies and spend our existence in a body longing to return to the heart of love, often believing we're separate from it. This separation can occur on multiple levels and throughout different phases of development.

These fractures often untether us from our bodies and the earth. In some way, it can feel as if we're living with one foot on the ground and the other in a perpetual state of homesickness. We might long to return to a place where compassion is a common language. Although we believe it to be foreign here on Earth, compassion is the essence and the driving force for our desire to heal. A state of dissociation can also be the basis for an underlying dissatisfaction and sense of not belonging anywhere, least of all in a body. The more we reject the palace of our soul, the less able we are to live fully and to experience the daily opportunities presented to us. This may seem impossible and frustrating, yet it's possible to begin the journey to reclaim wholeness, befriend grief, and reignite joy while learning to love your powerful human form.

MY STORY

AN AWAKENING

The day was clear with a refreshing early winter breeze and the promise of new beginnings. I didn't know any of the people on the bus heading to the art museum, but I needed something new. I had just returned to my hometown after 15 years away, five of which I spent in Guatemala. Being back in the United States was already a culture shock, and I was doing my best to find remnants of familiarity. Finding a window seat towards the front of the bus, I sat and closed my eyes, allowing the sun's warmth to filter through. Little did I know that this day would mark the beginning of a remarkable life change.

As I walked through the galleries, I noticed that the paintings felt extra potent, bright, and alive. I attributed it to years without seeing any such work, but the quality was something different altogether. I felt like I was a part of the art, with each painting offering me a message. I noticed a woman who seemed to be walking a few steps behind me, and she drew me in. I stood in front of a portrait, my eyes widening.

There is definitely a face looking at me within this painting! Am I losing my mind? Is this a ghost, or are spirits in all of these paintings?

She must have seen something on my face because she introduced herself. We walked a bit, and then she invited me to sit outside with her. I was overwhelmed and grateful for the reprieve.

Her face was worn and wise, and it felt as though she was reticent to be with me but felt obligated. We sat side by side on a bench, and I turned to her expectantly.

"You are ready, Maura," she said. "It's time for you to remember."

I felt tingles throughout my body and a deep level of discomfort. It was similar to what I felt before leaving Guatemala and returning to my family. It wasn't pleasant, and it held deeper fear underneath it.

She explained a bit more about what I was experiencing with the paintings, expressing that my heightened sensitivity was necessary to move closer towards my life purpose. I was already gifted at reading energy and understanding people. My studies of religion and spirituality, coupled with my years of experience as an educator, kept me highly attuned. Yet, I always felt that I didn't belong, and I had a strong desire to escape my body. Even after years of therapy, I was not satisfied with a generalized anxiety and depression diagnosis. There had to be a reason. My soul knew it.

We agreed to meet at her home in the coming days. On my way there, I couldn't help shake the sense that I was about to transform. Not in any way that I could prepare for; rather, something was "coming."

After an afternoon of talking about energy and sharing, I noticed I felt an urgency to leave. However, something stronger was keeping me there. Tears filled my eyes, and I became aware of the acute pain I had in my joints for several months. Despite practicing yoga daily for close to seven years, I encountered deep physical pain that I attributed to weather change, stress, uncertainty, or maybe the early signs of arthritis. The pain was getting more pronounced, and months earlier, during a yoga training, my teacher said to me:

"There is so much that wants to come through your body, and your body is not big enough. Yet. You will need to clear space for it so that this light and energy has a place to reside. Don't worry. Be at peace."

These words played through my mind like an omen. My fearful part was holding hands with my warrior.

The woman then motioned for me to lie down on the carpet. She told me she sensed my resistance and fear and that it would be okay. It was time.

How many times have I heard, "It's time, Maura." What could this possibly mean? The shaman in Guatemala said the same thing. What am I so afraid of?

As I lay down, I felt my muscles contracting and the tears rising to the surface.

"What is happening? Why am I so nervous?" I asked her.

She offered her hand and told me we would breathe together. She introduced a specific cyclical breath that would require me to tighten my Muladhara bandha, which is the root lock in yogic terms. This simply meant that I would tighten my pelvic floor as I breathed in and out. As I did this through several cycles, I felt a searing pain race through my body, as if a knife was being driven into my sacrum and up through my belly. As I stared at the ceiling, I began to see images: my childhood, teen years, adult years, flashes of men, moments that had once been frozen in time.

The images came flooding forward from the depths of the abyss that I had locked up. This deep remembering brought images of disrespect to my very vessel, of violence and disgust. I heard the taunting and teasing, and oversexualizing language. I heard the dismissive words that kept me silent, belittled my own wisdom, and made me feel less than human. I became aware of my father and brother's abuse that I'd erased. I was drugged throughout some of these experiences and not even aware of what was happening. My body was reliving it all in rapid succession. It was overwhelming. It was a tsunami. The shock of it caught me by surprise, and I struggled to find my steady breath. The truth of a life I thought I'd once lived shattered around me like shards of glass, piercing my fragile heart.

This can't be true. And yet it all makes sense now. How can I survive knowing this? What do I do with all of this? I am so shameful and disgusting. Who am I?

I looked at her with my grief-stricken face and curled into a ball. All at once, the world felt dangerous, and I felt defeated. I had been living a lie, and I was most definitely making up more lies. That was what my mind wanted to tell me to survive. I wanted to die, for to have to endure the truth of what I lived through, to carry the weight of this shame felt as though it would destroy me.

I struggled to lift my body, still in shock and unable to comprehend. She told me I would need to go slowly. I would have to be gentle with myself as I unraveled the threads and found a way to accept what was. She also told me that this was where our journey together ended. It felt as though I woke up to a nightmare, and there was no way I could live in the world again. This was only the beginning of a cataclysmic series of events that came as the aftermath of my remembering. While this felt like death, it was truly the beginning of my birth into the wholeness of who I came here to be. It required fortitude and courage, but most of all, willingness.

As I drove through the midnight hour, heavy and wet flakes of snow battered my windshield. My hands gripped the steering wheel as hot tears blazed trails down my cheeks. I comforted myself by singing Snatam Kaur's, Ong Namo on repeat and visualizing the face of my beloved dog, Blue.

Upon arriving back to my parents' house, my childhood home, my legs felt unstable as I crawled up the stairs to the bathroom. I crumpled to the floor and wept. The titanic loss of innocence I felt engulfed me. After what felt like hours, I heard my mother's footsteps and felt her standing on the other side of the door.

"What's wrong with you?" she demanded. Perhaps she meant to ask from a place of genuine care, but all I heard was exasperation. I realized that this simple phrase was the catalyst for my deep loathing throughout my life. I believed I was inherently flawed and that my body and emotions were a target for bad things; therefore, it would be much better if I did not live in it or feel.

I made it into my room, where I wept all night, saturated in the broken pieces. I wasn't held in the compassionate space I so desperately needed to be able to begin to process the abuse and trauma finally surfacing into my conscious mind. My story was not validated by those who were part of it, even after sharing my pain. While excruciatingly painful, this invalidation became a major portal into learning to validate myself.

My mind did a tremendous job of protecting me for many years, yet my body knew all along. I had no concept of how much this pain was limiting me, nor how I sought to care for others at the expense of loving myself. I was unaware of how disconnected I was from giving myself the fullness of what life was offering because I believed I wasn't worthy. These imprints written on my body seeped into my blueprint of expression, and all shackles holding these lies came undone.

It was at that moment I knew I needed to begin the great work of my life. It was time to begin to chart the course back into my body and choose to be here.

This journey required me to say "yes," to allow for the doors of support to open, and to tend to myself with patience.

THE HEALING JOURNEY

I'm so sorry that it hasn't been safe to be in your body. I'm so sorry that you don't want to be here on Earth. I'm so sorry it's so hard to be a human. I'm so sorry that this pain feels like it will never end.

These words, spoken to myself from the depth of my heart, saved me. I never knew that I could give myself what others did not or could not provide.

Learning to forgive myself and have compassion for all of my perceived flaws was the beginning of a powerful journey into my body. It was almost as if all moments before had left me undecided about life. Through self-directed compassion and giving voice to my beliefs about myself and my body, I also began to dissolve the physical pain I carried in my joints and muscles. My body wanted to be spoken to and listened to. This dialoguing became the foundation for my evolution.

I began the journey of reclaiming my parts, magnetizing the fractured aspects stuck in the painful experiences, and calling them home. I pieced together the parts of my story and learned what to release to write a new one. I retrieved aspects of my soul through journey work, dreams, singing, connecting with nature, EMDR therapy, movement, bodywork, energy work, writing, drawing, and honesty with myself and others who held a powerful container.

The path was always illuminated. This truth was illustrated by the fact that everything I had done up until the moment my repressed memories were finally released and given air to breathe gave me strength. I would no longer hold my breath.

Releasing shame and blame brought so much liberation, and I can now see the experiences and the people involved from a place of compassion. I learned to trust my body, even if I couldn't retrieve details. I let go of needing change or apologies from others and focused on the results I wanted from myself. The more I desired to love myself, the less I found myself gripping to the past and what had both done to me and for me. I honored the human part of the pain first and then endeavored to understand the deeper lessons.

It is a miracle that I am in a human body. I count each breath as a blessing. I'm grateful for my internal renovations, which are reflected by the life I now live. There is space. And in that space, there is love. I accept my work in progress with my body as my ally, and I am consistently met with opportunities to reclaim more of myself which leads to surprise, awe, and wonder.

THE MEDICINE

I acknowledge that it can be hard to know how to take the first step towards reclaiming your sovereignty, your body, and your choice to be here on Earth. The unraveling is tender and powerful. Let your body be your teacher. All that lives within you is precious. I offer you this compassionate body reclamation process.

Before beginning, be sure to give yourself at least an hour alone.

Materials needed include three sheets of blank paper, something to write with, some pastels or colored pencils, a candle, and a glass of water.

Throughout this process, take notice of sensations in your body and any tensions or releases that may occur. Notice and allow your emotions to be felt.

Listen to your bodily wisdom.

Begin by sitting in a comfortable position—light your candle.

Place both hands over your heart and take three long breaths, in through the nose and out through the mouth.

Bring both hands forward and switch hands, replacing them over your heart. Take another three breaths.

Do this one more time, replacing hands and taking three breaths.

Imagine or sense that there is a warm golden glow within your heart. This is your safe space and where you can speak freely and openly.

On the first sheet of paper, write *My Hurt Body.*

Draw an outline that represents the shape of your body, or it can simply be a large circle or oval. Begin to free write all of the things that you perceive as flaws about your physical body, including experiences that have occurred.

Examples: I was hit. My legs are ___. I hate my stomach.

From your heart space, begin to offer yourself compassion for all that you have written, beginning each phrase with "I'm so sorry you___."

Continue to use the pronoun 'you' rather than I.

You are working with an aspect of self.

Examples: I'm so sorry you were hit. I'm so sorry you believe your legs are too big. I'm so sorry you hate your stomach.

Take several breaths as you acknowledge the process.

On the second sheet of paper, write: *If I were to say yes to life and my body, then...*

Allow for a stream of consciousness to come forth. Do not filter yourself. You may be surprised about what arrives. This can be both positive and negative.

Offer yourself compassion once again for all that arose.

Examples: I'm so sorry that if you say yes to life, you will be destroyed. I'm so sorry that you are afraid of your body. I'm so sorry that if you say yes to your body, you will be free.

This process may take you to new levels of understanding, and you may also feel as though you want to write and process a bit more.

When you are ready, write the word: *Yes* at the top of your third piece of paper. Begin to make a list of all you are willing and ready to experience in your body, even if you haven't known it yet.

What does it mean for you to be here on earth? Speak from your heart.

After you are complete, you can burn your papers or keep them in a journal.

Welcome home. Thank you for saying yes.

Maura A. Finn is a poet/writer, educator, energy psychology, crisis and trauma support specialist, shamanic practitioner, expressive arts facilitator, yoga instructor, and multi-dimensional empowerment guide. Her passion for healing the human heart has led her worldwide, where she has gathered experience as medicine. She is dedicated to helping others achieve their maximum potential through integrated creative mind-body-soul healing approaches, starting with deep inner knowledge. Individuals who work with Maura are held in a safe space to explore and heal traumas and limiting beliefs and find their own answers, which often leads them to find authentic direction in life. More than anything, she endeavors to inspire humans to reclaim their Divine Spark so that it shines within their human form.

Maura chooses to live her unconventional life with integrity and authenticity. She finds inspiration in the little things and beauty in everything. Her nomadic life takes her all over the globe. She currently resides on a beautiful island in Thailand and can be found writing, laughing, singing, hiking, enjoying waterfalls, and ecstatic dance. She loves animals and can be found nurturing dogs all over the island. She believes in the power of dreaming and synchronicity and is so grateful that she gets to live in a human body, learning, growing, and shining.

Connect with her on the following sites:

Website: www.finnevolutions.com

Facebook: https://www.Facebook.com/FinnEvolutionsLLC

Instagram: https://Instagram.com/mfinnevolutions

LinkedIn: https://linkedin.com/in/maura-finn

VAYA CON DIOS... UNTIL WE MEET AGAIN

May this book be a messenger of hope for your heart.
May it awaken you and be an answered prayer in the dark
May it serve to remind you that sometimes the pain
Is a sacred initiation the rainbow after the rain
Don't give up. Reach out You are never alone
Within your wound is the medicine so chisel out your soul

I want to begin with thanking the 26 Shaman Heart authors and one bad-ass publisher who said yes to bringing this seed of a dream to life. Your brave words, courage, and commitment have inspired me and will no doubt inspire and touch the world. This tribe of transformation is now forever connected by the red thread and the sacred journey we took to birth our book and shaman hearts together. Viva la Vida!

To the readers, thank you for choosing this powerful collection of stories. I hope these words will inspire you to dive deep into the well of your own wisdom, follow your heart down into the dark, and mine it for gold. Your pain is an invitation into an initiation of transformation for your soul.

If any of these authors have inspired or touched you in any way, reach out to them. These stories are just a glimpse into the work that each and every one of them is doing in the world.

In closing, I offer this song I wrote years ago. It came long before I knew how to live and has been a road map to joy and freedom. I encourage you to keep chasing those far-fetched dreams, following your shaman heart and chiselin' out your soul. Within each of us is a masterpiece.

CHISELIN OUT MY SOUL

I once knew a wise old man Maximillian was his name
He was an artist of life a sculptor by trade
I used to sit and watch him work ask him questions try to learn
About the magic that he made but he'd just smile and say

I'm chiselin out my soul
Like Michelangelo
Found spirit in the stone
I'm chiselin out my soul

I used to go and visit him maybe once or twice a week
I drank in every moment I was thirsty for his kind of peace
He said let love be your discipline girl carve out your experience
Be authentic and be real that's how my piece was revealed

By chiselin out my soul
Like Michelangelo
Found spirit in the stone
I'm chiselin out my soul

Like a precious piece of treasured art
I'm not for sale I've worked too hard
To find out who I am
And at my age I don't give a damn

I'm chiselin out my soul
Like Michelangelo
Found spirit in the stone
I'm chiselin out my soul

Well my friend Max died a few years back and I think about him every day
You see his words of wisdom they guide my heart when I've got a tough choice to make
He said everyone's got an artist's eye painting pictures with their lives
Everything you say and do is a framed canvas of your own truth

So keep chiselin out your soul
Like Michelangelo
Found spirit in the stone
Keep chiselin out your soul

All my love,
Stephanie

Lyrics from *Chiselin Out My Soul* by Stephanie Urbina Jones

Messenger of Hope poem (above) by: Rev Annie Mark and Stephanie Urbina Jones

BITTERSWEET GOODBYE TO A FRIEND

As I was writing my chapter in the book *Sacred Death,* I read a post that my friend Diana Kenney had made on Caring Bridge as she pondered what her life's purpose was now that she was dying.

She was grateful that her journey through the painful loss of her beloved partner, Deb, had sent her diving into her own grief work that then became her life's work and passion.

Diana and I had a couple of profound conversations before she transitioned. I was moved by her curiosity and excitement about the next adventure of life after death. She shared that she was "grieved up" and ready to go. She was passionate about what she learned and reminded me that to really live, we have to grieve it, feel it, heal it, and release it.

As the lead author of this sacred journey of a book, I felt called to close with these brave words she wrote just before her passing. Thank you, Diana, for sharing your life and death and for turning your pain into passion and purpose. We can all learn and live from your journey. Vaya Con Dios— Until we meet again.

Stephanie

REFLECTIONS ON LIFE AS I AM DYING

By Diana Kenney

8/13/2021

I am dying.

In early spring 2021, I have warning symptoms of shortness of breath and a one-day episode of a racing heart. On April 8, I find out I have a blood cancer. On April 22, I'm told I have high-grade MDS (Myelodysplastic Syndrome), a kind of blood cancer that has a typical survival time of two and a half years with targeted treatment. Then a bone marrow biopsy, and I find out on May 13 that there is no hope for a targeted treatment; my counts are too low. My doctor tells me that my case is the worst he has seen in 15 years.

Now I wait to die.

I begin transfusions of packed blood cells. I start with a transfusion every three weeks, and now it's every two weeks. I decide I will not go to once a week. It takes a whole day to transfuse two units of blood, and then there are two days of not feeling well as my body integrates this blood. I live from transfusion to transfusion. I cannot do this once a week.

Once I stop the transfusions, I will most likely die within a month.

I consider myself lucky. While I do have a few symptoms—foggy brain as I get closer to the transfusion and shortness of breath when I walk— I'm not in pain. I don't have difficulty breathing when I'm sitting or lying down. I have blood clots in my mouth at times and some fevers and chills, but that is all.

I'm in control of when I will die. I have time to reflect. I've been using the free website CaringBridge.org as an avenue to reach my friends with updates on my health. What follows is an edited journal entry from that site.

Many people have commented on how strong I am, how good my attitude is, and how inspiring I am in the handling of this disease and dying process. I remember saying the same thing to Deb, my partner of 12 years, as she lived with non-Hodgkin's Lymphoma. She was given five to seven years and lived 17. Deb had a fantastic attitude toward her life and the process of dying, and I learned so much from her.

In describing my journey, I need to start with Deb. The first time I saw her receiving a chemo infusion, I literally saw her eyes filling up with grey liquid-like matter. It was horrifying. After seeing that two more times, I knew chemo wasn't for me. Deb's doctors told her she could only have chemo three or four times when the cancer had advanced too far or when the pain was too much. Deb spiraled back and forth between remission and illness, but in spite of this, she maintained a wonderfully positive attitude. She taught me how to be her advocate when she could not speak for herself.

The days leading up to Deb's death were awful. Three months earlier, I had a kidney stone episode. I was told I needed a follow-up chest X-ray, but I delayed. The day after she died, I found out I had kidney cancer. A month later, I moved into the Colorado strawbale home that Deb and I had designed together. Four days after that, I had kidney surgery. An encapsulated cancer node was removed with no further treatment required. I did, however, have a six-to-seven-inch incision that was going to take several months to heal. The pre-surgery anesthesia medication caused memory loss for numbers for 14 months. If I was given a phone number while on the phone, I could not write it down. No info from my brain flowed to my fingers to write the numbers. It was very odd.

I was grieving Deb's death, going through the fear and stress of my own cancer surgery, moving into a new home, and experiencing memory loss in an area that had always been reliable for me. It was winter; I was alone and dealing with three feet of snow. I was in mourning, exhausted, and even considered suicide. I came to understand that if I died via suicide, I'd have to repeat this life again. That would not happen, so I never let my sad feelings get to that point again.

Deb was writing a book on her experience of living with cancer. She described her journey and shared tips, tools, and techniques for dealing with the medical bureaucracy. She shared information on hiring and firing doctors, preparing for going to the ER, having chemo or any treatment for the first time, and lots of other information from her own experience. She asked me to edit and publish her book. I never thought it would happen, but then the Universe brought me to my knees, and a door opened that had always been shut.

After Deb's death, I attended a weekly hospice grief support group in town. This group was a Godsend. We used a book, *Understanding Your Grief,* by Dr. Alan Wolfelt, studying one chapter a week. Learning about grief, the myths, misinformation, and what griefwork really entailed was eye-opening.

During the day, I edited Deb's book, and at night I did my griefwork by going over things that meant a lot to her. I looked at her beading, woodworking, manuscript, and pictures and listened to her favorite music. This is called conscious grieving. I cried deeply every night while doing this. I then talked about my grief in the weekly support group.

After a while, seeing those things didn't make me cry, but I still cried. Now I was crying for everything I hadn't yet grieved, although I didn't always know what that was. I experienced overwhelming waves of grief; this went on for a year and a half. One night, the motion detector came on, and I could see it was snowing outside. I went into a deep trance. It seemed like I was going back in time like dark waves upon waves. I trusted Spirit and kept going back further and further until I reached a place where I was told that my grief was all current and dealt with. I understood that when I could not stop crying but did not know why, I was mourning forgotten experiences from further back in this lifetime and in past lifetimes.

I finished editing her book and added a section on caregiving based on my experiences. I self-published the book, and it was cathartic.

A few years later, I realized I wanted to be trained in griefwork to help others as it helped me. I looked at some griefwork workshops online and selected one that appealed to me as the most credible. Later I found out it was Dr. Alan Wolfelt's Center for Loss and Life Transition, the man who wrote *Understanding Your Grief,* the book used in my support group. I took several week-long classes and received a Death and Grief Studies Certification. This griefwork education has been critical to my positive attitude about life, death, and the process of dying.

Grieving isn't just about death; it's also about change. There are so many things to be grieved; the loss of a beloved person or animal, loss of a job, moving to a new city, a change in health, limitations due to aging, divorce, a life-threatening disease. Any change in your life needs to be grieved.

Grieving adds meaning to our loss and allows us to integrate major changes in our lives. It allows space for transition and transformation so that we live more fully. When we have major change and loss, we are scared of the many feelings associated with it. Because we are afraid, we try to control our feelings of helplessness and hurt. As C.S. Lewis famously said, "No one ever told me that grief felt so much like fear."

Prolonged avoidance of grief will always be destructive. In moving away from our grief, in repressing, denying, or deadening our feelings, we destroy our capacity to enjoy life fully. How can we relate to ourselves and others if we don't feel? If we don't grieve our losses, we will distract ourselves in some way, ranging from excessive busyness to addiction.

I think of grief as an emotional circle. There are others: mental, spiritual, religious, physical. The emotional circle is divided into grief and love. What we don't grieve fills up part of our emotional circle and prevents us from loving fully. If you haven't dealt with grief from a loss or a change, then you're using energy to push it down. This interferes with living life in joy and love. We all know people who seem uptight, afraid to live fully, fearful of all the things that "could" happen to them. They have shut down a crucial part of themselves.

Society has taught us ways not to deal with grief. My father dealt with the death of his 90-year-old mother by putting her memories on a shelf and closing the curtain. That is the quiet, stoic response to grief which is called "handling the death situation" by refusing to allow tears, suffering in silence, and "being strong." How many times have you heard someone characterized as handling the death of a loved one well because they don't cry or show emotion? Grief is not something to be overcome, let go of, or resolved, but rather needs to be fully experienced. Our animals understand this. When they lose someone special to them, we see them not being themselves—not eating, playing, being non-responsive. They're grieving. After a while, they resume their old habits.

The healthiest way to deal with grief is to approach it head-on. Surrendering to loss gives birth to self-compassion and grace, which leads to the integration of the loss into your life. You come to embrace the loss, creating a new you. There is wisdom in living life fully, including the pain. This is hard work that we do only when forced to but do it we must. Helen

Keller, who lived deaf and blind, said, "The only way to the other side is through it!"

You may ask, "How do I grieve?" The real question is, "How do I mourn?" Grieving is the intense sorrow caused by the loss of a loved one, thing, a way of life. It's an inward process. We grieve alone in our thoughts. We get stuck in a loop saying the same sad things to ourselves over and over again.

Mourning is "when you take the grief that you have on the inside and express it outside yourself" or "grief gone public," as Dr. Alan Wolfelt expressed it. It can be scary—we don't know where this journey is leading. Some people fear that once they start crying, they'll never stop. They bottle up the pain, stuff it, letting it slowly build up inside themselves until they finally blow. It takes a lot of energy to constantly wall up your grief and hold it captive inside.

You can do this outward expression of grief by talking and showing your emotions with friends, counselors, grief support groups and by doing something creative—art, painting, carving, dancing, singing, journaling. A major way is being in nature—taking walks, sailing, boating, appreciating how small we are in the big scheme of things. What a gift to let go and just be!

The magic of mourning comes when we understand that we are on a journey into the unknown. When we have embraced our sorrows, we begin the healing process, and we will change. This is a spiritual journey of the heart and soul.

You will naturally grieve, but you must make an effort to mourn.

You need to feel it to heal it. Mourning is the only way to heal our losses, to become the new you, never forgetting the memories but incorporating them into our psyche. We become whole again.

"Catch-Up" mourning: When you haven't mourned life's losses, you bag them up inside of you and lock them away. We do not live in a "death-free" society. People die, pets die, we have other losses. If you don't mourn your pain, it will keep coming back, building up inside of you. We must mourn our past losses! Instead of drowning in regret and guilt, anger and fear, sadness and loneliness, take a risk and come to the surface.

Symptoms of grief avoidance: Difficulties with trust and intimacy. Keeping people at a distance because you need to protect yourself from getting hurt. Depression and a negative outlook on life. Some people have anxiety and panic attacks as they are afraid to let go and live life. Others become irritable. Many people go into addictive behaviors such as drugs, alcohol, food, sex, or becoming workaholics.

Good grief symptoms: You may be surprised. At the beginning of your grief journey, you will feel sadness, shock, numbness, disbelief. Later you may feel disorganized and confused. You may lose your sense of time. You may even feel like you are going nuts with so many feelings coming to the surface. There may be anxiety, panic, fear, rage. Then there are the two most painful feelings to go through, guilt and regret. These emotions do not come in a specific order or way for everyone.

The main ingredient of healthy griefwork is understanding that we are not alone. You need people around you who understand what you are feeling. An acquaintance can become a confidant because they have been through an experience of grief. You are now part of a special group of people you didn't know existed until you shared your grief. Find these supportive people.

Let go of those people who say hurtful things such as, "It's only a dog; you can still have other children or another husband/wife." Or, "It's only a miscarriage, aren't you over it yet?" Drop these unsupportive people.

I'm so grateful I found griefwork as a tool to live my life more fully. If I find myself crying without knowing why I let the emotions flow. Some part of me needs this letting go so I will honor my body, spirit, and emotional self. Now I can process hurt, sadness, disappointment, and loss much faster and get back to an even track. Due to griefwork, I have very few unexpressed feelings left in me. As I consciously approach my death, I do so without fear and regret—what a gift.

Diana Kenney died in the early morning hours of August 30, 2021.

ADIOS MIS AMIGOS

There's a season for hello and a season for goodbye
That's the way the world goes round on this wheel of life

Adios Mis Amigos
Adios My Friends
Adios Mis Amigos
Until We Meet Again

Over the horizon is a new frontier so we must be on our way
With the spirit of pioneers head on west of yesterday

Adios Mis Amigos
Adios My Friends
Adios Mis Amigos
Until We Meet Again

Your love has left an imprint on my soul
I'll take you with me wherever I go

Adios Mis Amigos
Adios My Friends
Adios Mis Amigos
Until We Meet Again

Lyrics from *Adios Mis Amigos* by Stephanie Urbina Jones

MUCHISIMAS GRACIAS Y'ALL

I want to start by thanking the great mystery of life, the God of my understanding, Tonantzin, the Great Mother, Jesus, all my ancestors and loved ones who have walked and guided me on this road of life. It has been a long and winding road, and I'm deeply grateful for every twist and turn, crash, and burn that humbly made me who I am. I know I was held and protected every step of the way. May I continue to be a messenger of love and instrument of joy, wisdom, and grace. I am forever grateful.

To my great-grandfather Manuel Anaya Urbina who had the faith and conviction to follow his heart and crossed the border in 1907 in pursuit of his religious freedom, his divinity, and for a better life for me, my daughter, and the generations to come. To my abuelita Virginia for being with me every day since her death and making holy magic happen. To my father, Charlie Urbina Jones, for being my person, loving me unconditionally, and teaching me to walk between the worlds. Thank you for seeing and holding my dreams before I could. I love you more. To my mother, who had me, and my stepfather, who raised me, taught me to two-step, and the joy of music. Thank you.

To my own daughter Zeta for choosing me as your mama. You are the greatest gift of my life and a fierce, wise, loyal, beautiful young woman inside and out. Don't ever forget who you are and where you came from Mija! Shine on!

To my beloved husband Jeremy who I met and married in a medicine wheel. Our marriage is sacred medicine. It has taught me the gift of true love. You are the foundation of our family, our life, and our tribe. Your gentle, kind warrior ways have grounded me so I could fly. Your humble leadership comforts and has given me and so many others guidance and strength. Every dreamer needs their match, and I have found mine in you. Te Amo mi amor.

To my ride-or-die soul sisters and midwives of my broken hearts and dreams. Sherrie Phillips, Annie Mark, Elaine Watson Torres, Bridgett McGuire, Anita Mandell. I'm so blessed to have each of you through it all.

To Laura Di Franco and her team at Brave Healer Productions, including Alex Nason and artist Dino Marino. It is a gift and honor to work with each of you and to be in life creating this masterpiece of love. Thank you for your integrity, massive dedication, commitment, and sacred yes!

To the 26 authors of this book: WOW! What an adventure of a lifetime. My red thread tribe of transformation, I have fallen in love with each of you. We seeded our hearts together and made a baby that will touch the world! What a gift to know and be on this ride with each of you. I'm humbled by your wisdom and broken open hearts. A special thanks to Atlantis Wolf for being our writing wrangler, watching over this project, and helping to deliver this baby!

To my dearest amiga de corazon, Emily Grieves, my Frida Kahlo. It's a dream come true to journey and create so much meaningful life and joy with you. The dream lives on! Muchisimas gracias for painting the cover of this book. It's truly amazing! I cherish and love your heart, art, and friendship.

To my personal deep-dive sisters and husband who spent night and day and to all hours of the morning writing, editing, questioning, and helping me find the words and the way to birth this book. Thank you, Annie Mark, Ruthie Souther, and Jeremy Pajer. I am so deeply grateful. Each of your souls are woven into each word of this book. Thank you.

To my music manager I have waited a lifetime to find, Preston Sullivan. You and Ramona Simmons were worth the wait. It is a joy to create magic with you both. To De Foster, Valerie Alvarez, Rick del Castillo, Patterson Barrett, Mike Hernandez and all the musicians and mariachis who have played with me and keep my heart singing down this crazy dreamers road... mil GRACIAS.

To mine and Jeremy's families, the folks behind the scenes that gave us life and support us always: thank you Fred, Terry, Kipp, Sheila, Nicky, Hendo, Larson, Annie, Uncle Brian, Uncle Rudy, Linda, and Marcus. To my uncle Mike and Aunt Carol who seeded the dream of Freedom Folk and Soul and helped us in opening our nonprofit doors and providing scholarships: thank you. To Randy and Anita, my God-parents, thank you for teaching me how to love.

To my dear friends, teachers, and guides, Ruby Falconer, Grandfather Mowgli, Carley Mattimore and John Malan, Deb Kotz, Pam Savory, Barb Westover, Jaguar Bear and Baroness, Sharri Starfire, Linda Star Wolf, Judy Red Hawk, Abuelo Alvaro, Heidi Steffens, Melba Clark, Boyce Bronson, Christy Pilkinton, Maia Williams, Windraven, Maura Finn, Sara and Terry Curran, Sarah Jane Fridy, Kathy Morrison, Eddie LeShure, Alberto Kreimerman, Jim and Wesley, Luz Maria, Billy, Cookie, Miguel Conseco, Wyman, Dr. Kathleen Hudson, Tina Green, Tara Backes, Hemali Vora, Lisa Asvestas, Janice Ballard, and Jennifer Harvard: thank you for supporting me and helping me become the teacher and healer I am today. To my deep dive Shamama, Pat Cummins, I adore you. Thank you for loving me.

To our familia and friends from the Dreaming House, mil gracias for feeding our hearts and holding the seeds of our dreams while we came undone time and time again to birth ourselves and this book. We are so grateful for each of you! Alberto Hernandez Fernando, Veronica Contla Galicia, Victor, Camilo, Carla and Francisco.

A big Toltec Thanks to don Miguel Ruiz, don Miguel Ruiz Jr, Jorge Luis Delgado and Lee McCormick, who first brought me to Teo. Thank you, James Nihan, HeatherAsh Amara, Frances Rico, Rebecca Haywood, and my Toltec teacher Dawn Zurlinden.

To our Freedom Folk and Soul team who keeps the dream alive and moving forward. Dana Gusoff and Mary Thomas, thank you for your dedication, time, love, and energy. We couldn't do what we do without you both.

To David, Jean Marie, and the Laughing Winds crew. Your love lives on. To my first counselors, Kathleen and Max Haskett, for holding me while I first chiseled out my soul, as well as my Pot Hole sisters Jewelie Hargrove, Alison Auerbach, and Judy Holman. To spiritual leaders and friends Denise Yeargin and Judy Blackwelder and dear amigas, Kelly Easter and Jess Leary.

To our Freedom Folk and Soul community, I love you! You all have been the true inspiration behind this book. Thank you for always showing up, laying your hearts on the altar, and courageously turning your wounds into your medicine. To our ministers, thank you for being sacred witnesses in life and bringing your light into the world one ceremony at a time.

There have been so many people that have touched my life and influenced my journey. To those of you not mentioned here directly, a deep-hearted muchisimas gracias y'all!

All my love,

Stephanie

MORE ABOUT THE AUTHOR

Stephanie Urbina Jones is a powerful dreamer and artist of life. Once this shamama sets her intent on something, she almost always brings it to life and has fun doing it. She is a visionary seer and regularly walks between the worlds. She considers this normal and believes she has an army of Mexican angels (led by her abuelita Virginia) that guide and guard her life and career.

Born in San Antonio and raised in small-town Fredericksburg, Texas, she has never met a stranger. Her first job was picking peaches, and her first date was coon hunting. She still loves the great outdoors and the simple things in life. She is living her dreams full tilt boogie every day, working on songs, albums, books, tours, ceremonies, time with her family, or journeys around the world. She is enjoying her life now more than ever.

Stephanie lives on the river outside Nashville, TN, with her beloved daughter Zeta, husband and firewalk instructor Jeremy, their little white buffalo medicine dog Lulu, and moody cat Bolt. She loves getting snowed in and or any chance to be with her family.

She wrote her first song when her high school boyfriend broke up with her, and she never looked back. She loves her dad, Uncle Rudy, everything mariachi, and her Mexican roots. She spends a few months a year south of the border making music, playing, trying on dresses, leading journeys, or just hanging with her family of friends.

She loves Besame red lipstick (just like her abuelita,) listening to music, eating nachos, daydreaming, meditating, going days without makeup, sipping coffee on the river in her pajamas, and leading sacred journeys. She believes in supporting the artists she loves and is always paying off some piece of art from her favorite painter Emily Grieves, sculptor Alberto Hernandez, or a designer piece of clothing.

She loves sweat lodges, healing massages, traveling, and fabulous hotels. She doesn't cook and is so grateful for Uber Eats all over the world. She has a passion for helping people and things grow. She is not afraid of her, or your, darkness. She was born to hold sacred witness for others as they bloom through their pain and find their purpose.

One of the greatest gifts in the last ten years was becoming a Toltec teacher and starting Freedom Folk and Soul. She cherishes her deep connection with her Tribe of Transformation. Stephanie made history on the Grand Ole Opry, had a song she wrote to win *The Voice*, travels and tours all over the world with her Honky Tonk Mariachis, and is just getting started. She is a junkie for healers and works with two mediums and several renowned shamans, and continues to learn and carry indigenous healing ways herself.

She is finally coming out of the shaman closet with *Shaman Heart*. She is a reiki master and loves to see how spirit moves through different healing modalities. Stephanie believes it all comes down to being a messenger of love. She spreads and makes magic everywhere she goes.

HOW STEPHANIE URBINA JONES SERVES THE WORLD AND HOW YOU CAN BE PART OF THE MAGIC

THE ADVENTURE IS ON

FREEDOM FOLK AND SOUL

A TRANSFORMATIONAL COMMUNITY OF THE HEALING ARTS

Guiding folks on their journey of self-discovery, healing, and transformation. Empowering those who seek to live a life of passion, purpose, and personal freedom.

Jeremy Pajer and Stephanie Urbina Jones have spent over 40 years in combined pursuit of their personal freedom. Each of them studied, prayed, walked, talked, worked, and turned over stones in the road and in their hearts to heal and create a life of humility, passion, and purpose. Having personally experienced the journey of continuous transformation, they were called to give back what they had been given and share their experience, strength, and hope with other souls on the path of wellness and higher consciousness. They feel called to be compassionate stewards, witnesses, and teachers supporting others with a desire to heal and find their own passion, purpose, and transformation on their chosen life path. In all their years of healing, these modalities and tools have become some of the most powerful for healing and spiritual growth. Both Jeremy and Stephanie are honored and called to share this powerful medicine with those ready to transform their lives.

https://www.freedomfolkandsoul.org

PROGRAMS

TOLTEC MEDICINE WHEEL OF TRANSFORMATION

**A Shamanic Journey of Personal Freedom
in the US and Mexico with Jeremy Pajer & Stephanie Urbina Jones**

Journey through the Seven Directions/Seven Initiations & the Medicine Wheel of Your Life / Transform Your Wounds into Your Medicine, Your Pain into Your Purpose & Create a Masterpiece of Your Life

If you are ready to change your life, heal your hurt, and turn your wounds into your medicine, you are at the right place. We are humbly grateful to hold this sacred container for those who are standing at the crossroads of their life. Join us as we dive deep into and through the seven directions and this map of transformation. Through sacred initiations, Toltec teachings and ceremony, Native American sweat lodge, firewalk, and breathwork, we will recover and bring home those pieces of our soul we had to leave behind. From that place of more wholeness, we will hear the calling of our heart's desire and step into our soul purpose. This training is designed to take you through the Medicine Wheel of Your Life. Seven directions and seven initiations. We will step through the rites of passage and consciously grow through old wounds to healing wholeness, connection, and communion with Great Mystery.

Our foundational program to becoming a Minister of the Healing Arts & Transformational Facilitator of the Healing Arts

FREEDOM FOLK AND SOUL MINISTERIAL TRAINING

Join co-founders and master facilitators of Freedom Folk and Soul, Jeremy Pajer and Stephanie Urbina Jones, along with Interfaith/Shamanic Minister Annie Mark, for this experiential training.

Journey and learn how to perform the most meaningful and sacred ceremonies in life. This hands-on intensive training will give you real-life experience and a map of how to honor and perform rites of passage, weddings, funerals, baptisms, baby blessings, baby naming, coming of age ceremonies, shamanic initiations, and more. Learn how to meet and minister to families during these holy and tender times, honoring differences and the unexpected moments in between.

In these experiential and interactive trainings, you will gather tools of wisdom and actual ceremonies to add to your toolbox as we support you to step humbly yet empowered into your ministry of the heart.

ADDITIONAL OFFERING

Sacred Journeys of Transformation All Over the World

Monthly Medicine Ministry

Spiritual Counseling

Facilitator Training and Certifications

Healing Arts Ministerial Ordainment

Freedom Firewalks

Shaman Heart Concerts

Toltec Sacred Journey Breathwork

Transformational Adventure Guides Available
for Your Next Workshop, Journey or Retreat

To learn more about Shaman Heart:

Website: http://www.shamanheart.org

**To connect with Stephanie and Jeremy
or learn more about Freedom Folk and Soul:**

Website: https://www.FreedomFolkandSoul.org

Facebook: https://www.facebook.com/Freedomfolkandsoul

Instagram: https://www.instagram.com/freedom.folk.and.soul

Or email them directly: freedomfolkandsoul@gmail.com

**To learn more about Stephanie Urbina Jones Music
and her Honky Tonk Mariachi:**

Website: https://www.stephanieurbinajones.com

Facebook: https://www.facebook.com/StephanieUrbinaJones

Instagram: https://www.instagram.com/stephanie_urbina_jones

Twitter: https://twitter.com/stephanieurbina

YouTube: https://www.youtube.com/user/StephanieUrbinaTV/videos

Or email her directly: SUJmusic@gmail.com

It's a bittersweet beautiful ride

An emotional rollercoaster we call life

We heal we hurt go from bad to worse

Come out better on the other side

Of this bittersweet beautiful ride

Lyrics from *The Bittersweet Beautiful Ride*
by Stephanie Urbina Jones and Wayne Kirkpatrick